The Assault on Elisha Green

The Assault on Elisha Green

Race and Religion in a Kentucky Community

RANDOLPH PAUL RUNYON

UNIVERSITY PRESS OF KENTUCKY

Scholarly publisher for the Commonwealth,
serving Bellarmine University, Berea College, Centre
College of Kentucky, Eastern Kentucky University,
The Filson Historical Society, Georgetown College,
Kentucky Historical Society, Kentucky State University,
Morehead State University, Murray State University,
Northern Kentucky University, Spalding University,
Transylvania University, University of Kentucky,
University of Louisville, and Western Kentucky University.

Editorial and Sales Offices: The University Press of Kentucky
663 South Limestone Street, Lexington, Kentucky 40508-4008
www.kentuckypress.com

Library of Congress Cataloging-in-Publication Data

Names: Runyon, Randolph, 1947- author.
Title: The assault on Elisha Green : race and religion in a Kentucky community / Randolph Paul Runyon.
Description: Lexington : The University Press of Kentucky, 2021. | Includes bibliographical references and index.
Identifiers: LCCN 2021026377 | ISBN 9780813152387 (hardcover ; alkaline paper) | ISBN 9780813152400 (pdf) | ISBN 9780813152455 (epub)
Subjects: LCSH: Green, Elisha, 1818-1893—Trials, litigation, etc. | Bristow, Frank L.—Trials, litigation, etc. | Gould, George T., 1842-1911—Trials, litigation, etc. | African Americans—Violence against—Kentucky—History—19th century. | African American clergy—Kentucky—Biography. | Maysville (Ky.)—Race relations—History—19th century. | LCGFT: Biographies.
Classification: LCC E185.61 .R95 2021 | DDC 305.896/0730769323—dc23

This book is printed on acid-free paper meeting
the requirements of the American National Standard
for Permanence in Paper for Printed Library Materials.

Manufactured in the United States of America

Member of the Association of
University Presses

For Augusta and Ezekiel

Contents

Illustrations

Introduction

Reverend Elisha Green was traveling on a Kentucky Central train from Maysville to Paris on June 8, 1883, when the president of Millersburg Female College and its music professor, wanting to make room for their students, rudely ordered him to leave his seat and then physically attacked him when he refused. He was black, and they were white. He sued them for assault and, surprisingly, won. This book tells the story of his life and traces the network of relationships that led to the events of that day, together with their repercussions.

Green was born a slave in 1818 but by the 1850s had earned enough from side jobs to buy a sister's freedom and then his own. He started a church in Maysville in 1845 and a second in Paris ten years later. Until his death in 1893, he pastored both, traveling first by stagecoach and then by train, as he was doing the day he was assaulted. After the Civil War, he made speeches for Republican Party candidates, fought for equal rights in the voting booth and the courtroom, helped found Kentucky's first African American college, and was instrumental in creating a neighborhood of black-owned homes in Paris.

Three Kentucky towns figure in the story. Maysville, on the Ohio River, was the least southern in more than geography, having greater commercial ties to Cincinnati than to Lexington; in commenting on Green's refusal to yield his seat, a Cynthiana, Kentucky, newspaper accused Maysville of being under a Yankee influence that placed blacks like him above their station. In the heart of the Bluegrass, Paris was surrounded by wealth built on slave labor; after the Civil War, its population was swelled by former slaves from nearby farms. Millersburg, eight miles away and one-fourth the size, was at that time a bustling community with two colleges that have since, along with the bustle, disappeared.

Green's life was not enriched by his assailants, but his story is. This is especially true with regard to the college president, George T. Gould, who was admired for his brilliance and oratorical power but whose career was marred by bouts of drinking and adultery. Green's character was so sterling and the attack on him so vile that Gould lost the community support that had enabled him to weather previous scandals. He resigned his prestigious post and fled to New Mexico, where he tried several times to reinvent himself, not always with success. Green was well aware that he had triumphed in the end, recalling in his autobiography that not long after he won his suit against Gould, the latter "was found guilty of immoral conduct and excluded from the church and conference of which he was a member."[1] He notes, no doubt with satisfaction, that he has a copy of the proceedings of the church trial where that happened.

Green suffered his own tribulations in both Maysville and Paris, but they were not entirely his fault. In the summer of 1884, he lost members of both congregations to breakaway churches. The one in Maysville was led by an unscrupulous young rival fleeing an unsavory past and subsequently in league with the pastor of the one in Paris.

There was no racial segregation on the train Green took in 1883. That would come in the next decade, thanks to the Separate Coach Act, inspired by an incident on a Louisville and Nashville train in October 1891. The precipitating incident was consistently misrepresented by politicians and the press, and the law was passed in ignorance of the truth. An appellate judge's ruling in 1895 finally told what really happened, but it attracted little notice.

Contemporary newspaper accounts have proved an invaluable resource, as have documents and letters pertaining to Gould's church trial in 1884 preserved at Kentucky Wesleyan University in Owensboro as well as his sermons and lectures archived at the New Mexico State University Library in Las Cruces. Green's autobiography, *Life of the Rev. Elisha W. Green . . . Written by Himself,* widely available on the internet, makes for fascinating reading but in places needs clarification. I have scoured the records of the Mason County Circuit Clerk's Office to piece together the names of slaves and owners to fill in the gaps in Green's account of his early years. One of the most significant gaps is the date he purchased his freedom, which I have discovered.

In two excellent articles in the *Register of the Kentucky Historical Society,* Charles L. Davis recounts what happened to Elisha Green on the Kentucky Central train and delineates Gould's scandal-ridden career at Millersburg Female College. I am hugely in his debt.[2]

My book is about both Green and his assailants. Chapters 1 through 5 chronicle his life from his birth in 1818 to just before the incident in 1883. Gould's story up to that point is told in chapters 6 through 9. Chapter 10 does the same for Frank L. Bristow, the Millersburg music professor who beat Green over the head with his brass-bound valise. Chapter 11 covers the academic year in Millersburg preceding that fateful June day. Chapter 12 looks in detail at the event and its repercussions. Gould abandons his college and his family in chapter 13, hoping to start over in New Mexico. Green in chapter 14 must deal with divisions in both of his churches but finds happiness with a new wife. Gould is called back to Kentucky in chapter 15 to face a career-destroying church trial. He tries to reinvent himself in chapter 16 in a venture that ultimately fails, though he does succeed in divorcing his wife, marrying a former student from the Millersburg College, and raising a second family. We return to Elisha Green in chapter 17, recounting his final years as a citizen of Maysville venerated by both white and black and the renewed struggle for human dignity that grew out of another incident on another train.

1

On the Auction Block

Elisha Green was born into slavery in Bourbon County, Kentucky, six miles west of Paris near the Georgetown turnpike. He did not know the day of his birth, the register with that information having been lost in a fire, but he evidently knew the year was 1818, for he said he was brought to Mason County in 1828 at the age of ten.[1]

One of the few things he could remember about his childhood in or near Paris was finding fellowship and religious instruction at a "Sabbath school," held in secret at various locations and always at night. Owners forbade slaves from meeting on their own for fear they would plot their escape. The owners were especially apprehensive in the summer of 1822, when news broke of a blocked revolt in Charleston, South Carolina, led by Denmark Vesey, a former slave born on the Virgin Islands. The plan had been to steal arms, kill slaveholders, and free their slaves. The authorities arrested the conspirators before the date the revolt was set to happen, but it gave rise, as J. Winston Coleman noted, to "much excitement and fear" among white Kentuckians. They formed slave patrols to scour the countryside and break up forbidden gatherings. Sometimes the slaves took defensive measures, Green recalled, tying grapevines across the road at just the right height to knock a man off his horse.[2]

One night Elisha had gone to one such Sabbath school event with some friends, and "about the time we had gotten in a good way enjoying ourselves, the Patrollers came and whipped all of the grown persons in the schoolhouse. But, being very small, when they came in I ran out,

Elisha W. Green, from *Life of the Rev. Elisha W. Green* (Maysville, KY, 1888) (Library of Congress)

passing under the arms of one that was standing in the door." He ran a mile home as fast as he could, all out of breath. "I often look back at that time and now, whenever I pass that place, I draw the scene fresh in mind."[3]

Unlike states farther south, Kentucky did not typically have plantations with large numbers of slaves. According to Lowell H. Harrison and James C. Klotter in *A New History of Kentucky,* most white Kentuckians owned none, for they could not afford to. A single slave cost more than a farmer could earn from his crops in two years. In 1850, only 28 percent of families possessed any slaves at all, and only five owners possessed more than a hundred. Yet the numbers were nevertheless not insignificant. In 1860, slaves made up 19 percent of the state's population, and Kentucky had more slave owners than any state but Virginia and Georgia. In Bourbon County that year, 858 slave owners held 6,767 slaves, an average of eight slaves per owner, and in Mason County 727 owned 3,772 slaves, an average of five each. Though hardly worth the investment for the average farmer, slaves were nevertheless of great intrinsic value because they could always be sold south, where the need for them was greater.[4]

Slavery in Kentucky, Harold D. Tallant writes, "meant a lifetime of racial oppression, dawn-to-dusk work, monotonous food, inadequate clothing, primitive housing, and harsh punishments. Nevertheless, both white and black Kentuckians voiced the opinion that the labor of slaves was easier in Kentucky than in the states of the lower South." Because of a diversity of crops, farm work was spread throughout the year. In addition, according to Tallant, many owners allowed their slaves free time after they completed their assigned tasks. Elisha Green, as we will see, used his to learn to read, to study the Bible, and to earn his own income in preaching and other trades. As Tallant points out, "Living on small farms with few other slaves and, hence, fewer potential mates, most slaves were forced by circumstances to find spouses on other farms and to maintain their families across farm boundaries. This fact, and the greater variety of jobs assigned to slaves meant that Kentucky slaves probably experienced greater mobility than slaves of the Lower South." Green walked many miles to visit his wife on weekends, and his freedom to travel to preach at church services, weddings, and funerals was remarkable, even for a Kentucky slave.[5]

But it was only the work load that was easier for slaves in Kentucky. Tallant points out that in other respects slavery in Kentucky and other states of the Upper South "actually appears to have been harsher" than in the Lower South. Being the only slave on a small farm or one of just five meant that the slave lived in close contact with his or her owner, which was not always a good thing. "While in some cases," he adds, "intimate contact probably humanized the master–slave relationship, in more cases it appears that it simply exposed slaves to the constant demands of petty, racist tyrants." A male slave in Kentucky was more likely to be separated by sale from his wife and children because two owners were involved, perhaps both of them small farmers living on the margin of profitability. A slave child born in Kentucky in 1820 had about a one-in-three chance of being sold out of the state before his death.[6]

Objecting to the myth put forth by J. Winston Coleman and others that slavery existed in its mildest form in Kentucky, Marion Lucas writes,

"Slavery in Kentucky was *not* a mild form of servitude, for, to the modern mind, no such condition existed. Slavery was a heinous evil . . . regardless of the degree of degradation. . . . To state that slaves fared better under Kentucky's slave system as compared to that of the Deep South does not exonerate the evil." And as Blaine Hudson points out, the fact that slavery was only of marginal importance to the state's economy "did not lessen the tenacity with which many white Kentuckians defended it."[7]

If slaveholders were afraid of their property fleeing north, slaves' greatest fear was of being sold south, where they would work under ever more dismal conditions. In 1822, the Reverend James H. Dickey, traveling from Paris to Lexington, began to hear unseen fiddles in the distance ahead playing a snappy tune. Then he saw Old Glory emerging from behind a hill and fluttering in the breeze. Taking it to be some sort of patriotic event, he pulled over to the side of the road and watched as forty men and women in handcuffs and chains shuffled by. They were the property of Bourbon County native Edward Stone, whose handsome mansion in Federal style between Paris and Millersburg concealed a dungeon to house them until he collected enough to take to Maysville. There they would board a vessel bound for southern slave markets. In 1826, Stone was on such a boat when just past Louisville his cargo revolted, murdering him and his nephew and fleeing to the Indiana side. Most were captured and hanged, though some may have made it to safety.[8]

Green twice recalls seeing a slave coffle pass. In May's Lick, Mason County, the enchained were preceded by an aged slave who sang. His music was nothing like the sprightly tune Stone made his slaves endure but instead a dirge of a hymn from the pen of Isaac Watts:

> Hark! from the tombs a doleful sound; My ears attend the cry:
> "Ye living men, come view the ground
> Where you must shortly lie."

But perhaps the real message lay in the second verse:

> Princes, this clay must be your bed,
> In spite of all your towers,
> The tall, the wise, the reverend head
> Must lie as low as ours.

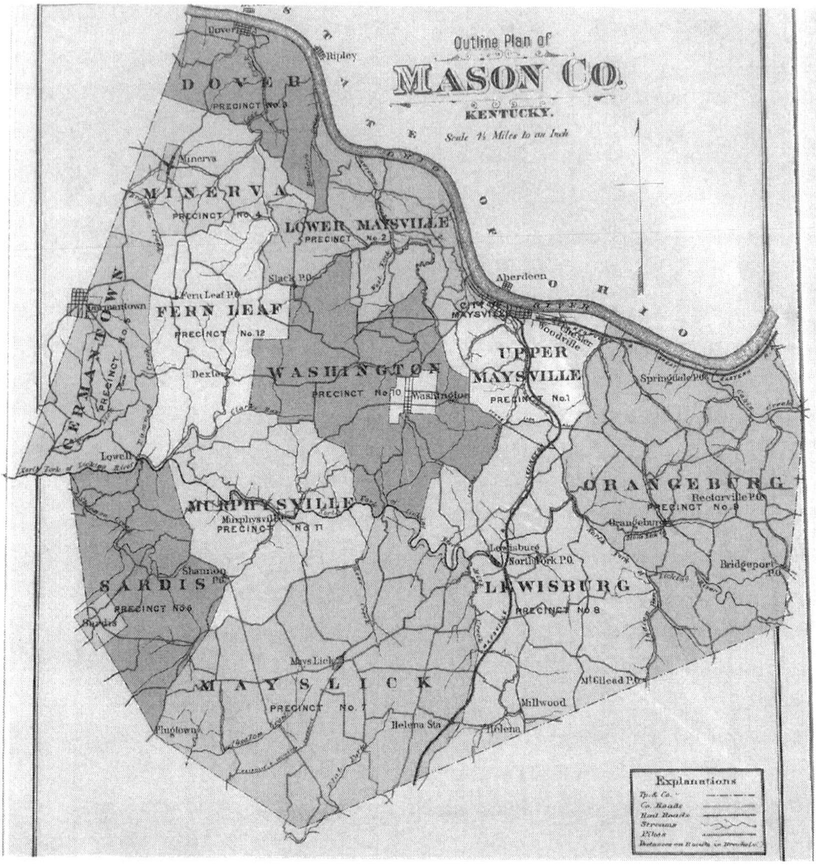

Map of Mason County, from *An Illustrated Atlas of Mason County, Kentucky* (Philadelphia, 1876) (Library of Congress)

Death is the great equalizer, and slave master and slave alike must go down to the dust. As the coffle went past, Green saw a white woman sitting at her window unable to hold back her sobs.[9]

He does not say when or where he saw the other procession, but the records indicate that it was in Maysville on November 4, 1849, a Sunday. Drawing on the account in the *Maysville Eagle* of November 6, Coleman writes that citizens of that town were shocked to see the steamboat *Herman* from Charleston, (West) Virginia, dock at the wharf with forty-four men, women, and children, who were then led through the streets in chains. They were going to Lexington, which surpassed Covington and Paducah as the biggest slave market because the risk of slaves escaping from those Ohio River cities was greater than in the landlocked Blue Grass. Green recalls hearing Thomas Young Payne (1802–1857), a noted Maysville attorney and a slave owner, declare that "a colored person should never again be brought through the city in that fix on Sabbath morning." It was apparently all right to do it on a weekday.[10]

Of his circumstances before the move to May's Lick, Green writes, "The name of the man I lived with in Bourbon was Judge Brown. My mother, sisters Charlotte and Harriet and the balance of the children were then [that is, at that period] divided among the heirs of Dobyns—sister Evaline to Silas Duvall; brother Marshall to the same man; brother Alvin to Thomas Parry; brother Henry to Thomas Dobyns; brother Elijah to Enoch Pepper." The Dobyns of whom those listed were heirs was Edward Dobyns, who had died in 1794. Born in Virginia in 1747, he had fought in the American Revolution and afterward brought his family to Mason County. Judge James Brown was an heir of Edward Dobyns by virtue of having married his widow, Frances Kay Dobyns, whom Brown outlived (she died in 1821). Silas L. Duvall was married to Elizabeth K. "Betsey" Dobyns and Thomas Parry to Mary Dobyns, both of them daughters of Edward Dobyns. It is not clear how Enoch Pepper was an heir, but the Peppers and Dobynses had intermarried in several ways. What Green says about Duvall owning Marshall and Parry owning Alvin is borne out by the slave records in the Mason County Court House compiled by Caroline R. Miller, which indicate that Duvall emancipated Marshall Green on February 13, 1837, as Parry did Alvin Green on December 14, 1846.[11]

The reason ten-year-old Elisha was brought from Bourbon to Mason County in 1828 was that Charles Dobyns, one of Edward's sons, had died in February of that year, and to settle the estate his slaves, one of whom was Elisha, had to be sold. That auction was held July 21, 1828, on the lawn of the Washington, Kentucky, courthouse, where Harriet Beecher (not yet Stowe) in the summer of 1833 would see another slave auction that impelled her to write *Uncle Tom's Cabin.* The results of that auction: "Sold to Asa R. Runyon, a man Harry $382; sold to William Greathouse, old Moses $101; sold to Silas L. Duvall, boy Elisha $421; sold to Berry Dobyns, one woman Charlotte $390; sold to Samuel Pepper, one girl

Mary $400; sold to William Greathouse, one girl Nancy $350; sold to William Mitchell, one boy Henry $335." An eighth slave appeared in the presale inventory but not in the sale. A notation in March 1829 explains why: "Man Joseph ran away before the sale of the said estate," perhaps a traveler on the underground railroad that ran through John Rankin's home on the hill above Ripley, Ohio, ten miles down the river from Maysville.[12]

The event was seared into Elisha Green's memory. "My sister and [her] four children and myself were sold in Washington. . . . When we were put up to be sold, Mr. Oliver Kale refused to 'cry' us off, and a man by the name of Charlie Ward supplied the place. . . . This act of selling colored people was considered by many as being of a low character, while there were those who thought it right, and to sell a negro was nothing more than selling a mule." His sister was the Charlotte named in the description of the auction; her children were Mary, Nancy, Henry, and possibly the adult Harry. We do not know if Moses and the runaway Joseph were part of Elisha's family, but they may have been. If so, Joseph may have been his father, Moses his grandfather. Elisha, his sister Charlotte, and her daughter Mary were sold to persons within the Dobyns circle: Berry Dobyns was Charles's brother; Silas Duvall, as noted, was married to Charles's sister Elizabeth; Samuel Pepper was married to a Nancy Dobyns. But Charlotte's children Nancy and Henry went to outsiders.[13]

Despite being sold to the Duvalls, Elisha names another family as the one in whose hands he soon found himself, that of "J. L. Kirk, who married my young mistress, Jane P. Dobyns." However it came about, he was evidently no longer the property of Silas Duvall but of Silas's sister-in-law, Elizabeth Porter Dobyns (1788–1871), the widow of Charles. Jane Porter Dobyns Kirk was Charles's daughter and had married John Lauderback Kirk in 1825. Kirk was coadministrator of Charles's estate together with the latter's widow, whom Green, as we will see, would call "my old mistress." His two mistresses were mother and daughter, but it was the mother who owned him and continued to as long as he was a slave. Her daughter was his mistress in function from 1828 until 1832, when he would leave the Kirk household for that of the mother, who by then had remarried.

That the widow sent him to live with her daughter could have been because Jane, who would soon be pregnant with her first child (Frances

Amanda, born October 23, 1829), had greater need of the assistance Elisha could render than did her mother, who had other slaves. But living with the Kirks was not a pleasant experience for him: "I saw very rough times. While there I cooked, washed, spun flax and yarn, and did all the house-work the same as a woman. Here was where a man became a woman if such ever were possible in the history of the world. I lived here about four years—from 1828 to 1832." By contrast, another young slave in Mason County, Francis Frederick, was happy to work inside because the food was better.[14]

Immediately after referring to his "young mistress," Green then alludes to his "old" one: "When Mr. Dobyns had been dead awhile, my old mistress married Mr. Walter Warder." His old mistress was his young mistress's mother and Charles Dobyns's widow, Elizabeth Porter Dobyns, who married the Reverend Walter Warder on December 15, 1830. Warder, a widower since October 1829, was pastor of the May's Lick Baptist Church, which Elisha attended. Elisha left the Kirks and joined the Warder household in 1832, which he found much more agreeable. He adored Walter Warder, finding in him a model to imitate.

When Warder first came to May's Lick in 1813, the congregation of the Baptist church was small, but by 1829 it grew to more than 800, the largest Baptist church in the state. But in 1830 it lost 383 members to Alexander Campbell, who was preaching a rival theology. According to Green, "Campbell's doctrine was, in substance, 'read, believe and be baptized.'" The boy Elisha followed events there closely, and throughout his own preaching career would continue to fight Warder's battle against the Campbellites. Warder found an ally in Reverend William Vaughan, who could more clearly than he articulate what was wrong with Campbell's theology.[15]

Green would still be fighting Warder's battles against the Campbellites fifty years later, quoting Vaughan at length about the points at dispute. Chief among them were Campbell's assertions that baptism was essential to salvation, that it brought remission of sins, and "that there is no direct operation of the Holy Spirit on the mind prior to baptism." But Baptists, despite their name, did not consider baptism essential to salvation. Conversion could come by the direct operation of the Holy Spirit, as it in fact did in Green's case. "When converted I was plowing" on Warder's farm, he distinctly recalled, adding that it was a

Friday morning between nine and ten o'clock. No one converted him; he did it on his own, with the help of the Holy Spirit, in classic Baptist style. Z. T. Cody notes in his history of the May's Lick church that Baptists were ridiculed by Campbellites for finding "religion out in the woods behind stumps and logs and bush-heaps"—and in Green's case while plowing a field.[16]

There is special significance in the declaration that Green's conversion happened when he was plowing, for his experience reenacts that of the prophet for whom he was named. God told Elijah to anoint Elisha as his successor. Elijah had to look for Elisha, eventually found him plowing a field, and cast his mantle upon him (I Kings 19:15–16, 19).

If Elisha Green modeled himself on the biblical Elisha, then he saw Warder as his Elijah. Both Green and Warder would prove to be great baptizers, but just as the biblical Elisha performed twice as many miracles as Elijah, Green baptized ten times as many as Warder. When Green arrived in May's Lick in 1828, Warder was holding a very successful revival that lasted for months, immersing five hundred converts. "I once saw Mr. Warder baptize forty persons before breakfast," Green says, truly impressed. In 1866, Green would hold a revival at his Maysville church, baptizing twenty-five in the Ohio River the first week, fifteen the second week, eventually seventy-five in all. On February 6, 1882, the *Maysville Evening Bulletin* reported that he baptized forty-five. They must have been hardy souls to brave the frigid waters of early February. Green was not sure how many he had baptized in the course of his career up until 1887, but a fellow preacher told him it must be close to 6,000.[17]

Both men founded churches, Warder in Millersburg, Carlisle, Pleasant Spring (Nicholas County), Bethel (Fleming County), and Sardis (Mason County); Green in Paris, Maysville, Flemingsburg, Mt. Sterling (Montgomery County), and Sharpsburg (Bath County).[18]

Warder preached in May's Lick only every other Sunday, spending the rest of his time at other churches in the area. This did not sit well with his home congregation, which "often expressed a desire for a larger portion than half his time, which was steadily and perseveringly refused." Nevertheless, they kept him on for twenty-two years. Green's time, as we have seen, was divided in a similar way, except that instead of spending his off Sunday at various other churches, he spent it at only one.

Green would eventually hear from both of his congregations the same complaint Warder heard for giving church members only half his time. Like Warder, he would refuse to yield.[19]

Green grew to adulthood in his years with Warder, undergoing his conversion experience and becoming increasingly convinced of a preacherly calling. He married Susan Young, likewise enslaved, in 1835; in their forty-five years together, they would experience much joy and sorrow.

2

I Desired to Read the Word of God

The Reverend Walter Warder died on April 6, 1836. But the situation for Green, still the property of Warder's widow, the former Elizabeth Dobyns, did not change until 1838, when her son John Porter Dobyns, twenty-three and recently married, decided to give up his Flemingsburg dry-goods business and try his luck in up-and-coming Maysville as a partner in Leach and Dobyns, merchants in grain and flour. Elisha was to go with him, and he arrived in the river town in February 1838, leaving his wife and children in May's Lick, where they were the property of Elizabeth Sisson.[1]

Maysville, named after landowner John May—while May's Lick was named for his brother William—had begun as a frontier settlement, incorporating as a town in 1787. It was originally called Limestone, after the creek that flows into the Ohio, and for many years was known by both names. Among its early citizens was Daniel Boone, who with his brother Jacob ran a tavern there from 1785 to 1789. Early growth was slow due to Indian attacks that persisted until the Treaty of Greenville in August 1795. It was a gateway for pioneers, who came down the Ohio in flatboats, of which thirty a day were arriving in 1789. But they didn't linger, preferring the relative safety of Washington, Kentucky, four miles inland and chosen as county seat in 1788. In 1800, Washington had a population four times greater than Maysville's 137. F. A.

View of Maysville from Germantown Road, from Lewis Collins, *Historical Sketches of Kentucky* (Maysville, KY, 1847) (Library of Congress)

Michaux observed in 1802 that one would have imagined Maysville, having been in existence for fifteen years, to have grown more than it had; Washington was much larger, with about two hundred houses and a brisk trade in corn shipped to New Orleans. Fortescue Cuming observed in 1807 that although Maysville was the greatest shipping port on the Ohio, that was all it had going for it, "not being a place of much business itself." Because so many travelers passed through, Maysville looked lively and bustling, "which might induce a stranger to think it a place of more consequence in itself than it really is." It was too hemmed in by the hills to allow further growth.[2]

But around 1817 Maysville began to look more prosperous. In that year, the Englishman John Palmer noted "the appearance of increase and progress." There were brick houses, stores, and taverns. In 1818, James Flint found there a ropewalk, a glass factory, stores, taverns, and a bank, whereas Washington was "not thriving." In September 1819, another Englishman, Adlard Welby, thought Maysville was "fast increasing in size and importance." There were many brick buildings and factories with machinery. The hills that Fortescue Cuming had thought would prevent growth gave Welby the opposite impression, offering building sites "that few places can surpass," with beautiful views looking down upon the river. In contrast, in Washington Welby found "little or no good land to sell."[3]

In the 1830s, the river town made rapid progress. In May 1830, more than 150 steamboats docked there, shipping commercial goods to and receiving goods from Pittsburgh, Cincinnati, Louisville, and ultimately New Orleans. In 1836, Samuel Cummings's *Western Pilot* counted 250 houses and a population exceeding 2,000. As the depot of merchandise arriving from Philadelphia and other eastern cities, Maysville had become "a very thriving, active town." Cincinnati was sixty-two miles downstream, and a turnpike connecting Maysville to Lexington, sixty-four miles south, was completed in 1835. It was a considerable improvement over the prior road, whose mud and mire in 1829 had obliged Henry Clay to spend four days getting from Lexington to Maysville.[4]

John Porter Dobyns left Flemingsburg because that small country town lacked "that excitement which his mind required," nor did it afford sufficient opportunity for his abilities. So he settled in Maysville, "advantageously situated on the Ohio River, one of the great thoroughfares of western trade," and the chief place of business for the northeastern part of the state. The surrounding countryside produced abundant crops and livestock, and channeling them to market would become his life's work.[5]

The weather was exceptionally cold when Elisha Green arrived in Maysville in February 1838, so much so that the Ohio River froze over. A young slave woman near Dover, in western Mason County, had learned that her master was planning to sell his slaves, including her two-year-old child. Having heard that the Reverend John Rankin in Ripley, Ohio, took in fugitives and forwarded them safely north, she decided to seize her chance. With the infant wrapped in a wool blanket, she ventured out onto the ice. It was breaking up, though, and she had to leap from floe to floe, but she got across and was later immortalized as Eliza Harris in Harriet Beecher Stowe's *Uncle Tom's Cabin*.[6]

That the underground railroad just over the river from Mason County was in full operation was made particularly clear in November 1838 at the trial of John B. Mahan of Sardinia, Ohio. He was charged with aiding in the escape of John, a slave belonging to William Greathouse. It may be remembered that Greathouse was present when ten-year-old Elisha Green stood on the auction block in July 1828, purchasing two other slaves, Moses and Nancy, from the Charles Dobyns estate. Thomas Y. Payne, who would later remark to Green that it was a shame for a slave coffle to be paraded through town on a Sunday morning, assisted in the prosecution of Mahan. After hearing six days of testimony and legal debate citing precedent going back to the Magna Carta, the judge directed the jury to find Mahan innocent if it could not be proved that he had committed the crime in Mason County. The state could not prove that, for he had not set foot in the county in twenty years; all the prosecution could argue was that he was a link in an extensive "chain" of agents reaching from Kentucky to Canada. After a few minutes' deliberation, the jury found Mahan innocent, and the courthouse was stunned into silence for several minutes. But he was not set free, for Greathouse was at the same time suing him for the value of his slave, so he had to stay in the Washington, Kentucky, jail for weeks to come and in fact lost that suit. He died in December 1844, a broken man. His widow would make sure that his grave bore the inscription "A Victim of the Slave Power."[7]

Now working for John Porter Dobyns, Elisha took full advantage of his opportunities, learning arithmetic from having to weigh salt, sugar, and hemp. "As I thought that I had been called to preach I desired to read the word of God. I spent all the time that I could spare from my work at night and the time I had during the day at reading. I kept my book in the third story. In the summer season, when work was slack, I would go up there endeavoring to study and read the Bible." He does not say when he learned to read, but it is probable that Walter Warder gave him some instruction because as a Baptist minister he would have agreed with Elisha on the importance of reading the Bible. Green elsewhere recollects, though, that slave owners generally did not want their slaves to acquire that skill: "I came up in an age . . . when books in a black man's hand were equal to a case of murder." He sometimes got in trouble for spending so much time on the third floor: "Being frequently called from my studies, they not knowing what I was doing, my boss would say to me, 'What in the h—l are you doing up there?' Well, I went on after this for some years, having been much benefited."[8]

To visit his family, he would take the stagecoach to May's Lick on Saturdays, but because it did not run on Sunday, he had to walk the thirteen miles back. He always carried a pair of saddle pockets in which he brought items for his wife and children. Several times when returning on foot, he was stopped in Washington as a suspected runaway because he was headed toward Maysville, where many fugitives crossed the river to freedom. A slave trader asked him where he was going. Green said he had just come from visiting his wife. He asked who she belonged to; he told him. Then the trader "said he had a great mind to put me in jail." Green replied that that was fine with him because he was so tired from walking he needed a rest and would be glad to sleep in the Washington jail while word was sent to Dobyns.[9]

Unfortunately, Elizabeth Sisson took a dislike to Green's wife and decided to sell her south. Dobyns intervened, buying Susan and her children and thus reuniting the Green family. But he could barely afford it, so he sold them to a Maysville friend, who lived nearby. Green no longer had to travel so far to see his family.[10]

Green recalls that he had not been in Maysville long before he began to hold prayer meetings at the house of "old sister Jennie Marshall, on Short street." One night he was going home when he was stopped by the night watch, which had the power to whip any black person out after 9:00 p.m. It was slightly past that hour. He recognized the captain of the watch, a man named Stephen Lee. "I told them that I knew them and would not run, because they would think that I was guilty of some act. With this explanation they let me go with threatenings of what they would do should they catch me again."[11]

The threats were real, and they came not just from the night watch. On September 8, 1841, a Maysville mob destroyed a black church and school, angered because the church was open at night. The mayor had in fact already ordered that it be open only during the day.[12]

That incident may have been inspired by events in Cincinnati a few days earlier. A black man had allegedly stabbed a white man; the next night, seven to eight hundred whites gathered to attack a black residence. The inhabitants fought back with gunfire, killing one attacker and wounding another. The whites found a cannon and fired it three times into the house. Several more were killed on both sides, and soldiers were called in to quell the disturbance.[13]

Whites imagined underground railroad conductors behind every bush. Earlier that summer, a visiting geologist from New York was nearly lynched because some Maysville citizens mistook him for an abolitionist. His perambulations on the hill above the town as he collected fossils and rocks with his black assistant excited their suspicion—all the more so because they found him there after dark: he had gone back after supper to pick up his specimens in the various locations where he had left them that afternoon. He led his pursuers back to his hotel, where they were finally talked out of lynching him by the bartender, who vouched for his character.[14]

As Green's prayer meetings continued, their numbers grew, and his followers had to rent a larger place. When that one in turn became too small, they took out a five-year lease on a house next to the newly built white Baptist church on Market Street. In addition to his duties at Dobyns's commission house, Green began a sixteen-year tenure as sexton of that Baptist church, which held its first service in its new building on November 17, 1839. "I was not only sexton of the church, but a worshiper in there among the whites," and "seeing different displays and other movements in church, hearing various men preach, I, of course, was somewhat struck with the idea of doing something for God." Eventually some of the white Baptists saw that he had a gift for preaching, and in 1845 they asked Dobyns's permission, which he gave, for them to give Green a preaching license. It granted "full liberty and permission from this day to exercise his gifts in the public before the colored population of this city or any others before whom in the providence of God he may be cast." Bethel Baptist Church, as the congregation that began in the house next to the white Baptist church came to be named, dates its origin from Green's pastorate.[15]

About this time, the white Baptist church began to be rocked by doctrinal differences. Green's former master John L. Kirk was one of the troublemakers, as he had previously been in the May's Lick church, objecting in both instances to the pastor's allegedly Campbellite tendencies. As a result, the Maysville church was without a pastor between 1845 and 1847, a state of affairs that correlates with Green's statement that "at this time, the Baptists had no regular preacher," and he consequently started attending the Presbyterian church.[16]

While there, he heard the Reverend Robert Caldwell Grundy announce his intention to open the Presbyterian church once a month for the purpose of preaching to Maysville's black community and wanted each white church to do the same. Green feared that this would prevent his own church from meeting. Grundy wanted to control what black congregants heard and especially to keep them from hearing unapproved preachers. "For who knows," Grundy asked, "what they are preaching into them?" Green was outraged. With two of his friends, he heard this from the gallery of the Presbyterian church, the seats reserved for blacks. As they all were coming out of church, Green said to his friends, "We ought not to stand such expressions as Mr. Grundy made this morning. We should meet and write him a letter and let him know that what he said is not true." His two friends at first said they would join him but then backed out. "I then told them that I would write to him, if I lost all my reputation afterward." He asked a fellow employee of John P. Dobyns, young J. M. Stockton (1827–1889), who "did all my writing," to do so on this occasion as well. Stockton had come to work at Dobyns's when he was just a boy and had long known and admired Green. He was at first reluctant to write the letter to Grundy for fear his handwriting would be recognized, but when Green told him that he, Green, would personally hand the letter to Grundy and say that it came from him, Stockton consented.[17]

Green found Grundy at the courthouse and told him he had a letter and wanted him to read it and then give him an answer. Grundy took it, but no answer came; however, Grundy gave up his project and told Green afterward that he hadn't realized the blacks had their own church. Green sums up with a note of triumph: "So this was the last of the white churches being opened in which to preach to the colored people."[18]

In Grundy's defense, it should be noted that on September 30, 1852, he was in a tailor shop on Front Street in Maysville when he overheard Colonel John Reid say he hoped that if the abolitionists Cassius Clay and George W. Julian were allowed to speak at the Mason County Courthouse, the county judge would catch the cholera. The judge in question was Lewis Collins, a pillar of the Presbyterian church Grundy pastored. Clay had made a speech in Richmond, Kentucky, on September 6 in support of Julian, who was running for president on the Free Soil ticket. After hearing what Reid said, Grundy told Reid that if he were a man, he would tell that to the judge's face, and added that his language was "illiberal, ungentlemanly and puppy-like." Reid immediately struck Grundy just below the ear, causing him to fall to the stone pavement, break his nose, and lose consciousness. He would bear the scars of the encounter for life. Grundy took a pastorate in Memphis in

Maysville Presbyterian Church and Mason County Courthouse, 2020 (Photograph by Elizabeth Runyon)

1857, and when the Civil War broke out, he was the only avowed Unionist pastor in the city. His congregation opposed him for that reason, and the church hierarchy removed him from the pulpit. When Ulysses S. Grant chased the Confederate forces out of the city in 1862, the Union army occupied the church. A church elder called on Grant to ask for the keys back, but he replied, "It will be at your service when you recall Dr. Grundy to the pulpit."[19]

While the Maysville Baptists were splitting for doctrinal reasons, the town's Methodists were doing so over slavery, as were their fellow congregants on a national scale. Baptists generally were undergoing the same scission at the same time, with the difference that Baptist churches were so independent of each other that there was no national Baptist hierarchy, but the Methodist Episcopal Church was, as its title denotes, governed by a higher authority, namely bishops. For the Maysville Methodists, the bone of contention was whether the pro- or antislavery camp would get to own the building. John Wesley (1703–1791), the original Methodist, had been unequivocally opposed to slavery, and for a while Methodists in America were as well. But little by little the church gave in to the demands of the slave owners in their midst and took the topic off the table. Things came to a head at the General Conference in New York in 1844 when a motion was passed calling on Bishop James O. Andrew of Georgia, who owned slaves, to either free them or desist from his episcopal duties. Andrew and his fellow southern Methodists falsely claimed that he owned only two, when in fact he owned at least fourteen. The two he admitted to, he claimed, had been forced upon him, one from his late wife's estate and the other by an unnamed wealthy woman from Augusta, Georgia, who at her death awarded him a young mulatto girl named Kitty in the hope that he would raise, educate, and set her free when she turned nineteen on condition she immigrate to Liberia. According to the story put forward by Andrew and his friend Augustus Baldwin Longstreet, Kitty refused to go to Liberia and instead remained Andrew's slave under his assurance that she would be treated as if she were free. She would live in a little house next to the Andrew residence in Oxford, Georgia.

As Mark Auslander has discovered, however, although the white citizens of Oxford today celebrate "Miss Kitty" for loyalty to her master, African Americans in that town tell a quite different story: that she was the bishop's lover and that her nearby house was convenient for his nocturnal visits. As a descendant of another of Andrew's slaves put it, "My grandmother told me, we were never angry with Miss Kitty. We just felt sorry for her, being his mistress as she was. She didn't have any say in all that, nobody did back then." If this is true, then the Southern Methodists, who took the demand that Andrew give up being a bishop as the casus belli that provoked them to form their own church, unwittingly based their institutional origin in an illicit affair between a white man and a mulatto woman. Andrew's accomplice Longstreet, a journalist, lawyer, Southern Methodist preacher, and celebrated apologist for slavery, is remembered today as a significant southern humorist, the author of *Georgia Scenes* (1850). Just before the New York Conference that would take up the case of the slave-owning bishop, with lawyerly skill he concealed Andrew's ownership of fourteen slaves by a deed conveying them to himself and then to Andrew's second wife. Longstreet may have invented the story of Kitty's origins, as Auslander speculates, so that no one would know that the mysterious woman who bequeathed Kitty to Andrew was actually Longstreet's mother and that he, Longstreet, was Kitty's father.[20]

The "Plan of Separation" adopted by the General Conference of the Methodist Episcopal Church in 1844 stipulated that if the northern and southern Methodist churches were to divide, the Mason–Dixon line separating slave from free states would prevail, although congregations on the border could vote to join either group. The schism became official when southerners met in Louisville in May 1845 to formally establish the Methodist Episcopal Church, South.

In the immediate aftermath of the events of 1844 and 1845, the battle between northern and southern Methodists raged especially keenly in the border states of Maryland, Kentucky, and Missouri. In Maryland, a pastor in Salem was dragged out of the pulpit by his coat and hair, and one in Guilford was in the middle of his sermon when a mob began shooting and throwing stones at the church. The preacher was forced from his pulpit and threatened with being ducked in a nearby pond if he returned. In Parkersburg, (West) Virginia, a preacher sent by the Ohio Conference arrived to find a mob blocking his way and a preacher from the South occupying the pulpit. He waited until the latter had finished his sermon, then announced that he would speak there at three that afternoon. The church building was locked against him, but his supporters let him in through a side door and filled the church to hear his address. Southerners showed up to object, making noise in the basement to interrupt the services going on overhead.[21]

The Maysville Methodist Church case has the distinction of being the first instance of northern and southern branches of a church fighting over who owned the building; many more would follow. After the General Conference of 1844 but prior to the Louisville meeting in 1845 that established the Methodist Episcopal Church, South, only two members of the Maysville congregation wanted to go south. John Armstrong (1779–1851), who had been instrumental in founding the Maysville church decades earlier, was among those who wanted the church to remain as it was. As a youth in Ireland, he had heard John Wesley preach; when he came to Maysville in 1798, he was the only Methodist there. In 1800, he built the town's first brick house and invited circuit riders to preach in his kitchen. In 1812, he built the church now the object of dispute. Pastor G. C. Light told Armstrong before the Louisville meeting that he had been opposed to joining the southern branch, but after attending it, he was all in favor; the same was true of the district's presiding elder. Of the approximately 260 members of the Maysville church entitled to vote, 139 had signed a statement affirming their desire to remain with the Methodist Episcopal Church, as the northern wing was styled. Unfortunately, they thought that meant they did not have to show up when a vote was taken on August 31, 1845. As a consequence, the vote was 109 to 97 to affiliate with the southern church. Part of what swayed those in favor of the southern church, in addition to the urging by their pastor and presiding elder, may have been the unfair way the question was put: "Do you prefer an abolitionist preacher from Ohio to one of your own kind from Kentucky?"[22]

The preacher whom Armstrong invited to address the church soon after the vote was indeed antislavery. Dr. Joseph Tomlinson was the president of Augusta College, located in the little village of that name nineteen miles west of Maysville. The Augusta church had successfully requested the Ohio Conference to allow them to join it, and Armstrong had hoped the Maysville church would follow their example. A notice was placed in the newspaper announcing that Tomlinson would preach the following Sunday. But Armstrong and his supporters were shocked to discover the same issue of the newspaper announcing that a Southern Methodist agent named Grubs was to preach there the same day. Armstrong's followers asked the opposing faction to allow one of the preachers to have the morning and the other the afternoon but were refused. Armstrong consulted an attorney, who recommended he lock up the church so that neither could preach. The southern supporters broke into the church and gave Grubs the pulpit; Armstrong sued. A local judge ruled that the two groups should meet on alternate Sundays. The southern faction rejected this solution and appealed to the state supreme court, which ruled in that faction's favor on July 27, 1847. Frustrated in his attempt to save the Methodist church from the slaveholders' grasp, John Armstrong donated a lot on Third Street for a new church to be built. It was dedicated in 1847; eleven years later Green would make his home in a tiny cottage behind the church and live there the rest of his life.[23]

3

More Than One Path to Freedom

Green was now the sexton at the white Baptist church, the pastor of his own congregation, and a frequent preacher at slave funerals, his eloquence often drawing white listeners. At Dobyns's commission house, he found ways to make money. He cleaned five kegs of nails that had fallen into the river as they were being offloaded from a boat and earned a dollar a keg. He devised traps baited with hemp seed and dried beef to solve a rat problem, earning twenty-five cents for every dozen caught. When Dobyns bought up a lot of bacon, so much that it was stacked six feet high and leaking grease onto the floor, Green was tasked every morning with changing the old sawdust that was there to soak up the grease and putting down new. It occurred to him that it would be profitable to save the grease, and he invented a way to do it, filling an empty nail keg with greasy sawdust and placing it upside-down over a kettle. This produced a barrel of grease that he sold to a soap maker for $37, affording him the luxury of ordering from a local silversmith the dozen silver spoons he had been dreaming of owning. He liked being able to say that "the way I obtained them I scraped them up off the floor."[1]

He was not the only Kentucky slave to create an income on the side. According to Marion B. Lucas, "Hired slave laborers frequently worked as janitors and handymen for businesses, stores, city governments, and white churches," as Green did for the white Baptist church.

"In numerous factories, skilled hired slave laborers worked with little supervision, lived on the premises in barracks, and ate their meals at a common table." Green enjoyed similar freedom from supervision, stealing away to read the Bible on an upper floor where he also slept. But unlike the factories Lucas describes, Dobyns's commission house may not have had many other slaves working there.[2]

That Green was eager to generate income is evident not just from these efforts but also from a remark he made when called to testify in court in June 1850. A slave named Spriggins had a disagreement with one named Burl. "Spriggins took up a small stove griddle and struck Burl on the head," and Burl died. Spriggins had been hired out to the Poyntzes, who did not want to lose him to the hangman. So they called in Green as a character witness. He said of Spriggins "that when I first came to Maysville he was the first to put me in a way of making money"—indicating that as early as 1838 the twenty-year-old Green was looking to earn extra cash. Of Burl, he testified that he did not know much about him except his fondness for whiskey, that "I never cared to know a man's bad traits except in cases of illustration, and that I loved no man better than I ought to." The jury found Spriggins guilty.[3]

As Green was prospering, so too was Dobyns. By 1844, he had abandoned his partner and set out on his own; that year an advertisement for "John P. Dobyns, Wholesale Grocer, Produce & Commission Merchant, Market Street," appeared in a contemporary business directory. The *Maysville Eagle* of June 2, 1845, reported that his commission house shipped 938 bales of hemp on two river steamers. He had at least one other source of income as agent for the Franklin Insurance Company of Louisville. In 1844, a satisfied customer wrote to the *Maysville Eagle* praising the promptness with which Dobyns settled a claim arising from the loss of $5,000 of goods on a ship from Pittsburgh that sank on its way to Maysville. The same fate befell one of Dobyns's own shipments in 1849 when a flat boat with 620 bales of hemp on its way to a factory in New Albany, Indiana, sank at the Maysville wharf. It presumably was insured.[4]

Margaret Walsh writes that in the 1840s Dobyns "built up an extensive knowledge of trade in northeastern Kentucky and acquired commercial connections and property in the vicinity." He set up a pork-packing plant in 1846. In 1850, he was named director of the Maysville

John Porter Dobyns, from John Livingston, *Biographical Sketches of Distinguished Americans, Now Living* (New York, 1853) (HathiTrust Digital Library)

branch of the Farmers' Bank. In 1852, he joined the board of directors of the planned Maysville and Big Sandy Railroad, which was intended to connect the town with Virginia (now West Virginia) and thereby the Atlantic coast with the Mississippi River. The project's popularity in 1852 was a major change from the widespread opposition in 1839 to a similar railroad for fear it would take away the income the town derived as a river port: "the Merchants, draymen, etc. of Maysville think it an imprudent interference with the designs of Providence to make a Rail Road to the Atlantic, whilst the Ohio River flows by that city," the *Lexington Observer and Reporter* noted that year.[5]

Maysville was thriving along with Dobyns. The population had grown to 5,000 by 1848; there were two newspapers, a bank, the world's largest hemp market, five ropewalks, five factories for tin ware, two for cotton, twelve for plows, three for tobacco, one for bagging, another for carding wool, a tannery, a flour mill, two saw mills, and fourteen houses in the wholesale grocery business. The following year brought a factory making linen from hemp.[6]

Dobyns was doing so well that in 1848 he built an imposing brick mansion of octagonal shape just outside Maysville, comprising 5,000 square feet and 14-foot ceilings, and it is still there today. He named it "Glen Alice" in honor of his daughter. There were marble mantels in the drawing room and the library as well as dazzling chandeliers. He had to order special furniture from New York to fit the odd angles of the house's corners. The kitchen and slave quarters were located in a two-story, six-room brick building behind the house.[7]

Green apparently lived in the slave quarters at Glen Alice instead of at the commission house for a period in 1851 or 1852, for he says that Dobyns's daughter Alice was eight or nine when she taught him to read, and she was born in 1843. While he was laid up with rheumatism, unable to work, Alice "would come up into my room to see me every evening when she had come from school." Since she lived at Glen Alice, at some distance from downtown Maysville, he, too, must have been at Glen Alice. "Uncle Elisha, you must learn to write," she said one day. He could read, having already read the Bible twice through, but could not yet set pen to paper. Normally, owners did not want their slaves to learn to write for fear they would forge passes and escape to the North, but Dobyns may not have objected. About this time, Dobyns was describing himself as having "become a large slaveholder by the purchase of slaves who, in working for him, had become so much attached to him as to beg him to buy them." Alice was a good teacher, for within a month Elisha was able to write a letter to a brother who lived in Missouri. A measure of his earning power was that he bought her a ten-dollar gold pencil to express his gratitude, asking her father's permission first.[8]

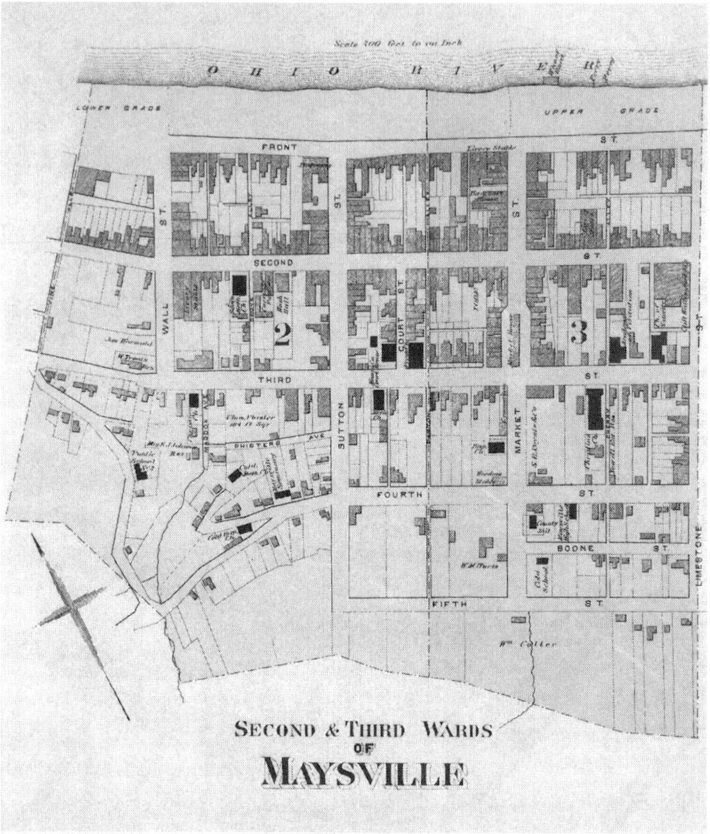

Map of Maysville, from *An Illustrated Atlas of Mason County* (1876). John P. Dobyns's Commission House was on Market Street between Front and Second. Green held prayer meetings at a house on Short Street, not on this map but located one block west of Wall Street; he was arrested by the night watch one evening when returning home from there. He was sexton from 1839 to 1855 for the white Baptist church on Market between Third and Fourth; a committee from that congregation granted him his preaching license in 1845. Beginning in 1858 he rented and in 1867 completed the purchase of the southernmost of the three small houses behind the Methodist church on the alley between Third and Fourth. In 1854, Bethel Baptist was meeting in a rented house on the Fourth Street site where they would later build their own structure. Indicated here as "Col. Bap. Ch.," it was a short walk going west on Fourth from Green's house. He performed baptisms in the Ohio River at the foot of Wall Street. George T. Gould was pastor of the Southern Methodist church on Second between Wall and Sutton for a year beginning in September 1871. (Library of Congress)

Despite Green's relatively comfortable circumstances, his ability to increase his savings, and his growing career as a preacher, he was doubtless aware of slave owners' increasing concern about escaping slaves. A Centre College student named Patrick Doyle had led an armed group of perhaps seventy-five fugitives from Lexington and Bourbon County in a bid for freedom in August 1848; most made it only as far as Bracken County. A more permanent fixture was the underground railroad station in Ripley, Ohio, where John Rankin and former slave John Parker were assisting thousands in their journey north. Parker ventured across the Ohio River into Kentucky almost nightly, meeting fugitives and taking them back over the river to Ohio. While still a slave in Mason County, Arnold Gragston rowed fugitives over to Ripley three or four times a month from 1859 to 1863.[9]

The Fugitive Slave Act of 1850 made it harder for Green to cross the river, even on legitimate business. When a member of his congregation died in Ripley and he wanted to attend the funeral, he procured a pass, but the ferry captain refused to take him because of the new law. Before he could board, he had to get a Maysville citizen to pledge to cover the cost (that is, Elisha's value as a slave) should he escape. As he told the captain, "I have had a dozen chances to run off. I do not want freedom in that way."[10]

There was another way, but that was beyond his control. His owner could simply have emancipated him, as Walter Warder did Edward G. Pines in 1835. Warder could not have done the same for Elisha, as it was his wife who owned him. Silas Duvall, who had owned Elisha at one time, freed his brother Marshall in 1837. Duvall's brother-in-law Thomas Parry freed Elisha's brother Alvin in 1846. Other members of the Dobyns family emancipated slaves: Charles Dobyns liberated a slave named Edmund in 1818, the probable year of Elisha's birth; Edward Dobyns emancipated a slave named Lucy in 1827; Enoch Dobyns freed John Tolliver in 1831; Berry Dobyns emancipated William Taliaferro in 1832. The Dobynses were not alone in this regard; in scouring the Mason County Court House records, Caroline Miller found at least 120 other emancipators.[11]

Escaping slaves were making life more difficult for free blacks. A letter to the editor of the *Maysville Eagle* in the spring of 1852 told slaveholders that free blacks are "an enemy to your interest, which if not abolished, must ultimately destroy the institution of slavery." Another letter to the editor later in the year warmly endorsed a mass meeting of slaveholders to be held in November in Minerva in western Mason County, complaining of the loss of seventy bondsmen in two months from Mason, Bracken, Pendleton, and Boone Counties. A number of free blacks were arrested in Mason County for enticing or enabling slaves to escape: Benjamin Gooch in May 1834, James Blackburn in August 1849, John Davis in November 1850, George Williams in August 1856, Charles (no last name given) in April 1857, and Benjamin Stokes in October 1858.[12]

A correspondent in Dover, across from Ripley, wrote to the *Anti-Slavery Bugle* on March 24, 1852, to report that the peace of a Sunday morning in the village had been disturbed by a someone shooting a gun. The shot was a call for recruits to join in crossing the river to hunt for a group of slaves who had escaped the night before. A man who had purchased his freedom a few years earlier had returned to get his wife and children. The fugitives stole a skiff in the dead of night and crossed to the other side. A dozen ruffians joined in the search, tracking the fugitives' footsteps in the snow and hoping for a share of the $800 reward. But by the time the hunters reached Ohio, the snow had melted, and although they searched two houses, the fugitives got clean away. The *Ripley Bee* complained about the home invasions by the hunters; the *Maysville Eagle* replied that the searchers were known for their gentlemanly behavior and if the citizens of Ripley wished to prevent future occurrences, they should "quit concealing property which belongs to other people."[13]

But stealing can work both ways. Isaac Hensley, who had been granted his freedom in 1832 and was living peaceably with his wife and children in Sardinia, Ohio, had his home broken into in September 1853 by a party of kidnappers. They knocked his wife unconscious, tied up Hensley and his four children, and loaded them all into a wagon covered with quilts. It was the underground railroad in reverse in that freedom conductors customarily hid their passengers beneath quilts, too. The kidnappers drove the wagon to the river, put the Hensley family in a boat, and rowed them to the opposite shore. They took them to James McMillen's private slave jail on West Second Street in Maysville. McMillen had advertised his "safe and commodious Jail . . . for the reception and custody of Negroes" at a daily charge of twenty-five cents per head. Hensley's Sardinia neighbors contacted a Ripley lawyer, who telegraphed Maysville attorney William H. Wadsworth, to whom McMillen confirmed he had the prisoners. He promised to keep them in safety and not to deliver them to anyone, including those who had brought them, until the affair could be cleared up. The Ripley lawyer arrived with Hensley's certificate of freedom, and Hensley and his children were quickly released. This time the *Maysville Eagle* condemned the Kentuckians: "There is no apology for this outrage—it is as bad as . . . slave rescues; it is on a par with the lawless acts of the Abolition banditti, and equally with such acts deserves the penitentiary."[14]

4

I Belong to Mr. Green

Elisha Green began preaching in Flemingsburg, Kentucky, eighteen miles from Maysville, in 1853 but could do so only in the daytime because he had to be home by nightfall. There was no Baptist church for blacks in that town, so he held services in the Methodist one. But then the Methodists became alarmed at the growth in the number of Green's Baptists, and he had to seek refuge with the Presbyterians and later with the Christian Church. At last, the white Baptists in Flemingsburg saw that he was a force for good and decided to let him use their church on a regular basis. He preached there for two years before being called in 1855 to the church in Paris. In the meantime, he often preached elsewhere in Fleming County and in neighboring Bracken and Lewis Counties. All this time, he was also preaching on at least alternate Sundays at his church in Maysville.

On December 13, 1853, Green purchased the freedom of his sister Harriet Lee, the slave of John Triplett, who had emigrated from Mason County, Kentucky, to Sedalia, Missouri. As Green later complained, "With $600 in my pocket I could not buy my own sister unless the bill of sale was made out in our mother's name. She herself [his mother] was compelled to own slaves to get my sister's freedom." His mother therefore by then must have been a free woman, for only free blacks could buy slaves and on condition the slaves were members of the buyer's own family. The bill of sale indeed states that Harriet was sold to her mother, Catherine Green, for $600; a copy was delivered to Elisha Green on January 31,

1854. A John Triplett is listed in the 1850 census as a Mason County resident, with thirteen slaves. Elisha, of course, could not have traveled to Missouri to effect the sale, nor could his mother. John R. Clarke, a Mason County lawyer, signed his name to the contract and may have been the go-between to effect the sale. Triplett had married Virginia Clarke in 1827, and so John R. Clarke may have been a relation as well. In any case, it is remarkable that Green could have amassed $600 to buy his sister.[1]

Despite so much preaching in Flemingsburg and other communities, Green was still pastor of the Maysville African Baptist Church (later called Bethel), and on February 15, 1855, he and the other trustees purchased from Daniel Spalding for $500 a lot on Fourth Street for the church's permanent home. Spalding had previously rented them a building on that site; the church, however, owned the pews and other furniture. The frame building had been damaged in a powder-magazine explosion that had wreaked havoc on many structures in that part of town on August 12, 1854.[2]

By 1855, Green had more freedom of movement, no longer having to come home at night. He spent three weeks in Louisville and four nights in Georgetown, preceded by a stay in Lexington. He was not the only slave preacher to enjoy such liberty; J. Winston Coleman cites the case of one in Lexington whose owner in 1856 allowed him to remain in Louisville for as much as three weeks.[3]

On one occasion while in Georgetown, Green had read the scripture, sung a hymn, and was about to start his sermon when a white man walked down the aisle brandishing a stick that he pounded on the floor and asked if there were any other white men present. There were not. He then told Green to leave the pulpit, which Green did. The stricture against blacks getting together on their own was still rigorously obeyed in Kentucky. "During the days of slavery," Green says, "I was frequently invited by the white folks to preach the funerals of their dead slaves. But the law would not suffer it without some white person present. I frequently had as many whites in my audience as colored." The next morning, the pastor of the white Baptist church came to call, asking Green not to go home yet but to stay and preach as long as he liked. He preached four more days.[4]

He then returned to Lexington to buy a train ticket for Paris, where he had been asked to preach. The ticket agent refused to sell him one, saying he did not know Green. He asked Green if any one there at the station knew him "and could be responsible to him for my purchasing a ticket." In fact, a prominent Maysville citizen known to Green was nearby, a judge, but the agent did not know him either. Green's friend Bishop Dupee told him to hop on the train once it started; he could get halfway to Paris before the conductor put him off and could walk the rest of the way. Green did this, and indeed halfway to Paris the conductor asked for his ticket. Green admitted he had none and asked how much it was. "Eight-five cents," said the conductor but continued his way down the car and didn't return to sell Green the ticket. Two years later Green happened to see the conductor again and told him he had been waiting since 1855 to ask why the conductor hadn't thrown him off the train. "He told me that my face satisfied him."[5]

The Paris invitation turned into a permanent position. His tenure there began in July 1855, while he was still pastoring the Maysville church on alternate Sundays. But there was an obstacle to overcome: the white Baptists in Paris wanted total control, so much so that, as Green put it, "the colored church was a slave to the white." Many of the whites, Green recalled, did not think him capable of doing more than preach, such as to carry out pastoral and administrative duties. But they did want him to preach, and Green bent them to his will. He told the white church that rather than submit to their opinions, he would take the next stagecoach back to Maysville. "They seeing in my actions that I possessed some quality of manhood, and that if I could not rule I would not be ruled, yielded to my purpose," allowing him to admit members on his own and to administer church discipline. The black Baptists in Paris first held services in a stable, standing beneath umbrellas when it rained. The stable was located behind what became the present brick structure at 128 West Eighth Street, which was erected in 1858.[6]

In July 1855, the same month Green started the Paris church, John P. Dobyns, having amassed enough money to retire from the commission house business, did so, while maintaining positions with the Farmers' Bank and the Maysville and Big Sandy Railroad. An indication of his wealth and perhaps of a desire to pursue new interests was his purchase in March 1853 of the most famous horse in Kentucky. Grey Eagle, though his racing days were past, could still win prizes as a show horse. Dobyns showed him off at agricultural fairs, attracting thousands of

First Baptist Church in Paris, KY, 2020 (Photograph by Elizabeth Runyon)

spectators, and put him out to stud on his Mason County farm, where he sired Traveler, the horse Robert E. Lee would ride in the Civil War. A measure of the esteem Dobyns enjoyed among Mason County farmers was the silver service they gave him and on which they had inscribed their gratitude for having "created for us a market."[7]

With the commission house now closed, Green's usefulness there ended, which may explain why he began to have greater freedom to be away from Maysville. But, like Dobyns, he had saved up his money, and on November 28, 1856, he bought his freedom for $500 from Elizabeth Dobyns Warder, who had evidently been his legal owner all the years he had worked for her son. "I, Elizabeth Warder," the document states, "do bargain and sell unto Catherine Green of Mason County and state aforesaid, Elisha Green, her son." In a speech to a Democratic group after the Civil War, Green said that he had not been able to buy himself but had to make out the bill of sale in his mother's name, as he had when he bought his sister Harriet's freedom in 1853. Elisha's mother, seventy-nine years old at the time he purchased his freedom, was living with his brother Marshall, who had been made a free man by Silas Duvall in 1837.[8]

Other Kentucky slaves were able to purchase their freedom—for example, John Carter and Henry Summerville of Louisville, Lewis Smith of Franklin County, and a man named Jim, who won $30,000 in a lottery and thereby liberated himself, his wife, and children. Slaves leased to manufacturers were able to rack up overtime, and some were able to save enough for this goal. Trimble County bondsman Isaac Griffin earned enough money working on flatboats to buy his freedom and that of his wife and one child.[9]

Until there was a railroad between Maysville and Paris, Green went to his second church by stagecoach. But he found it more difficult to do so after gaining his freedom. "Many freemen," Marion B. Lucas writes, "ran into problems on stagecoaches," and that was certainly the case for Green. Unlike trains with their conductors, coaches had no representative of authority to resolve difficulties between passengers. Green recounts an example:

> As I was not a slave I had some difficulty in traveling. Frequently I would be riding among slaves that were hand-cuffed going south. The "negro traders" and other persons would ask me:
>
> "Boy, where are you going?"
>
> I would tell them to Paris.
>
> "What for?" continued they.
>
> Said I: "To preach."
>
> "Does your master allow you to go from Maysville to Paris to preach?"
>
> "Yes, sir."
>
> "To whom do you belong?"
>
> "I belong to Mr. Green."
>
> "He must be a very good man."
>
> Said I: "He is, sir; a very good man."
>
> The explanation of my belonging to Mr. Green is this: That I had, previous to this, bought myself from my master. I was now my own master.[10]

His use of the auxiliary verb *would* in telling this story suggests he resorted more than once to this reply.

Stagecoach in Lexington, KY (J. Winston Coleman Jr. Photo Collection, Transylvania University Library)

Blue Licks Hotel, from Collins, *Historical Sketches of Kentucky* (1847) (Library of Congress)

The stagecoach stopped at the Arlington, a hugely profitable resort hotel at Blue Licks, and for fifty cents Green would buy his dinner. But on one occasion after dining among five hundred other guests, mostly southern planters, he was standing outside on the steps waiting for the stagecoach when he heard someone calling, "Boy! Boy! Come here. Did you eat your dinner?" He had to prove he had paid and did so by calling on the steward, who "handed Mr. Holiday the money which I had paid him. . . . He never charged me any more afterward. This was the result of being honest. He thought that I had slipped in there and eaten without having paid for it."[11]

On another occasion, after the bridge at Blue Licks burned, the stagecoach had to ford the Licking River. Green and the other passengers were then obliged to walk up a hill. A drunken passenger grabbed him by the collar, cursed, and demanded to know where he was going. Another passenger told him Green was a preacher and to leave him alone. Green did not say a word. The drunk, with his hand still on Green's collar, cursed again and said he would make him speak. Green then told him to take his hand off his collar. The drunk refused. "I then knocked him about twenty feet backward. This was shortly after I had bought myself. I will say that I was more of a slave after I bought myself than before. Before this I could go many places without interruption, but when I became a freeman I could not cross the Ohio river." Ferry captains would refuse to carry him for fear of running afoul of the Fugitive Slave Act. The Civil War, through the Union occupation of Kentucky, appears, however, to have made it easier for Green to travel, for he was able to take a riverboat to Cincinnati in 1864 to participate in a series of religious meetings and then continue to Louisville.[12]

Not every journey by stagecoach between his two churches was an unpleasant experience for Green, at least after the war was over. It was probably then that he traveled from Paris to Maysville with two Kentucky gentlemen who for some time had been discussing divine omniscience. One of them turned to Green and very politely asked him if he was a preacher. Green said he was, and the man asked permission to pose him a question: "When God made Adam and put him into the garden did he know that Adam would sin?" Green said yes. Then the man asked why God let him sin and then punished him. Green replied, "God never made Adam a slave, but a free agent." Green, in an aside to the reader, states that was the first time that thought had ever occurred to him.[13]

John Porter Dobyns was riding the crest of his business success in 1855 and 1856. But in the fall of 1857, the national financial panic brought him ruin. A Maysville banker recalled sixty years later that the Maysville and Big Sandy Railroad, in which Dobyns was deeply invested, as well as the Maysville and Lexington Railroad "were disastrous failures, leaving the whole community stranded. Property shrank to nearly nothing." Dobyns was even forced to sell his beloved Glen Alice, the beautiful octagon house.[14]

His downfall had consequences for Green, for Dobyns still owned his wife and three of his children, and they were now at risk of being sold. To prevent this, Green "was induced by the advice of many friends to become the purchaser of his wife and two of his children, at the price of $850." The two were Thomas and Catherine, but Dobyns, as we will see, held on to Green's son John. "His [Green's] means (although he and his wife labor faithfully and live economically) will not enable him to meet the payments as they become due, and he has been counseled to seek assistance. . . . We commend him to the kind consideration of the Christian public, and particularly to the members of the [white] Baptist Church." Dated November 1, 1858, this statement was signed by thirteen Maysville citizens, including the church's pastor and two particularly prominent figures, A. M. January (1797–1877) and Lewis Collins (1797–1870). January was a commission merchant, banker, and part owner of the January and Wood Cotton Mill; Collins was a Mason County judge from 1851 to 1854, a former editor of the *Maysville Eagle,* and the author of *Historical Sketches of Kentucky* (1847). The signers, Green comments, "were very generous, shown from the fact that when I told them I could not purchase my wife and children, they drew the money from the bank and said it was for me" and added, "'If you never pay it, we will never trouble your family.' I worked and made the money and paid it back."[15]

Green's son John was not among those he was able to purchase, though. "After Dobyns's misfortune," Green recalls, "he kept John for his own use, and failed to pay for him. Therefore he was sold to Roe Pearce. Pearce in turn sold him south." Had Dobyns not tried to evade the inevitable, perhaps John would have figured among those whom

Green's benefactors bought and then offered him, though John's value was likely so high that it would have considerably increased the cost to Green. Even if Green could not have afforded to buy him with the others, "the court gave me the liberty of selecting them homes" when his family members were put up for sale, and he might have been able to keep John in Maysville.[16]

That is precisely what Elisha tried to do when by chance he and his wife, having stopped for dinner at the Blue Licks hotel on their way to Paris in December 1858, were horrified to discover their son John, tied up and shivering coatless in the winter cold, being transported south, forced to ride outside the coach. "The sight of this act I thought would break the heart of my wife. When the stage drove up to the steps, the [hotel] proprietor came and opened the stage door. My wife was crying. He told her to hush. I said to him that that woman was my wife and that we had seen our son tied in ropes going south. Then said he: 'Old lady, get out.' It was my son that I saw tied, sold and taken from me."[17]

The stage driver, who, it turns out, had grown up in Maysville and had been John's playmate there, urged the slave traders to untie him and let him come inside the coach. He promised to take financial responsibility should John escape. Parents, son, and slave traders continued on to Paris, where John was lodged in the jail while Green sent a desperate telegram to Pearce's father in Maysville, begging him to keep John until he could find a home for him. But this request was refused, and the Pearces went ahead with the sale. Green later traced his son to a livery stable in Memphis, then to Texas, from where he may have been sent with other slaves to Cuba. After that point, Green had no idea what became of him.[18]

In November 1859, John Porter Dobyns mysteriously disappeared. He had gone to St. Louis, then one evening crossed the Mississippi with some acquaintances to East St. Louis, Illinois, to see them off on the train going east. Because it was too late for him to catch the ferry back across the Mississippi, he checked in to a hotel. At about 2:00 a.m., he fell—or more likely jumped—from his window thirty feet to the ground. He never recovered consciousness, dying a few days later in the Belleville County, Illinois, hospital. Documents in his pockets enabled the authorities to learn his name but not where he was from, so his family did not know what had happened to him. It was not until March 1860, when his widow began placing notices in newspapers around the country asking for information, that the Belleville authorities were able to inform her of her husband's death a few months earlier.[19]

On June 19, 1860, the census taker registered Elisha Green, forty-five, a "Baptist Clergyman" with an estate worth $150; his wife, Susan, forty-four; their son Thomas, eight, who had attended school in the past year; and their daughter, Catherine, six. They were living on Bugle Alley, between Third and Fourth Streets in Maysville, directly behind the Methodist Episcopal Church (the northern, not southern, one) and a short walk to Green's Bethel Baptist. Lewis Collins had begun renting the house to Green in late 1858 for $4 a month. Green would have bought it outright had he not been paying off the $850 he owed for the freedom of his wife, Thomas, and Catherine.[20]

5

The Interests of My People

With the Civil War came an increase in salary from the Paris church. When Green began to preach there in 1855, the church had paid him $8.50 per trip from Maysville, out of which he had to pay $6.50 for the stagecoach and $1 for meals; in other words, his expenses nearly equaled his income. "I preached on in this way until the war," when the church raised his remuneration to $29.15 a month. The war itself did not pose much of an obstacle to his fortnightly journeys from Maysville to Paris, though one might have thought the five-week Confederate occupation of central Kentucky in the fall of 1862 would have done so. Yet a Maysville newspaper reported that travel was uninterrupted and that the soldiers in gray were readily granting passes "to all classes of citizens to go where they please," perhaps even former slaves preaching at church services.[1]

That is all Green says about the war's impact on him, from which we may conclude that it did not affect him very much. He pastored his two churches as best he could, just as he had before the outbreak of hostilities, and both Maysville and Paris were for the most part spared the destruction others suffered, thanks to the large Union army presence. The Emancipation Proclamation of January 1, 1863, did not free any Kentucky slaves because the state was not in rebellion. Freedom for them did not come until the ratification of the Thirteenth Amendment on December 18, 1865. Kentucky did not ratify the amendment when it should have, on February 24, 1865, and in fact put off ratification for more than a century, until 1976. "Stubborn slaveholders persisted in believing that slavery would somehow survive, and slaves in Kentucky continued to be traded through most of 1865, even after the fall of the Confederacy."[2]

But General John M. Palmer, appointed the military governor of Kentucky by Abraham Lincoln, took measures on his own to end slavery there, issuing orders in May 1865 for Louisville and in July for the rest of the state that granted blacks the freedom to travel. Army officers issued "Palmer's passes" on demand. Other federal officials also saw the need to protect the life and liberty of the newly liberated slaves, among them General Oliver O. Howard, head of the US Bureau of Refugees, Freedmen, and Abandoned Lands. The "abandoned lands" were the property of rebels the federal government could confiscate. The Freedmen's Bureau, as it came to be known, originally had jurisdiction only over former Confederate states, but after Kentucky failed to ratify the Thirteenth Amendment and because of increasing violence directed against blacks there, Howard extended its domain. The Tennessee Freedmen's Bureau was enlarged to cover Kentucky on December 26, 1865. From Maysville, bureau superintendent C. J. True complained on September 30, 1866, that violence against blacks went unpunished by the civil authorities, who made no effort even to arrest the perpetrators.[3]

By August 1, 1865, Green must have paid off the $850 he owed for the freedom of his wife and children, for on that day he contracted to purchase the house behind the Methodist church on the west side of Bugle Alley, where he and his family had been living since 1858. He paid Lewis Collins $200 in cash and took out promissory notes for the remaining $300, which he paid off by August 8, 1867. The lot was twenty-five feet square and later (in the 1900 census) given the address 311 Bugle Alley. The house no longer exists, but the stone wall behind the neighboring Fourth Street house that marked the Green lot's southern boundary is still there.[4]

That same August, Green went to Louisville to help organize the Convention of Colored Ministers of the State of Kentucky, which then drew up plans for an institution of higher learning for "the rising generation." It would be called the Kentucky Normal and Theological Institute. Green was so proud of his work for the school that the first thing he says about himself on the title page of his book is that he was one of its founders. In 1869, a site overlooking Frankfort was purchased but later proved unsatisfactory, and it was not until 1879 that the school was built in downtown Louisville. It exists today as Simmons College of Kentucky, renamed after one of its early presidents.[5]

Green's constant alternation of Sundays between Maysville and Paris eventually caused some dissatisfaction for church members who had to make do with not having a preacher every Sunday. In addition, his regular absences made it more difficult for him to know exactly what was going on in either church when he wasn't there and prevented him from responding immediately to issues as they arose. Just such a problem emerged early in 1866. "In January, after the emancipation of the slaves"—that is, after the passage of the Thirteenth Amendment in December 1865, even though the Kentucky legislature voted against it—"I told the brethren [in Maysville] that the Lord had in reservation for us a blessing. I then expressed my feelings in starting a series of meetings. . . . Everything went on very agreeably till I went to Paris and came back. I felt as soon as I came back that there was something wrong in the church." In other words, an unfortunate event had transpired in the Maysville church when he was away at the Paris church: one member had insulted another. Green brought them together, ironed out the difficulty, and persuaded them to shake hands. But about the same time, he began to feel fatigued from conducting the series of revival meetings he had called for to celebrate African Americans' newfound freedom. "I went to Paris and secured the assistance of the Rev. Clay, of Xenia, [Ohio]"—that is, Clay preached in Green's place in Paris. Then Green became seriously ill, underwent an operation under chloroform, and "when they began operating I commenced preaching. . . . My wife and children rushed up in the room, supposing that they were killing me." Susan Green wrote to their son Marshall to come home immediately. She also wrote to his Paris congregation, and two of those members came to Maysville. As his health improved, they turned their visit into a prayer meeting, perhaps of thanksgiving. Once again on his feet, Green conducted another revival, resulting in the conversion of at least sixty new members, whom he baptized in the Ohio River.[6]

In that same year, 1866, although slavery had in theory, if not in fact, ended, Green had to fight to free his children. John C. Reid claimed to still own Green's daughter Amanda, and when she returned to her father, Reid told Green to send her back, or he would charge him with harboring slaves. Green said he would do no such thing. Reid had him arrested. The judge listened to Reid's lawyer, then announced he had reached a decision and refused to hear Green's lawyer: Green was liable for $30 damages, and if he did not pay, he would go to jail. In response, Green announced he could not pay and would willingly be incarcerated. "I left the Sheriff by the Courthouse and when I got a little way beyond the Presbyterian Church, he said 'Oh damn it, come back.' I came back. and we went up into the Courthouse together. When we had been there a little time, he went to some one and whispered. I told them that the whole thing was rascality, a cheat and fraud. They then told me that I might go home." Green went to see a Captain Larrell, the head of the local office of the Freedmen's Bureau, who told him to get a copy of the trial proceedings, which were forwarded to General Palmer in Louisville. Two days later, orders were given preserving Green's property from seizure. Larrell suggested that Green see if he could compromise with Reid. He did, and Reid settled for $7 in court costs and gave up all claim on Amanda.[7]

Soon another daughter, Mariah, showed up on Green's doorstep with a bundle of clothes, saying she wasn't going back anymore to her (former) owner, John P. Dobyns's widow, who somehow still claimed to own Mariah. The widow sent for Green, demanding Mariah's return.

He refused but would not stand in his daughter's way if she wanted to go back. Mrs. Dobyns said in that case Mariah must leave Kentucky. George A. Orr, the husband of Elisha's writing teacher Alice Dobyns, went with him to the ferry to take her across the river. But the captain refused because Orr was not her owner. He would take her if Orr got permission from the mayor of Maysville. As Green and Orr were walking back up the river bank, Orr became so angry, he said "he wished every negro was in hell." Permission was obtained from the mayor, and Green found a friend in Aberdeen, Ohio, opposite Maysville, who offered Mariah a temporary home until Elisha could find a permanent one.[8]

His daughter Caroline was the slave of Robert Andrews, who lived around the corner on Fourth Street, just up Bugle Alley from the Green residence. "She wanted to leave but was afraid. A squad of soldiers went there and got her"—in effect, she was rescued by the Freedmen's Bureau. "I went down and took her to Portsmouth, Ohio" by steamship up the Ohio River, states Green. "From there I took the train and went up to

Jackson, about twenty miles above Portsmouth. I left Caroline with her sister Charlotte."[9]

Mariah and Caroline must have eventually returned to the Green household, for they appear in the 1870 census together with Elisha, his wife, and their children Catherine, Elisha Jr., and Thomas. To earn money, his four daughters and his son joined him in making chair seats; each could make one seat a day at fifty cents per seat, earning a daily three dollars for the family. Mrs. Green had lost an eye and the use of one hand to sickness, so she could not contribute to this cottage industry. Elisha added to his work repertoire shoemaking, carpentry, broom making, whitewashing, and house painting, in particular for Christian Shultz (1788–1867), a noted local businessman who had a formula for making whitewash in more colors than one.[10]

At some point in the Civil War, Green's teenage son Elisha Green Jr., born around 1849, had run away from his owner, apparently with the help of some of the Union soldiers who frequently visited, according to Green, the farm where Elisha Jr. was a slave. "The people with whom he lived treated him very bad." Green spent many a sleepless night worrying about the youngster, who had evidently fled to Ohio, for he was discovered six miles from Columbus by an acquaintance in Xenia, who sent Green the good news on May 19, 1866, and Elisha Jr. was soon returned by train and steamboat to Maysville.[11]

In early 1866, Green learned "that a great many colored people had been driven from their masters and had come to Paris for protection." Some had crowded into an old stable for which they paid $10 in monthly rent. When Green visited them, he saw that they were venting their cooking stove through a hole in the roof. It happened that landowner Samuel H. Clay (1813–1872) had a large plot of land he wished to sell, having failed to obtain permission from the city to build a shipping pen there. It was on the southeastern edge of town, on the other side of the railroad. Green persuaded members of his Paris church to accept Clay's offer to sell lots on which he would build cottages for displaced former slaves. The terms for each were $500 cash or $100 down and the remainder to be paid off at 6 percent interest. Clay had first approached the pastor of the black Methodist church, but the minister turned him down, saying that his sole business was to preach the gospel and that he had no interest in "political matters." Green held a different view, assuring Clay that it was "as much my duty to look after the interests of my people as to preach the gospel, for that to some extent is a part of the gospel."[12]

The first sale was recorded September 16, 1868. The purchaser was "Jackson Moore, of color," and the price $500 in cash. Few blacks could have bought outright, so Moore and probably most other purchasers took the finance option. Subsequent sales recorded in Bourbon County Deed Book Number 5 consistently refer back to the plat shown on the page next to the one where Moore's sale is recorded. It shows 115 numbered plots fifty by ninety feet in extent. Samuel H. Clay showed some generosity on December 17, 1870, selling for just one dollar lot number 8, "to be used for building a schoolhouse and keeping a school therein." The neighborhood became known as Claysville and over the decades developed its own businesses, stores, churches, and school. Fearing the political power of Claysville's expanding population, the city of Paris wrote a new charter in 1870 that placed it outside the city limits. The last building of the original neighborhood was torn down in 1972, as "blacks moved into new, attractive housing projects in Claysville," according to Paris historian H. E. Everman.[13]

On February 14, 1866, a state law was passed legalizing marriages between former slaves, and on November 14 Elisha and Susan Green reaffirmed their vows before the Mason County circuit clerk and were granted a certificate.[14]

Green was one of three Mason County delegates sent to the State Convention of Colored Men held in Lexington on November 26–28, 1867. He was chosen at the convention to be one of its four "adjunct vice-presidents," and he reported on the condition of blacks in Mason County: "four Churches and four Schools in the county, with aid from Bureau of $40 per month; considerable suffering; no tax drawn"—that is, no tax revenue allotted to the black schools. This is not surprising because the education tax was levied only on black citizens, who as yet had little or no income. The convention passed resolutions asking for the right to vote, the right to testify against white people in court, and the right to equal treatment on stage coaches, railroads, and steamboats. Green gave the closing benediction, a measure of the respect he enjoyed in that company.[15]

From September 1867 through June 1868, he collected $20 in monthly rent on behalf of his church from the US Freedmen's Bureau

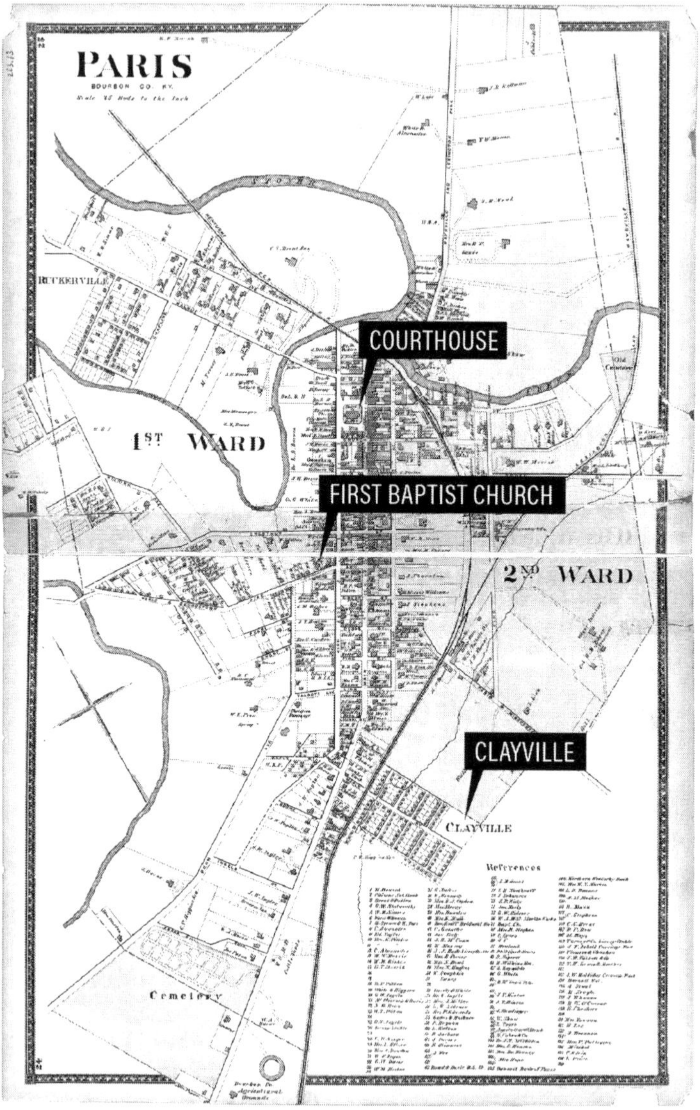

Map of Paris, in *Atlas of Bourbon, Clark, Fayette, Jessamine, and Woodford Counties, Ky.* (Philadelphia, 1877); labels added indicating Green's church, the Bourbon County Courthouse (where he won the case against his assailants in March 1884), and Claysville, a neighborhood of African American–owned homes that Green was instrumental in establishing. (Library of Congress)

for providing a one-room schoolhouse that was probably the church itself to educate the freed children of Maysville. The rent was used to pay teachers because the bureau could not legally hire them. Similarly, Fielding Fant, a trustee of the African American Scott Methodist Church, located on the same street as Green's church, a few blocks east, collected the same amount for another school. But such schools were the target of white violence throughout the state. In March 1867 in neighboring Fleming County, a notice was posted on the black schoolhouse door threatening to assassinate the teacher if the school did not close. In 1868, the schoolhouse in Germantown, on the Mason–Bracken County border, fell victim to arson. Yet, as Diane Perrine Coon writes, Green's Maysville school was more generally accepted: "Augusta, . . . Maysville, and Washington were quick to embrace the education of freemen."[16]

In October 1868, Green was attending a Republican campaign event when Maysville attorney and former congressman William H. Wadsworth (1821–1893) urged him to address the crowd. Wadsworth was campaigning for Ulysses Grant in that year's presidential election. Wadsworth and Grant had been classmates at the Maysville Academy in 1836–1837, and now they were united by politics. Wadsworth had been a presidential elector on the Constitutional Union ticket in 1860, pledged to John Bell, and carried it for Mason County. He served in the US Congress from 1861 to 1865 and as a colonel in the Union army, fighting under General William Bull Nelson at the Battle of Ivy Mountain in November 1861 and later defending Mason County against Morgan's Raiders and other invaders. Though he had voted against the Thirteenth Amendment in Congress in 1865, he had undergone a change of heart by 1868. On June 13, he gave a speech at Flemingsburg that shocked the local correspondent for the *Louisville Daily Courier:* "I never before heard a man come out so fully and explicitly for negro suffrage and negro equality in a public speech." Wadsworth said it was God's will that the South lost the war. He welcomed black votes and predicted that one day former Confederates would do the same, would "confess their faults and ask forgiveness." That day never came. It took enormous courage to make such a speech in rural Kentucky.[17]

Green was at first reluctant to address the assembly, but Wadsworth insisted that he go up and just say anything at all, even if only "I am a Republican, from head to foot." Wadsworth knew that Green was a loyal Republican and that newly enfranchised African American voters were essential to the success of the party. Green did speak, beginning by thanking Wadsworth for the invitation and joking that although he was more than fifty years old, on election day he would turn twenty-one, the age of a new voter.[18]

Then he told the audience what he had heard a Democratic speaker say a few days earlier: "that he did not believe the negro was human; that he was of a species between the baboon and the monkey; that God had foreordained that he should be a slave . . . 'How would it look for a great, big, black negro buck sitting beside your daughter?' These are his exact words." As for baboons and monkeys, said Green, "you know it is customary for those animals to have tails. Had I a tail next Tuesday I would curl it upon my back and go to the polls and vote the Republican ticket." The crowd broke out into cheers.[19]

Elisha was as combative in church as he was on the stump. On Saturday, November 11, 1871, Elder Paris Fisher, pastor of St. Paul Methodist, a black church in Paris, invited Green to accompany him to the black Christian church to witness a public debate between him and its pastor, H. M. Ayres. But the invitation was more in the nature of an ambush because when the debate began, Fisher was nowhere to be seen, and Ayres directed his thunder at Green. He began by saying there was no scriptural basis for the "mourner's bench." As a follower of Alexander Campbell, who had split the May's Lick Baptist church when young Elisha was a member there, Ayres thought the Bible the only valid basis for faith and practice. Among both Methodists and Baptists at that time, people wishing to better their spiritual condition would come up to kneel at a bench at the front of the congregation and mourn their sins, although the custom has since then fallen into disuse. In reply, Green drew Ayres's attention to the Sermon on the Mount: "Blessed are those who mourn, for they shall be comforted" (Matthew 5:4).[20]

Ayres brought up other issues, eventually arriving at the biggest difference of all between Campbellites and Baptists: whether baptism grants remission of sins. The former say yes, the latter no. In the Baptist church, one works through one's salvation first, then undergoes baptism, which is a public demonstration of faith and of adherence to a particular Baptist congregation, not a means of salvation. Following Campbell, Ayres asserted that "there was no promise of salvation this side of baptism." Green countered with the case of Cornelius in Acts 10, who received the gift of the Holy Spirit while Peter was talking to him, no water required. Likewise in Acts 19:6, Paul was similarly converted. That seemed to end the debate, for the congregation was dismissed.[21]

Green published a pamphlet about the encounter. Though it has not come to light, he quotes enough in his autobiography *Life* for us to hear his real voice in a way we cannot in *Life* because, as he says, if the latter has any "elegant diction of speech," Brother Butler, the man who wrote down Green's autobiography, is responsible. "I had no idea of the discussion until I reached the church"—that is, he had no idea it would be a debate between him and Ayres instead of between Ayers and the Methodist pastor who had extended the invitation; he thought he was going to be a spectator, not a participant. "I believe his object was to kill me off, but he waked up the wrong passenger. If Mr. Ayers wished a discussion why did he not do as I would have done? I would have invited him to my room." Green here alludes to what Jesus said in Matthew 18:15 about how best to deal with disagreements within the church: "If thy brother shall trespass against thee, go and tell him his fault between thee and him alone." Only if that doesn't work should you bring other members into the discussion. "But I suppose he did not consider me worthy, and therefore he thought he would kill me off in the Christian Church. . . . I heard an elder once say that if a man fooled you the first time it was his fault and the next time it was your own fault. Elder Ayres will never fool me again in his church."[22]

Green's own voice came through again when he published a reply to a personal attack by another minister, E. W. S. Hammond, pastor of St. Paul Methodist Church in Paris from 1873 to 1876. The attack appears to have had its origin in a difference between Baptists and Methodists over how to baptize. Baptists immerse, as Green frequently did in the Ohio River in Maysville or perhaps in Stoner Creek in Paris (and as May's Lick pastor Walter Warder had done in the North Fork). Methodists more often sprinkle or pour but will immerse if the candidate desires. Neither church believes that baptism has a saving power, as other Christians do, but Baptists, as opposed to Methodists, never baptize infants, for whom immersion, of course, is dangerous. Hammond held a successful revival, garnering four hundred new members. "Many of these desiring," says Green, "to be immersed or baptized" (implying that sprinkling was not really baptism), "the church had a pool dug." Hammond immersed some and sprinkled others, as they wished. The following Sunday Green was in Paris and remarked to his flock that "baptism by immersion had planted a battery at the M. E. Church." To "plant a battery" meant to set up artillery pieces in anticipation of battle, so Green's words were provocative, even warlike, suggesting that Hammond's church was in danger from new converts who had a little Baptist in their soul.[23]

In response, Hammond wrote in a church paper he edited: "There is quite an extensive movement on the part of the younger and more progressive members of the Baptist Church in Paris in favor of a change of pastors. They want an educated minister. We hope their wants may be gratified. Paris needs more light." Green was livid. He demanded a retraction, which never came. He subsequently published a response in which he admitted he was not as educated as Hammond but denied there was any dissatisfaction in his church.[24]

Hammond, born in Baltimore in 1842, had never been a slave. He came from an educated family: his father had a doctor of divinity degree. Young Edward spent a year in the navy before studying theology at the Ashmun Institute (renamed Lincoln University in 1866) in Pennsylvania. In early March 1872, he was appointed to a pulpit in Cincinnati but appears to have quickly gotten into trouble, for at the annual conference of the Ohio African Methodist Episcopal Church "the committee to whom the case of the Rev. E. W. S. Hammond was referred brought in a report finding him guilty of all the charges and specifications brought against him. This action, of course, settles the fact that Brother Hammond has been guilty of 'gross immorality.'" In reference to a Methodist pastor, that term often meant sexual misbehavior. But the guilty verdict did not derail Hammond's church career; his next assignment was Paris, where he felt free to criticize Green in print, as we have seen. Perhaps because he left the Ohio Conference for the Lexington one, he felt confident the odor of scandal would not attach to him there.[25]

Green, probably unaware that he could have used such a weapon against his assailant, readily admitted that "I have no education." Fearing that Hammond and perhaps others might suspect "that I did not write this"—that is, his printed reply—"I will be good enough to tell him how I learnt to write. My young mistress taught me to write when

I was a slave. Her name was Miss Alice Dobyns. . . . You don't think the colored people of Paris and the south have any sense, because they have never been to college. Why, Elder, I did not know that all the books were in college." The Bible, he goes on to say, is just such a book. Brother Hammond would do well to read his Bible and leave others alone. "You have just as much as you can do well. There are some men that have a little learning and they are so afraid that the people won't know it that they have to keep meddling with other people's business. I reckon you think that I have been in Paris long enough. But you are not the judge."[26]

Having paid off the loan for the Bugle Alley lot in August 1867, on December 2 of the following year Green purchased a lot on West Fourth Street across from his Maysville church. He paid $150 for it, $50 in cash and the rest to be paid off in two years. On September 18, 1871, he purchased two adjoining lots also across from the church for $273 under a similar arrangement.[27]

He was politically active again in 1876, when he was a delegate to the state Republican convention held in Louisville on May 18. Black voices played a prominent role in the convention's decision to give its twenty-four votes to Benjamin Helm Bristow (1832–1896) in his effort to become the party's nominee for president.

A native of Elkton, Kentucky, Bristow had most recently been Grant's Treasury secretary. In 1866, as US attorney for the State of Kentucky and in 1871 as US solicitor general, he prosecuted the Ku Klux Klan. In 1871, he argued unsuccessfully for Kentucky to ratify the Thirteenth Amendment and in that same year inveighed against the state law prohibiting black citizens from testifying against whites in court, a cause dear to Elisha Green. Bristow declared in a letter to John G. Fee, "If I had the power I would not allow any local prejudice or racial etiquette to stand in the way of every child in the Commonwealth. Regarding as I do the education of the youth of all races as the paramount duty of the state, I would not hesitate to place the facilities within the reach of every child of the State, of whatever color. . . . I regard all laws discriminating against colored people on account of color or previous condition as antagonistic to the spirit of the age." This letter, according to Bristow's biographer Ross A. Webb, "did much to win Negro support for his candidacy." But Bristow lost to Rutherford B. Hayes, who then lost the popular vote to the Democratic candidate, Samuel J. Tilden, but won the Electoral College after promising to withdraw Federal troops from the South, thus ending Reconstruction.[28]

Beginning in 1855, Green took the stagecoach on his frequent journeys between his two churches in Maysville and Paris, traveling the turnpike through Washington, May's Lick, Blue Licks, and Millersburg. The Kentucky Central Railroad finally started running trains between those two cities in March 1872, taking an entirely different route through Helena, Ewing, and Carlisle before paralleling the turnpike for the distance between Millersburg and Paris. On May 19, 1876, Green was returning by train from the Convention of Colored Ministers of the State of Kentucky in Louisville. About to enter Millersburg, the train was crossing Hinkston Creek when the bridge collapsed. The engine made it across, but the coupling pin connecting Green's car to the one in front of it broke, and the car was suddenly tilted back so severely that a stove broke loose and slid down the aisle. Green was seated at the extreme rear of the coach, which was now four inches deep in the water. A Methodist preacher came over and pulled Green's leg out from under the stove. It was at this point, that Green realized it was broken. "I lifted my right leg out of the water and tried the left, but it appeared as heavy as if there were a log attached to it." A woman sitting in front of him was screaming because her ankle was stuck. Green told her to stop struggling, or she would break the ankle for sure. A man across the aisle was lying on his back with seats piled up on top of him. He kept throwing them off, and they kept falling back. Green told him to cease that fruitless effort, and he did.[29]

The conductor called out to Green to get up and exit the car. Green replied he couldn't because his leg was broken. The conductor asked how he knew. "I told him that I was holding it together." Would-be rescuers then excitedly rushed to carry him out and in their disorganized haste would likely have injured him further. He told them to stop, and they did. He instructed them to place the bad leg over the good one before carrying him out. At the house of a Millersburg acquaintance, seven doctors stood by his bed vying to set his leg. Green was shivering from the shock. Whiskey was brought, but "I told them . . . that when I died I wanted to die sober." They started to cut his boots to remove them, but the boots were new, and he refused to allow it. What are we going to do? they asked. He told them to raise him up, and he held on to his broken

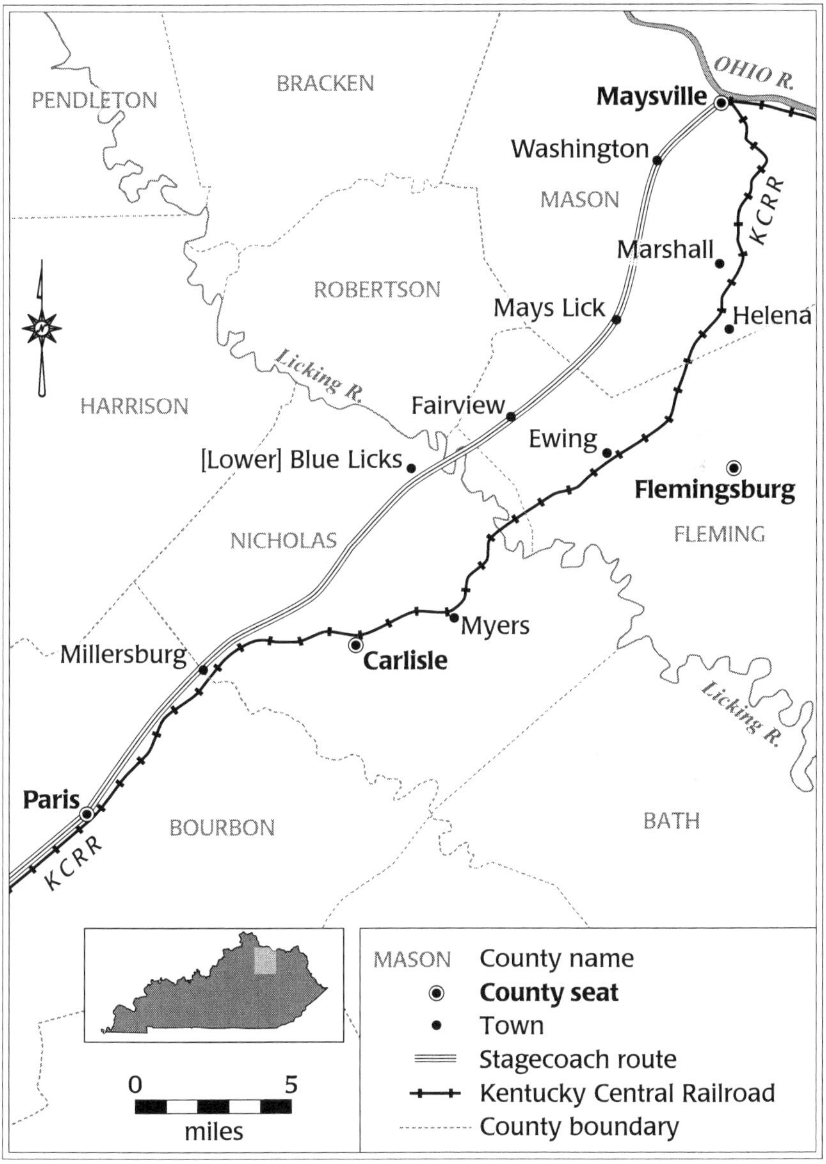

Green's routes from Maysville to Paris. From 1855 to 1872, Elisha Green took the stagecoach between Maysville and Paris, stopping at the Blue Licks Hotel for dinner. From 1872 to 1893, he took the Kentucky Central Railroad, a few miles to the east. Gould and Bristow's assault on Green began at Millersburg as the train departed for Paris. Map by Dick Gilbreath.

leg while they pulled off the boot. His leg was broken in two places.[30]

Susan Green traveled all night from Maysville to visit her husband. When she appeared at the door, Elisha told her not to cry, that he wasn't dead yet. This brought a smile to her lips, and she entered the house. The Paris church sent a deacon to look after him; the Maysville congregation sent $37 via William H. Wadsworth, the former congressman who had persuaded Green to address an electoral gathering in 1868. Millersburg citizens made frequent visits and brought food throughout his six-week recuperation.[31]

The superintendent of the Maysville and Lexington Railroad came to see Green and told him that whatever he wanted, he simply had to ask for it. When Green was able to get about on crutches, and the bridge had been repaired, he revisited the site where the accident happened. The train had just left for Paris and was crossing the now-repaired bridge. "When they saw me they [the train] came back. I mention this to show the feeling they had for me." The railroad was grateful that he did not sue, as did Mrs. Herrick, who was awarded $5,000. He settled for a modest $500.[32]

In four years' time, the roles were reversed, and now it was Elisha who rushed to his wife's bedside. He had received a telegram in Paris informing him she was gravely ill and not expected to survive. He left immediately for Maysville and arrived a short time before she expired on September 13, 1880. They at least had time to talk about "her prospects for heaven." Surely they were good. She told him, "My time is at hand, and all is well." For the hymns to be sung at her funeral, she requested "Come, Brothers and Sisters That Love One Another" and "On Jordan's Stormy Banks I Stand."[33]

Elisha Green soon had to withstand another heavy blow: "Not long after the death of my wife my daughter Mariah was stricken very severely, which resulted in her losing her mind and thus having to be taken to the Lexington Asylum, where she died in a short time." It was Mariah who had appeared at his door with a bundle of clothes one early morning in 1866 saying she was not going back to be a slave of John Porter Dobyns's widow. She didn't have to go back, for slavery was over. But it was going to take a while for that reality to sink in for people such as Elizabeth Dobyns, who made Green take his daughter out of the state.[34]

Elisha kept preaching. In the Maysville church, a revival was held in early 1882, with a harvest of forty-five new members for him to baptize in the icy Ohio on February 5.[35]

That summer, a special train was arranged for those of Green's parishioners desiring to attend the state meeting of the Colored Baptist Association in Cynthiana. They would board at six in the morning and be back by five in the afternoon. There would be an additional coach for white persons wishing to go.[36]

On June 8, 1883, Green would again board the train, as was his custom, for the biweekly trip to Paris. But before he gets there, let us make the acquaintance of two men he would meet on the journey, George T. Gould and Frank Leslie Bristow.

6

The Confederacy or the Church?

The Reverend George T. Gould, the Millersburg Female College president who with Professor Frank L. Bristow would engage in a violent attack on Elisha Green in 1883, began his ministerial career at the tender age of thirteen by conducting the graveside rites for his uncle's illegitimate child. This inauspicious debut took place in March 1856; he would not actually begin his theological studies for another three years. The brother of Gould's mother, Thomas M. Oliver, still had a wife in North Carolina when he began fathering children with Mary Ann McCaffrey in Louisville. He had moved to Kentucky because it was easier to get a divorce there, but the longer he lived with McCaffrey, the less he was inclined to marry her and never did. He left her in 1860 and successfully sued for custody of their second child in 1867. In 1879, McCaffrey would sue former Pennsylvania senator Simon Cameron for breach of promise, saying in court that she was the widow of Thomas Oliver, whose wife she had been in Louisville. Her assertion was doubly false, for they had not married, and Oliver was not dead.

For reasons unknown to us, Gould, born on December 17, 1842, in Beaufort, North Carolina, was closer to his uncle than he was to his father, George L. Gould. Oliver stated in 1884 that young George lived with him and his mother (i.e., George's grandmother) more than with his parents, and it was there that George learned his ABCs from his grandmother's big family Bible. "When a little fellow not more than four years of age he would leave his father's home and come down to . . . where I was living and my mother keeping house for me and stay with us as long as his father would let him, and he would have stayed forever if he had been permitted." This is borne out by the US Census of 1850, which shows him living with his uncle and grandmother in Raleigh, North Carolina, while his parents and siblings were living at another address in the same city.[1]

Oliver was a well-established tailor and taught Gould's father the trade, though his pupil never prospered. In October 1851, Oliver announced that he was selling out and leaving Raleigh for Louisville; his brother-in-law would continue working in the shop. In 1853, young George T., with his mother, siblings, and grandmother, left his father behind and went to Louisville to live with Oliver. The father finally joined them in January 1854, but in August they all were forced to move out so that Oliver could install his mistress, Mary Ann McCaffrey, in the house.

Instead of joining his brother-in-law in the tailoring business in Louisville, George L. began preparing to be a Southern Methodist clergyman, obtaining his license in October 1856. In 1859, he had a church in Harrodsburg, where his son in September enrolled at Kentucky University. The school had a church connection, but it was with the Disciples of Christ, more theologically liberal than the Southern Methodists. Robert Milligan, the school's president and the younger George's professor in biblical literature and moral philosophy, had converted from the Presbyterianism of his native northern Ireland to the Disciples of Christ when running his own school at Flat Rock in Bourbon County, Kentucky. He later became a professor at Bethany College, now in West Virginia, a Disciples school. Kentucky University grew out of Bacon College, another Disciples institution, which had relocated to Harrodsburg from Georgetown, Kentucky. "The name of the College," writes Richard M. Pope, "suggests the admiration that its founders had for Francis Bacon and the methods of science. This is of course consistent with the early Disciple affinity for the British empirical tradition." Milligan later became president of the College of the Bible in Lexington, a Disciples theological seminary.[2]

In the course of study Milligan oversaw at Kentucky University, he emphasized that anything with "a tendency to create in the mind a sectarian bias is carefully avoided . . . and the Bible is, as far as practicable, made its own interpreter." Textbooks included, in addition to the New Testament in Greek and the Old Testament in Hebrew, J. H. Merle d'Aubigné's *History of the Reformation*, Gibbon's *Decline and Fall of the Roman Empire*, Locke's *Essay Concerning Human Understanding*, Coleridge's philosophical works, Kant's *Critique of Pure Reason*, as well as works attempting to reconcile science with the Bible and books on archaeology, ecclesiastical history, biblical exegesis, and pulpit eloquence.[3]

Young George needed to spend only two years in Harrodsburg before securing a preaching license from the Southern Methodist Church in April 1861. Of Kentucky University's six schools, George was most likely enrolled in "Biblical Literature and Moral Philosophy," which required only two years to complete, but he may not have completed his course of study there, for he "was recalled from college on account of his father's illness." Gould's father was ordained in September 1861 and assigned to Simpsonville in Shelby County, but after a brief illness died on January 27, 1862.[4]

The Civil War came to Kentucky, and in August 1862 young Gould saw the fighting up close. Major General Edmund Kirby Smith of the Confederate army defeated Brigadier General William "Bull" Nelson of the Union army at Richmond, and the Union soldiers retreating to Louisville passed through Simpsonville, where George was living with his mother. "For five or six hours they streamed through our little village," he recalled, "officers, privates, teamsters, horses, wagons, pieces of artillery, all jumbled together and pressing forward as though death were at their heels." Three soldiers died from exhaustion in his front yard. His sympathies were with the South, as he would tell a reunion of Union soldiers in 1892:

> I had been born in one of the cotton states, where my people from the time of the revolutionary war had been born, had lived and had died, and I was more proud of being a southerner than I was of being an American. In fact, we of the south, being taught the divine origin and rightful perpetuity of slavery by our churches, and looking on the slavery agitation not as the demand of the advancing civilization of the age but as a sectional and unconstitutional attack upon our pros-

> perity and our guaranteed rights—very naturally we came to love the state more and the union less, till the mass of the people were ready to be swept out of the union by the secession movement. I was, then, a southern sympathizer. With all my heart and soul, I wanted the south to succeed; I believed that she was right, that her cause was just, that the God of battles would hear her cry and send her the victory.[5]

He recalled seeing Confederate army general Braxton Bragg's soldiers pass by his house that fall of 1862 after the Battle of Perryville. He decided to join them, but in his hurry forgot to bring any blankets or food. After a chilly night in a corn shock, hunger sent him home.

Gould told the Union veterans of his visit to Perryville a few weeks after the battle. He did not tell them, however, of his other attempt to join the Confederate army, which he soon abandoned in favor of resuming his career with the Southern Methodist Church. John W. Cunningham in 1903 wrote of running into Gould in Lexington on September 15, 1862, when the city was under Confederate control. Cunningham and a number of other Southern Methodist preachers were stymied in their efforts to attend a Kentucky Conference meeting scheduled for Flemingsburg, which was then under Union control, on September 17. Pulpits for the coming year would be assigned, and the pastors were anxious to negotiate their future assignments. Cunningham went to Confederate general Kirby Smith for permission to leave Lexington. Smith refused: "My army is thundering at the gates of Cincinnati, and I cannot allow any person to pass through my lines."[6]

The presiding bishop urged Cunningham to try to run the blockade and get to Flemingsburg. Cunningham ran into Gould near the Lexington courthouse. "I knew that he came alone from Simpsonville in his buggy and desired to join the Confederacy," Cunningham recalled. So they drove north to Paris, then on to Millersburg as dark fell, seeing a few pickets along the way but never challenged. After spending the night with a friend, they left the main highway for less-traveled roads. They saw some Union soldiers, who said nothing to them, and concluded they were scouts sent to look for rebels from Kirby Smith's army. They arrived in Flemingsburg by midmorning. Given their laudable defiance of the order not to leave Lexington, Cunningham was invited to help make the pulpit assignments, and Gould was awarded the Simpsonville church.[7]

Gould considered his options. Should it be the Confederate army or the church? But, of course, becoming a Southern Methodist preacher was in itself a way of fighting for southern values, that denomination's raison d'être being the defense of slavery. So Gould began his church career at the Simpsonville church where his father had served. The succeeding years found him at posts in Lawrenceburg, Bedford, North Middletown, Bloomfield, Danville, and Maysville. They were, as he put it, "various appointments in increasing importance." Indeed, for the most part his yearly salary increased, from $900 in North Middletown in 1867 to $1,200 in Bloomfield in 1868–1869, dropping to $1,000 in Danville in 1870–1871, before rising in Maysville to $1,250 in 1871–1872.[8]

During his Lawrenceburg pastorate, Gould married Ella Fullenwider of Shelbyville on September 7, 1865. Her great-grandfather, Peter Fullenwider, had left Switzerland for America in 1752 in the hope of converting Indians to Christianity; he came to Shelby County in 1783. His son Jacob, by contrast, was known for fighting the Indians under General Mad Anthony Wayne in 1794. Jacob's son Henry Winter Fullenwider (1815–1900) apparently prospered, for he would later lend his son-in-law, George T. Gould, $7,500 to buy a financial interest in Millersburg Female College. Mary Ann McCaffrey, Thomas M. Oliver's mistress, would later remark, "George Gould married a rich girl, so I have been told, an only child of a rich German." Ella did have a sister, though, and her father was of Swiss descent, not German, but he was relatively rich.[9]

The marriage soon turned sour. "I think we loved each other" in the beginning, Gould would later recall, "and for a short time were happy, but too soon it began to appear we had made a most fearful mistake. We were unsuited to each other in every particular. She was cold, phlegmatic, gloomy, despondent, suspicious, unsocial; I very quick, hasty, impetuous, ardent, hopeful, cheerful and fond of society. . . . My wife has ever been cold, unimpassioned, and utterly disinclined to the embraces of the married bed. When not actually repulsing my advances she had submitted to them with a manifest disinclination that has robbed them of all pleasure."[10] Their first serious quarrel arose from her objecting to his supporting his mother, whom Ella insulted to her face by calling her a liar, a thief, and a hussy. "I threatened if she had no more respect for me than that I would cause her to hold her peace through fear, for I would fasten her up in the closet. I did not attempt to put the threat into execution, as it had the desired effect." Ella remembered it differently, not as a threat but as the real thing: "He snatched me from his table and dragged me off and locked me up in the closet." By her recollection, this occurred in the fall of 1867, which would have been about the time of their second wedding anniversary.[11]

Somehow, despite Ella's reluctance in bed, the marriage produced four children, beginning with George H. on January 19, 1869. A few months later she woke up in the middle of the night and realized her husband wasn't there. She sat up and could see him crouching on the bedroom floor near the black nurse girl, who was sleeping on the floor to care for the newborn. When Ella asked him what he was doing, he at first denied having anything to do with the girl. "I told him that my eyes could not deceive me. Then he said he had read that the negro race was not like the white and that he was simply making an examination to find out." He later denied everything.[12]

Two years later, according to Ella, he again attempted to have sexual relations with a black woman. This time she was not in their employ but in that of the family with whom they were lodging, and as a result the woman lost her job. It occurred in Danville in the summer of 1871. The Goulds and the Gentrys were about to drive in two carriages to a Lexington park. George left momentarily to go back to the house, saying he would be right back. As he returned to the carriage, the Gentrys' cook followed him. She went up to Mrs. Gentry, and from the Goulds' carriage Ella could see that she was speaking excitedly and that George was getting increasingly nervous. He told Gentry to drive on and not listen to the cook. When they returned home at the end of the day, the servant went up to Ella and said, "I told Mr. Gould I was going to tell you what he said to me this morning": he had asked her to let him sleep with her in the hall that night. Ella asked George if it was true. He denied it. When Ella brought it up with Mrs. Gentry, Mrs. Gentry fired the servant. Gould's version of the story was that he had left the carriage to get a drink of water from the bucket on the back porch but was enraged to see the woman drinking out of the dipper he had intended to use. "I said something to her about the impudence of negroes and that she ought to have the dipper stuck down her throat." He imagined she was complaining to her employers about the way he had spoken to her.[13]

In Maysville, he again aroused Ella's suspicions by leaving her bed for a possible tryst. They had two young female servants, a nurse and a cook. The younger one told Ella that she saw a man come in and out of in her room and then realized that the other girl was missing. Both of these servants were white.[14]

In September 1872, having been in Maysville a year, Gould claimed he could not continue preaching because his throat hurt too much. But it would later emerge that the whiskey he was taking to calm the pain had itself become a problem. He had tried to do without it for the past year but claimed that as a result he almost died. It was in the midst of this struggle to give up the bottle that he gave a well-received temperance lecture at the Maysville Courthouse on December 29, 1871. The *Maysville Republican* reported that the room was well filled considering the wintry weather and that the lecture was said to have been excellent. Even if his heart wasn't in it, Gould could always give a good speech.[15]

7

Millersburg Beckons

Gould set his sights on a new venture, leaving the pulpit for the professor's chair and ultimately the presidency of a women's school in Millersburg, thirty-seven miles southwest of Maysville. But the second of these goals would require a significant financial investment. On September 9, 1872, while still a pastor at Maysville, he took out two $1,000 loans from William H. Savage, who owned Millersburg Female College, toward the eventual purchase of a half-share in the school. Both loans incurred 10 percent annual interest; one was due in one year, and the other in two. On October 21, 1873, with $3,000 in hand and $2,000 to be paid later, he bought that half of the school from Savage, paying off the remaining $2,000 by April 2, 1877. But he was able to do that only by mortgaging two-thirds of his half in 1875 to W. H. Abbett, who had already bought a third of a half from Savage in 1874. Savage conveyed a third of the college to Gould for $3,000 cash on June 30, 1875. Gould bought out Abbett in 1877 through a succession of one-year mortgages that he never succeeded in paying off.[1]

At some point, Gould borrowed $7,500 from Ella's father. When he did so and whether it was all at once or at different times are unknown. All we know is that in October 1884 his uncle Tom Oliver stated that Ella told him in the summer of 1878 that her parents had lent George the money, that he had never repaid any except by giving the Fullenwiders free room and board at the college from October 1879 until June 1884 as well as by giving free tuition, room, and board to a Fullenwider niece and nephew and free room and board to another nephew who attended Kentucky Wesleyan in Millersburg.[2]

Millersburg was named after John Miller, a Pennsylvanian who had built a grist mill on Hinkston Creek at the future town's southern edge in 1788 and was the original owner of the hundred acres on which the town was laid out in 1798. It was and still is an oblong rectangle pointing northeast to Maysville. The original Limestone Trace, also known as the Maysville Road, is its central axis.

Eight miles north of Paris, Millersburg lies at the northern edge of Bourbon County. As one travels south from Maysville, Millersburg marks the beginning of the inner Bluegrass. To the immediate north is the Eden Shale region, with inferior soil. When in 1880 seventeen-year-old Alma Bridwell traveled in a covered wagon from her native Lewis County to attend Millersburg Female College, she noticed the difference: "I had never seen anything but the hill country . . . and now the broad blue-grass fields, with fat cattle grazing everywhere, greeted my vision. I had never seen the rural mansions of the rich land and stock owners, with their surroundings and equipments, and could feel the hardening influence of wealth. . . . These rich men with their thoroughbred horses driving along the turnpike and coming in and out of the gates of their estates made quite a contrast with our humble mode of traveling." Fifty years earlier, the same line of demarcation between rich and poor was already apparent; when a traveler from Lexington arrived at Millersburg, it was the last town where he could find a decent tavern, and after it "the refined landscape and architecture of Fayette and Bourbon Counties faded," giving way to the rough country and humble farmhouses of the Eden Shale hills.[3]

A town of 675 inhabitants in 1870, Millersburg was located on the Maysville–Lexington Turnpike, a stroke of luck it owed to Governor Thomas Metcalfe, who in 1830 decided to route the turnpike past his Forest Retreat Inn instead of by a more logical route through Carlisle, three miles to the east. As a result, Craig Friend writes, "Forest Retreat flourished, Millersburg received the benefits of being the major village between Paris and Washington, and Carlisle floundered." Millersburg's citizens in 1870 included several doctors, dry-goods merchants, preachers, pharmacists, grocers, painters, carpenters, wagon makers, saddlers, blacksmiths, tailors, a milliner, a shoemaker, a cabinetmaker, a tinner, a

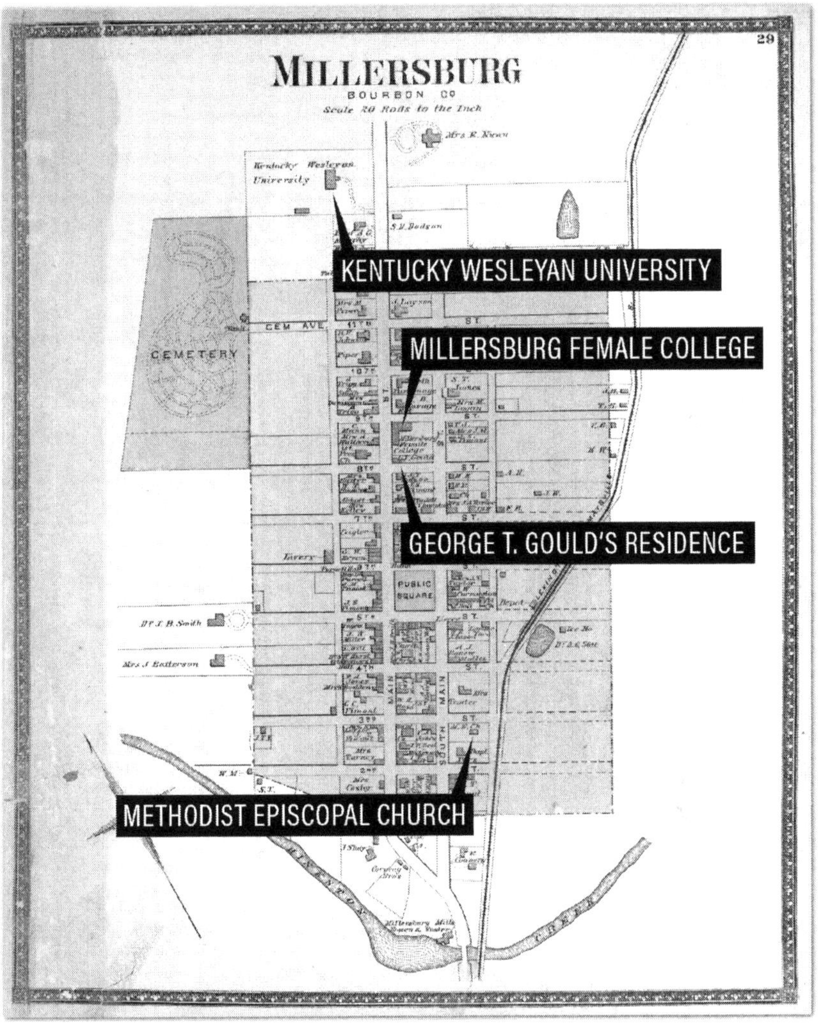

Map of Millersburg, in *Atlas of Bourbon, Clark, Fayette, Jessamine, and Woodford Counties, Ky.* (1877); labels added indicating the Female College campus, Gould's residence, Kentucky Wesleyan College, and the Methodist church (site of the church trial of Gould in October 1884). (Library of Congress)

whiskey dealer, an undertaker, a postmaster, two livestock traders, two butchers, two hotels, and one police officer.[4]

Millersburg Female College began as a girls' school in 1849, became coed in 1852, and in 1854 passed into the hands of Reverend George S. Savage. When Kentucky Wesleyan College, a males-only school, opened in Millersburg in the fall of 1859, Savage's school became a female-only institution once more. Savage was succeeded by J. W. Hamilton in 1866, who was replaced by J. A. Brown in 1869, who ceded the college to Judge William H. Savage (no relation to Reverend Savage) in 1870. There were a number of competing institutions in the Bluegrass region: Bourbon Female College in Paris, Harrison County Female College in Cynthiana, Georgetown Female College, Lexington Female College, as well as Hocker Female College and Sayre Female Institute in Lexington.[5]

Gould and Judge William Savage, cosuperintendents of the school from 1873 to 1875, were not on good terms. "He and I were trying each to destroy the school of the other," Gould later said. Nor did Gould and his wife get along, as we know. Ella concluded he was having an affair in 1876 with a mulatto woman named Lucy after seeing them standing too close together and later overhearing the janitor repeat to the cook some remark Lucy had made about Gould that could have been an allusion to his sexual prowess.[6]

With the strain of living with his wife and of having to deal with Savage, Gould sought relief in whiskey. On Christmas 1874, Ella found him lying on a bench in the school chapel. "I knelt down in his vomit and put my arms around his neck and said, 'Oh my God, has it come to this?'" He kept a jug in the closet and resorted to it when they had an argument one night in the winter of 1875–1876. Then he walked out, and she didn't see him until the next morning. He was coming from the stable, crossing the yard with the help of his mother and the janitor, shaking like a leaf. The janitor told her Gould had spent the night in the stable loft, where he had hidden another jug.[7]

Nevertheless, Gould made steady progress toward acquiring academic credentials worthy of a college president. In 1873, he received an honorary master of arts degree from Kentucky Wesleyan, a men's college in Millersburg. The two schools were on opposite ends of town but cooperated in various ways and were both sustained by the Kentucky Conference of the Southern Methodist Church. Even more helpful to Gould was the honorary doctor of divinity granted him June 7, 1877, by what might seem an unlikely institution, the Kentucky Military Institute. Located six miles southeast of Frankfort, it had become more than a military training school. Students learned Latin, English grammar, American history, architecture, political economy, physiology, and international and constitutional law. It may not have taught religion as an academic subject but did practice it. The Education Committee of the Kentucky Conference noted that the institute had a "religious tone," with daily prayers in the chapel and services every Sunday, and praised its head, R. T. P. Allen, for his "frequent gospel ministrations to his pupils."[8]

Gould's school received positive reviews in successive years of Kentucky Conference annual meeting minutes. It particularly shone when compared to Kentucky Wesleyan, which was finding it hard to make ends meet. The conference's Education Committee in 1878 complained that the men's college was in such financial difficulty that it was having trouble sustaining a competent corps of professors, but at the same time the committee praised Gould's intellect and energy in building up a school of which the state's Methodists could be proud.[9]

The editor of the *Paris Kentuckian* listened to a sermon Gould preached in 1877 and found it "a treat indeed." Gould was maintaining there was no real conflict between science and religion, only between false versions of the two. Christianity encouraged the progress of knowledge, and some of the best scientists had been devout men. "The audience was remarkably attentive considering that the sermon was necessarily long and to a certain extent above the average listener."[10]

But then disaster struck. On the night of December 28, 1878, a fire broke out at Millersburg Female College. The building was a total loss, all the furniture, desks, and pianos going up in flames. It had been insured for $8,000, but Gould still had to take out a $3,500 loan to rebuild and had to rent rooms to house the students and conduct classes for the rest of the academic year. Reconstruction began in the spring, and the new building was dedicated on September 26, 1879.[11]

As if this were not bad enough, in the midst of raising money to rebuild in March 1879 Gould had to drop everything to go with his uncle Thomas M. Oliver to Washington, DC, and testify at a trial so salacious it riveted the eyes of the nation. A woman was suing former senator Simon Cameron of Pennsylvania—who had also been Lincoln's first secretary of war—for breach of promise of marriage. She claimed to be the widow of a Thomas M. Oliver, who she said had died in the service of the Confederate navy. When Gould's uncle, who bore that name but had never gone to sea and was very much alive, learned of this claim, he asked a lawyer in Washington if the woman was from Kentucky. Yes, she was, and Oliver's suspicion was confirmed: she was none other than Mary Ann McCaffrey, with whom he had cohabited in Louisville from 1854 to 1860.[12]

Cameron's legal team asked Oliver and Gould to testify, promising to cover their expenses. If the plaintiff's husband were to appear at the trial, then she would be caught in a lie and as a married woman have no standing to sue the senator for not marrying her. Oliver was willing to go but not to say he was her husband, for he was not. He could not have married her without committing bigamy, for until 1859 he still had a wife in North Carolina. He had told McCaffrey when they were living together in Louisville that his wife was dead, but in fact she was alive, confined to an insane asylum.[13]

Oliver testified that in 1850 he had traveled from Raleigh, North Carolina, to New York City on business and had visited a Masonic regalia factory, where a young female employee caught his eye. Several months later he returned to New York and was disappointed to learn that Miss McCaffrey no longer worked there. In the spring of 1851, he was again in New York, where he was waiting in the parlor of a bordello when he saw her again as she came in with the other prostitutes. He spent that night with her and the next six as well. He offered her a job making vests in Raleigh and promised that if she came to North Carolina, he would never expose her past life. She consented, but after two or three months he took her back to New York and left her there. In 1852, after he moved to Kentucky, he traveled again to New York, looked her up, and arranged for her to join him in Louisville. He had her placed in a boardinghouse and directed his foreman to give her a job.[14]

In August 1854, as we know, he decided to install McCaffrey in the house where he and his sister's family, the Goulds, had been living and forced them to seek other lodging. The boy George addressed her as "auntie." As noted, he presided at the funeral for her and Oliver's first child in March 1856. On March 12, 1857, Oliver and his mistress had a second child, named Alice in honor of his mother. Oliver got custody of her in 1867 and kept her away from her mother, hiding her in a succession of convent schools. For years, McCaffrey was desperate to find her daughter, bombarding both Oliver and George Gould in Millersburg with letters demanding that Oliver reveal the daughter's whereabouts or that Gould as Oliver's employer (Oliver was at that time employed at the Millersburg Female College) force him to do so and threatening to bring scandal to the Gould family by revealing that Oliver, who had remarried in 1874, was a bigamist. She also pestered the Millersburg postmaster, hoping to bribe him to spy on the mail to see where Oliver sent letters. At the time of the Cameron–McCaffrey trial in 1879, Alice, then twenty-two, was in fact Mrs. Willie D. Harget of North Carolina.[15]

One day at the trial, McCaffrey came into the courtroom carrying a huge book. It turned out to be the family Bible belonging to Oliver's mother, with which young George had learned his ABCs. She had stolen it. The judge at the trial had asked her to bring it, hoping to find inscribed within it some indication of her age and that of Oliver's mother, for McCaffrey had made the ludicrous claim that before she met Oliver, she had been adopted by his mother and that was how they had met because it made a better story than his finding her in a house of prostitution. Neither item of information was there, certainly not McCaffrey's date of birth because she was never a member of the family. The judge ordered the Bible be returned to Thomas Oliver.[16]

When Gould was called to the stand, a reporter described him as "a dark complexioned man, about five feet six inches tall, weighing about one hundred and thirty-five pounds, and about thirty-seven years of age. He is inclined to be bald, and uses heavy gold spectacles. He claims to be a minister of the Gospel." There were some who doubted he could be, given his association with a man who had frequented prostitutes and made one his common-law wife; worse, he had given that man a job in a church-supported school. Gould became indignant when asked if Oliver was the right kind of person for a clergyman to think well of. An Alabama newspaper was shocked to learn that Oliver "has been for some time a professor in a high-toned female college at Millersburg, Ky., the trustees of which never thought it worthwhile, we suppose, to make any exhaustive inquiry into the character and social position of a man selected to mould the intellect and influence the morals of young ladies placed under their care."[17]

When Gould testified, he avoided looking anyone in the eye, preferring to gaze up at the ceiling or down at the floor. McCaffrey shifted her chair so that she could stare at him, and reporters thought that made him hesitate. He would pause to think and several times corrected himself. This made the spectators roar with laughter, but then came "the stern voice of Fred Douglass demanding 'Silence!'"[18]

Yes, that Frederick Douglass. Escaped slave, abolitionist, writer, and national figure, he was living in Washington, DC, as US marshal of the District of Columbia. He had been faithfully attending the trial, regaling his friend Ottilie Assing with tales from the courtroom. "I should certainly not miss a single day in the Oliver trial," she replied, "if I could reach the Court House" as easily as he could by simply passing over the bridge from Anacostia; she was then living in Hoboken, New Jersey.[19] The phony widow lost her suit and lost as well a subsequent appeal. As Cameron's biographer Paul Kahan explains, between the time McCaffrey filed suit in 1877 and the trial itself, the press had been sympathetic to her and with gusto ridiculed the aged senator for playing the Lothario. But her conduct at the trial put a stop to that: "The tone of the coverage changed dramatically, in large part due to 'Mrs. Oliver's' testimony, which was inconsistent, vague, and downright bizarre."[20]

When news of the trial reached Millersburg, the inhabitants were astonished. People there had had no idea what lurked in genial Tom Oliver's past. The local correspondent for the *Cincinnati Commercial* reported that "the quiet town . . . is rampant at the notoriety that has been given their village by the publication of Oliver's testimony, and much indignation is expressed at the management of the college." Oliver had told the court he taught calisthenics there, earning an annual salary of $150 plus room and board. In addition, he was in charge of the business department, as the *Commercial* reporter noted, referring to the school's catalog.[21]

The townspeople's indignation, directed at Gould's management of the college, meant that his association with his uncle reflected poorly on him, as it already had done at the trial. Gould took the hint and ceased to employ his uncle in any official capacity, though he continued to allow him to take his meals in the dining hall. "School Girls Dream," a piano piece published in the summer of 1880 by J. C. Meininger, the college's music professor, lists the school's personnel on the cover, and

Oliver is not among them. Asked in 1884 if he had held any professional position at the school, Oliver appeared to have forgotten what he had said at the Cameron–McCaffrey trial in 1879 about being a professor of calisthenics: "I did have a nominal position in the Female College. I have forgotten what it was. It never amounted to anything. I think it was Professor of Etiquette and Commercial Law, or something of the kind. It never amounted to straw. I never exercised any of the privileges and never wanted to." When asked "Was that position ever discontinued by request or notice of Dr. Gould in any way whatever?," he replied, "It was not. It was discontinued at my own request. I never wanted the position. And never knew that it was assigned me until I saw the Catalogue that contained it." By November 1880, he had found another job, that of Millersburg's city marshal. The office had frequent turnover, and he may not have lasted long. Indeed, it is hard to see that he was at all qualified in light of the ease with which his pockets were picked by three professionals in April 1879 as he was returning from the McCaffrey trial. They struck up a conversation with him at the Harrisburg train station, "freely mingled in his company, and when he boarded the train west he found his pocketbook, money and passes gone."[22]

8

An Accusation Dodged

The energy and speed with which Gould rebuilt the college by September 1879 saved his job, which seemed to be on the line after the McCaffrey–Cameron trial. And he continued to burnish his reputation as a pulpit orator. A sermon he delivered on February 29, 1880, at the Paris Methodist Church, "The Soul and Its Immortality," impressed the editor of the *Paris Kentuckian,* who observed that it was "grand and impressive" and the ablest refutation to date of the doctrine that man has no soul. Materialists, Gould affirmed, believe that man is a mere automaton, that all mental activity is the result of molecular changes caused by heredity and environment, and that freedom of the will is impossible. He countered this argument by observing that we are often able to restrain our automatic responses when they would be socially inappropriate, such as "sneezing in church, laughing at a funeral, yawning in the face of a bore, belching in company." Such restraint is an effort of the will and therefore "of the willing soul." This line of thinking, of course, made absolutely no sense except to those of his hearers already committed to belief in a soul. We could just as easily conclude that it is the conscious mind, not the soul, that keeps us from sneezing in church. But though his logic was slippery, it did allow him to move to an eloquent conclusion:

> Would you still further see the value of man's immortal part? Look out over the world and see the wonders it has wrought.

> See the palaces it has built, the canals it has dug, the bridges it has erected, the vessels it has constructed, the monuments it has reared, the discoveries it has made, the contrivances it has invented. See it giving to the world the only value it possesses. See it tunneling the seas, see it mining the mountains, see it girdling the oceans, see it weighing the hills, see it driving the lightnings; see it fearlessly flinging itself across the untrodden skies, that it may tell the distance of the farthest star that wheels its burning coursers upon the very confines of creation. See it, in a word, the very image of God on earth![1]

This gives us an idea of his theology, which was far from the fire-and-brimstone preaching of others. Man, it seems, according to Gould, does not need saving; just by being his expansionist, imperial self, he is the image of God.

But his reputation was about to sustain another blow. Just a week or so after he preached that sermon, Professor Joseph Young of Kentucky Wesleyan College brought before the Kentucky Conference of the Southern Methodist Church the accusation that Gould had been visibly drunk on more than one occasion. The editor of the *Paris Kentuckian* backed Gould: "There is no real foundation for the charge, more than that Prof. Gould, who is consumptive, as was his father, also a Methodist minister, has been advised to use cod liver oil and liquor, but has never done so to great excess." In the course of the trial, Gould would actually allude to a different ailment, chronic diarrhea, as the reason for the taking of whiskey. Gould somehow managed to persuade those running the investigation to reduce to merely one day—February 21, 1880—Young's original charge that Gould had been intoxicated on several occasions. That reduction would make it easier for him to elude conviction.[2]

Nevertheless, several teachers and students at the college said they had seen Gould drunk that day. Young testified that when he saw Gould on the street, he "noticed redness of eyes and stupidity of appearance," that he smelled whiskey on his breath, and that Gould "reeled and staggered." Miss Nettie Platte, one of the teachers, testified that when she saw him in his office that day, she could tell from his face that he had been drinking, and she could smell it on his breath. Then when he got up to walk, her suspicion was confirmed, for "he was limber in his knees."

Millersburg Female College, date unknown (Hopewell Museum, Paris, KY)

She had come in with a question to ask, and he began talking "in a very ungentlemanly manner. . . . I thought it rude for him to speak to a lady so loud and excitedly when she is not deaf." Another teacher, Mrs. Crouch, saw him in the dining room and was troubled by his appearance. "He lingered in conversation. I was afraid he was intoxicated," but she would not have spoken of it were she not compelled to do so. Some of the students, she added, were talking about it and "seemed distressed and excited." Miss Jennie Stillman, the music teacher at the college, was looking out her window and saw him leaning against a fence, his hands in his pockets, his head to one side, and his feet oddly apart. He looked drunk to her. Miss Jennie Benton, a student, was in Mrs. Crouch's room and saw him as well. She had heard he was drunk, and what she saw through the window gave her that impression. "He staggered as much as he could not to fall." She gazed at him through the window for a full five minutes. He was leaning against the fence "like he couldn't support himself; if nobody had said anything to me, what I saw from that window convinced me Dr. Gould was drunk." Later that day she went into his office to discuss an essay she had written. He "laughed a great deal, and I'm sure I smelled whiskey on his breath; next saw him in the dining room; noticed him stagger when going around the table. I thought he faltered in his blessing."[3]

Gould then took the stand. He began with an extremely detailed, indeed tedious, account of his every moment on the day in question. He had risen late because, having strained his back the day before in lifting a piano, he had hardly slept all night—the general import being that this would account for his looking a little under the weather. He supervised the removal of benches from the dining room, where there had been "an entertainment" the previous night. He went to see his uncle Tom Oliver and walked him over to breakfast; after breakfast he continued to speak with him outside at the corner gate. He spoke with his mother. He gave twenty-five cents to a tramp and told him not to spend it on whiskey. He went to his office, where he received "the negro Methodist preacher," who told him of his troubles; Gould gave him $5 and accepted his invitation to come preach. At 11:00 a.m., he went over the plans for a gymnasium with Charles McCormack. He examined the grocery bill with his father-in-law, Mr. Fullenwider, and inspected the quality of two barrels of sugar. He received payment for coal from a Mr. Demaree. Dr. Hunt came in, and Gould got him to make a contribution for the black preacher. He discussed changing the venue for a temperance lecture with Professor Murphy. He sent Joe Corrington to see about posting a notice for the lecture. He went to the house of the ailing Reverend James E. Letton and told him he would send him a load of coal. He had a conversation at the fence with Brother Chamberlain. He spoke with some persons who passed by in a buggy; he conversed with Dr. Hunt, who was a local banker as well as a physician, about an important business transaction; he asked his mother for advice on choosing a speaker for the commencement in June and talked to his wife about that as well. Colonel Oliver came in to ask when dinner would be.[4]

There is more. This description takes us only to four o'clock of Gould's day, and there is a whole evening to come. But he apparently wanted to let it be known that he could not possibly have been drunk that day if he could remember everything he did in such detail. "I am thus minute because the whole day is imprinted on my memory like a book."[5]

Then he got to the interview with Miss Platte. When he returned to his office, she was there. Mr. Fullenwider came in and was a witness to the encounter. It seemed not to have occurred to the investigators that

Fullenwider, his wife's father, had an interest in Gould's escaping conviction. Perhaps they did not know that this interest was not just familial but financial. Gould was deeply in debt to Fullenwider, from whom he had borrowed the money to buy his proprietorship of the college several years earlier, a loan he had not yet repaid. If Gould were convicted of drunkenness, he would lose the presidency, and his father-in-law would lose his money. Platte had come to ask permission to be away for a few days to take a trip. Gould refused. "She insisted that she could put Miss Mary Hughes in her place. I replied that if I had desired Miss Hughes I could have obtained her services for about half of what Miss Platte's cost. Still urging, I told her that further conversation was useless, for I would not consent. She immediately arose and flouted out of the room, muttering as she went." Gould told the investigators he was surprised she had asked for such a favor at such a time because just a few days earlier he had twice rebuked her and his other chief accuser among the faculty, Jennie Stillman, for not being punctual at meals, "the last time telling them that if they could not observe my rules they must seek another place."[6]

Thus, he impeached both witnesses. But he still had to do something about his official accuser, Professor Young. The latter's status in the Southern Methodist Church did not permit Gould to impugn his motives. Before the trial, he interviewed Young to see if he could get him to change his story or at least his certainty. "The burden of the conversation was to show that he [Young] was mistaken in his impression, and it was his statement alone that gave any semblance of truth to the report. Endeavoring to convince him that he was mistaken, I asked him whether in my coming to him" in their encounter on February 21 "he noticed any peculiarity in walk." Young answered no. Any peculiarity when I walked away? No. Was I thick-tongued? No. Was I incoherent? No. Gould assured him he was not drunk that day. Young then retreated to the position that he would help him out as long as his own truthfulness was not questioned. Gould had learned that Young had spoken of Gould's drunkenness in Maysville and other places. He thought that if the accusations rested on Miss Platte's testimony alone, "the thing could be lived down," but he decided to call for an official investigation so that he could clear his name.[7]

After two days of testimony, the investigating committee took just an hour to declare Gould not guilty. The verdict came at midnight. At morning prayer in the college chapel the following day, Gould announced that the three teachers who had testified against him, Miss Platte, Miss Stillman, and Mrs. Crouch, were fired. None of the six students, however, would be expelled, Gould saying that "their minds had been poisoned against him" by those teachers.[8]

The *Paris Kentuckian* of March 31 reported that Crouch, Platte, and Stillman left Millersburg for their respective homes and editorialized that it was time for the community to move on as well. But the same issue also contained this statement:

> We the undersigned, teachers of the Millersburg Female College, do hereby pronounce as false all statements in published reports of Dr. G. T. Gould's trial calling in question the honest intent of certain members of our faculty. We refer to Mrs. Crouch, Miss Platte and Miss Stillman, who appeared as witnesses for the prosecution. We also earnestly protest against Dr. Gould's action in dismissing them from his faculty, since we know them to be Christian ladies of unapproachable veracity and dauntless moral courage. We believe that circumstances forced them to the stand they took in the recent trouble. As they leave us we bid them God speed wherever they may go and commend them to any community so fortunate as to secure their professional services.

It was signed by ten members of the faculty, including four who were also recent graduates of the college, evidently familiar as students as well as teachers with Gould's occasional tyranny.[9]

The list of signers begins with Professor A. G. Murphy, who had already submitted his resignation on March 23. Gould wanted to accept it immediately, but cooler heads persuaded him to wait. He did so until April 13, when he found a replacement for Murphy: the Reverend J. C. C. Newton, who coincidentally had been "one of the principal witnesses for the defense" at the church trial from which Gould emerged victorious.[10]

John G. Craddock at the *Paris Kentuckian* asserted that the trial had taken place because Gould had demanded an investigation of the charges to clear his name. Although Gould may well have told Craddock that, in reality Gould thought Murphy was behind the accusation. "I had told my wife that I believed him to be a scoundrel of the deepest dye," he reflected in a statement for yet another church trial of him four years later, "that I was confident he had gotten up the whole matter of my trial in February 1880 for the purpose of ousting me from the school and succeeding me as the principal." He may have been right to fear that, for not long after the trial Craddock indicated that Millersburg citizens had thought such a turnover was going to happen: "The rumor of the sale of the Millersburg Female College to Dr. Savage and Prof. Murphy is, like many another rumor, without foundation. In fact, Dr. Gould assures us there is no intention on his part to sell to anybody, that he owns the school and intends to keep it." In other words, Craddock did not deny that Murphy and Savage wanted to buy the college.[11]

Gould was enraged to learn from his wife that she had told Murphy of her husband's intention to fire him. "I had made up my mind in March [1880] to dismiss him and was looking for someone else to fill his place," he wrote later. She told Gould he ought not to do it, going, as Gould stated, "on a rigmarole about [Murphy's] virtues and standing in the community until in my wrath I could stand it no more, but jumping out of the bed, I flung myself into my own room, saying that for my life I could not understand why she should take up for the old hypocritical scoundrel, unless she was too intimate with him, as I was almost inclined to believe." The following month, she suffered a miscarriage and blamed it on Gould's kicking her when he leaped out of bed that night.[12]

Gould hated Murphy because he feared him. "Professor Murphy is my enemy, and has every motive to expose me that one man can have to expose another." Murphy could have exposed him for his addiction to drink, but in fact when some of the students discovered Gould's jug of whiskey, Murphy swore them to secrecy and took steps to have the jug hidden in a more secure place. When Gould learned this, he asked for the names of the girls. Murphy refused, and then Gould demanded of Professor O. P. Moore, who also knew about the jug and to whom Murphy had told some of the names, that he reveal them. "Prof. Moore became a little agitated," Murphy recounted, "and raised his arm, saying 'I will suffer this right arm to be cut off before I will make known the names of the girls.' The Doctor [i.e., Gould] manifested some feeling and said if he could ascertain who the girls were he would expel them from the school." As a result of his refusal to give the students' names,

Moore lost his job, if not his arm. He had begun teaching French and German at Gould's college in September 1878, but a year later was in Stanford, Kentucky, trying to interest students in a class in German.[13]

Six months after his resignation from the college, Murphy sold his ninety-acre farm near Millersburg and a year later was teaching at the prestigious Science Hill women's college in Shelbyville, Kentucky. The *Paris Kentuckian* mourned his loss: Murphy "has been a citizen of our town for the past twenty years. His time was devoted to the instruction of the young in our institutions of learning, where he won many life-long friends. He is a man of a highly moral and intellectual character, dignified in his bearing and a noble Christian. We regret very much his departure, and congratulate Shelbyville on receiving a man of his power in her midst."[14]

In the wake of the public letter from Murphy and other faculty at the college condemning Gould for firing the three teachers who had testified against him, the correspondent for the *Cincinnati Commercial* wrote that "many rumors have been afloat" since the trial and that "nothing has excited the people of Millersburg and vicinity more in the recollection of our oldest citizens than this case. . . . It is conjectured by many that other resignations will now follow. There can be little doubt but the majority of the teachers are against Dr. Gould." The editor of the *Paris Kentuckian* did not agree. He wrote that if the account in the Cincinnati paper "chanced to leave the impression that the school was in a perfect tumult and uproar let it be understood that such is not the case." Most citizens accepted the outcome as just, "though a few are left who still gossip and no doubt they often petition the Almighty to give them some light on the subject which others have not yet obtained."[15]

9

Let the Past Be Buried

At the Millersburg Female College commencement in June 1880, medals were awarded for elocution, music, English literature, Latin, mathematics, philosophy, natural science, neatness, and deportment, and selected graduates read aloud their essays, performed musical selections, and recited poetry. J. F. Wight, father of two students, honored Gould with the gift of a gold-headed cane. Gould responded with his usual eloquence, promising that when classes resumed that fall, the school would have the best teachers in the state. Editor John Craddock of the *Paris Kentuckian* wrote that Gould "voiced the sentiments of everyone present and the community at large when he exclaimed, 'Let the past be buried.'"[1]

One way to bury it was to fire all the dissenting teachers. By September, every single teacher who had signed the letter of March 31 protesting the firing of Crouch, Platte, and Stillman was gone. As Gould later explained, "It was . . . my custom not to permit my teachers to dictate to me any line of policy or to protest against any of my management. For so protesting . . . I dismissed Murphy and refused to employ a single teacher I had in the school." He overstated the case because he did not fire all the teachers, just those who signed. One he kept on was J. C. Meininger, professor of music. That same year, 1880, as noted earlier, Meininger published a waltz dedicated "to the Young Ladies of Millersburg Female College" with the title "School Girls Dream." An engraving of the college building graces the cover page, together with a list of the school's teachers and administrators. None of the ten teachers who signed the March 31 statement is there. Mrs. S. F. H. Tarrant, who would join the faculty in October, is not on the list either, which indicates that it was drawn up before her arrival but after the departure of the principled ten. Gould's wife appears as both lady principal and art teacher. Other family members on the payroll are her father, H. W. Fullenwider, as the college's purveyor, as well as her mother, Mrs. H. W. Fullenwider, and George's mother, Mrs. E. B. Gould, together composing the Health Department.[2]

Though Gould fired ten faculty members, he could not bury all his troubles. In the fall of 1880, Professor H. K. Taylor of Kentucky Wesleyan College went public with a grievance with him over money. The funds to rebuild the college after the 1878 fire were generated by Gould's creating a stock company in which Taylor had purchased a share for $50. Reverend James E. Letton also bought a share, but when in the spring of 1880 he checked with the county clerk, he learned that his share had not been registered. Letton told Taylor he had better do the same, and he did, with the same distressing result. Around May 15, Taylor went to see Gould about it. Gould assured him he would correct the oversight but did not do so. Taylor let some time pass and then sent Gould a note desiring an immediate settlement. Taylor wrote to the *Paris Kentuckian,* "He did not reply, but about this time Rev. W. T. Benton went to see him about Brother Letton's mortgage, and my name being mentioned, Gould flew into a rage and said if I [Taylor] did not watch out he would kick me all over Millersburg, at the same time using vulgarity characteristic of the veriest blackguard." The vulgarity lay in Gould's saying what part of Taylor's anatomy he would kick.[3]

Taylor brought the matter before the Kentucky Conference of the Southern Methodist Church. A committee was formed before which Benton, Taylor, and Gould appeared. Gould satisfied Taylor with regard to the mortgage, but Taylor still pressed charges over the abusive language. Benton raised the issue before the committee, and Gould responded: "Yes, if I said it I meant it, and I mean it still." And added: "If you deprive me of the right to kick a fellow whenever I want to, the sooner we sever our connection the better for both." He meant the connection between himself and the Southern Methodist Conference, a remarkable threat to make, for without that connection he could not continue to run the college. But he must have thought, and apparently was justified in thinking, that his stock was so high with the conference and that the college brought the conference such prestige, he could make that empty threat to get his way.[4]

Gould eventually acknowledged the "impropriety" of his language, and the committee accepted his excuse that "he had been so set upon by parties who seemed desirous of his overthrow, with that of his school, was so harassed, vexed, worried and aggravated, that at that time he scarcely knew what he said" and "that other men thus situated would have done no better, perhaps worse." Taylor pointed out in a letter to the editor of the *Paris Kentuckian* that although Gould may have felt set upon back in March, when he had been obliged to fight a charge of drunkenness, he could have had no such excuse in September. Summer vacation had come in between, and a new school year had begun.[5]

But the committee still faced a problem that one of its members put this way: "How shall we get over Dr. Gould's intelligence of improper words and tempers?" In other words, how can we get over the scandal of his knowing those dirty words in the first place? Nevertheless, Gould persuaded them not to bring up the matter before the whole Kentucky Conference in September. But the scandal lingered, for Taylor and the committee chair debated each other on the point in the columns of the *Paris Kentuckian* as late as November 17. Taylor accused Gould of being "a man who protects his diabolical deeds with the mantle of the ministry," those deeds being his threat of violence, his obscene language, and his attempt to avoid paying the $50 he owed Taylor. The latter accusation Taylor revealed only in his final volley, to which neither the committee chair nor Gould could manage a reply. Gould had left town before the November 17 installment of the paper anyway, off to Texas on a recruiting trip. He returned in early January, bringing nine new students.[6]

Ella once complained to George's uncle Tom Oliver about those trips, as he later testified: "Any man that will travel around as Mr. Gould does spending his wife's substance ought to be hung." Oliver asked what she meant by substance. "She replied that he owed her father $7500.00 and that he was not supporting her and her children." Oliver answered that he thought Gould supported them pretty well, that no lady in Millersburg dressed more elegantly than her, and no girl as well as the Goulds' daughter, Mamie (born January 23, 1872).[7]

Marital discord induced Gould to stay away more than he had to. He later admitted as much, saying that "under the stress" of his unhappy marriage, he "commenced going to Texas and being absent two or three months at a time. But a few trips of this sort convinced me that my school would go to ruin if I kept it up." Yet he probably enjoyed the attention he received on such an occasion as his appearance before the Ladies' Missionary Society of Corsicana, Texas, where he was praised for his "chaste, scholarly, and timely" address. With only ten minutes' notice, "to our surprise and gratification he spoke as if he had studied nothing else for ten years, and had been sent by the Ladies' Missionary Society to travel and speak alone in this interest. . . . Dr. Gould has thus won a welcome to Texas, for whomsoever the ladies make welcome is welcome indeed. We can't help thinking the girl happy and fortunate who shares with her comrades his instruction in Millersburg College."[8]

Just before Gould left for Texas in November 1880, he had scored a major success in both student and faculty recruitment, having enticed Mrs. S. F. H. Tarrant, principal of Tarrant College in Crab Orchard, Kentucky, to close her school and join his, bringing six of her students with her. "Mrs. Tarrant has been at the head of female colleges for thirty years, and Dr. Gould says she is the most accomplished lady connected with female education in the State." But there is a risk in hiring someone better and more experienced than you, as Gould would learn the following year.[9]

Susan Frances Hale Tarrant was born on April 16, 1834, in Cumberland, Rhode Island. When she was fourteen, her family moved to Prattville, Alabama, where her father became superintendent of the cotton mills and gin manufactory built by New England industrialist Daniel Pratt. She attended school in Prattville, then returned to Rhode Island to continue her education at the Providence Seminary, graduating with honors in 1852. Gould's claim that Tarrant had been at the head of female colleges since 1850 was a slight exaggeration. She did not begin to teach until the fall of 1853 and probably did not start out as the head of her school. On September 14, 1864, she married Reverend John Frederick Tarrant, four years her junior. It was actually her second marriage; her first, to a Dr. Custer from Tennessee, had caused a scandal. "I have some news to tell you that I know will shock," a Pratt family member wrote to her husband in November 1872. "Sue Hale's husband has a *wife* and *four children living*. Mr. Hale"—Susan's father—"received a letter last week from someone in Shelbyville, Tenn. telling him all about it." Dr. Custer, she continued, is "a villain indeed. . . . He thought . . . that the Yankees had Tennessee and would probably hold it and there would be no danger of Sue's ever hearing of his wife." It is likely that neither George T. Gould nor anyone else in Kentucky ever heard of it at all.[10]

Apparently, the marriage was annulled because Miss Hale became free to wed again. At the time of her marriage to Reverend Tarrant, the latter was principal of a female college in Dayton, Alabama. He was originally from Danville, Kentucky, and he eventually returned with his wife and growing family to that part of the country, taking charge of the Crab Orchard Springs Female College, twenty miles away, in the fall of 1872. In 1874, the Tarrants and their five children moved to Danville, where he was to serve as principal of the Caldwell Institute for Young Ladies. But on October 14 he died of a sudden illness. Mrs. Tarrant and a daughter continued on as teachers at Caldwell until the end of the spring term. That fall she returned to Crab Orchard to found Tarrant College for Girls, where she remained until Gould enticed her to Millersburg five years later. Her decision to leave Crab Orchard may have been prompted by a difficulty that arose in finding a suitable building to house her school. The owner of the property that for several years had been its home died; the heirs sold it on August 16, 1880, and she was unable to rent it from the new owner. She appears to have found another location, but it may have proved so unsatisfactory that she accepted Gould's invitation. Another contributing factor was that Gould was so desperate to restore some excellence to the faculty he had decimated that he offered her the significant incentive, though he could ill afford it, of assuming a debt she owed.[11]

The Crab Orchard correspondent for the *Stanford (Kentucky) Interior Journal* reported "with deep regret" on the part of the town that Mrs. Tarrant was leaving for Millersburg. She would be missed, "for she has been as a light upon a hill." She had done much for the cultural life of the town and had trained a dozen young women teachers then serving within a twenty-five-mile radius. "We congratulate Dr. Gould and his school, and heartily wish for Mrs. Tarrant more sunshine than has been her lot. May the shadows that have darkened her life since her residence in Kentucky be the last that she may be called on to experience." Those shadows were the deaths of her brother in May of that year and of her husband six years earlier.[12]

After the public dispute with H. K. Taylor, no new scandals involving Gould erupted to entertain readers of the local press. At the Millersburg Female College commencement in June 1881, the citizens of Millersburg, or at least some of them, prepared "a grand illumination" in Gould's honor. Hundreds of burning candles adorned the college's windows and as many Chinese lanterns bedecked the grounds. An arch spanned the entrance gate with illuminated letters proclaiming or predicting the "Success of Millersburg Female College." Major Hiram Bassett spoke for a grateful town when he praised Gould as "the only man in Kentucky who could, under the circumstances, achieve the wonderful success which his indomitable will and untiring industry have accomplished, by establishing, not only one of the best, but the largest College for young ladies in the State." The "circumstances" to which he alluded may have been the obstacles posed by one church trial for drunkenness and Taylor's attempt to instigate another for theft and aggravated menacing as well as the loss of ten teachers through firing and resignations. Bassett was hardly a disinterested observer, however, for since the fall of 1880 he had been a member of the faculty and Gould's fellow Mason in the Millersburg Lodge.[13]

The 1880–1881 school year appears to have gone off without a hitch for the teacher from Crab Orchard, but in October 1881 a chain of events was set in motion that caused Mrs. Tarrant to sever her connection to Gould in a disagreeable way. Mattie Couts, who at twenty years of age was older than most of the other students, was walking with a group that included Gould when she asked to be excused to go into the bookstore to buy a piece of music. Gould forbade her to do so. She tartly replied that she would do whatever she had a mind to do. Enraged that a student would openly defy him, Gould told her to pack her trunk and go home.

At the next chapel service, Gould told the assembled students and faculty, "I have to announce to the school this morning that I have dismissed Miss Mattie Couts, for impertinence." Mrs. Tarrant spoke up: "Dr. Gould, do you intend to say that Miss Couts has been expelled from this school?" "None of your business!" Gould replied. "She has not been expelled," said Tarrant, "for no young lady can be properly expelled without a meeting of the Faculty and the majority agreeing that the offense is sufficient for such disgrace." Gould's reply: "You may follow her." After recounting these events in a letter to the *Paris Kentuckian,* Tarrant wrote: "And I followed her. Thus it happens that a very serious beginning ended in a ridiculous farce."[14]

Craddock, the editor of the *Paris Kentuckian,* was normally eager to back Gould whatever he did, but on this occasion he seemed to regret Gould's course of action, for Gould "loses an excellent teacher." Craddock had also regretted the loss of Professor Murphy. Gould had a long-standing animus toward Murphy, but his firing of Mrs. Tarrant was an impulsive act.[15]

She would not go quietly. On December 7, the *Paris Kentuckian* featured all on the same day "A Card from Mrs. Tarrant," one from Gould, and then another from her. In the first installment, she argued that his treatment of Miss Couts was inconsistent with what he wrote in the college catalog about behaving toward his pupils as if they were his own daughters: "Eating with them at the same table, visiting them in their rooms and during sickness, counseling them in their little troubles, and assisting them in their studies, the President and his wife endeavor to fill the place of father and mother to each young lady committed to their care." He would not refund one dollar of Couts's tuition but sent her penniless out into the world when she was hundreds of miles away from her Texas home. This was not a very fatherly thing to do. Tarrant recounted the scene in the chapel where he announced the student's expulsion and fired Tarrant when she objected. She closed by announcing that on January 2 she would be teaching at another school, one "where the principal and teachers will sacredly perform all they promise."[16]

Gould responded with a personal attack. The violence of the abuse, he wrote, that a fired employee heaps on her employer is usually "proportioned to the indebtedness of the employee. At the time I discharged her she was largely and hopelessly in my debt." Tarrant replied: "I don't know how he has come to the conclusion that I am so largely in his debt—we have had no settlement; he assumed a debt for me, but he has not paid it, and I presume, will not do so very soon." This appears to allude to a financial inducement he had made to persuade her to leave Crab Orchard for Millersburg but had apparently never followed through on.[17]

Gould maintained that he dismissed the student "for telling me to my face that she would do a certain forbidden thing whenever she wished to do it." No school in the country would put up with such behavior. "It is bad enough for a pupil to secretly disobey those in authority over her, but when she openly and defiantly places herself in rebellion against the very head of the school, her dismissal becomes imperative." He had not refused to refund the money. He told her she could have it in the morning, but she was leaving on the train before the banks opened. She asked him to entrust the money to Mrs. Tarrant, which he was unwilling to do. He later sent her a check. She was not going off alone in the world but to a school in the very next county and "had the largest abundance of means to carry her there." She was not "the usual school girl, young, timid, inexperienced, and committed to my care by her parents." If that were the case, he would have telegraphed her parents to come get her, and he would have housed her with his own family until they arrived. But her parents had not put her in the school; she herself had done that. "She was her own mistress. She had money at the bank in her own name." She paid her own bills and selected her own course of study. Although he did not mention her age, his characterization of self-sufficiency was correct, for she was born in 1861 and therefore past her teenage years.[18]

Besides, all she had to do was apologize, and he would have forgotten the whole thing.

Tarrant had argued that he could not expel a student without the consent of the faculty. Gould pointed out in reply that he owned the school. In other schools, the president might be elected by a board of trustees, but that was not the case here. He paid the teachers to do what he told them, no more and no less. The entire control was in his hands. In concluding, he returned to his initial barb about Tarrant's being in his debt, snidely commenting that the news that she had a new job lined up in another school would no doubt make her many creditors rejoice.[19]

Tarrant in reply ridiculed Gould for "living in a house"—the college—"that has a mortgage of thousands of dollars over it, and at the same time so hopelessly in debt that he says no one can make anything out of him by law." Her accusation was accurate. He had mortgaged the property to pay for rebuilding it after the fire three years earlier. Before that, he had borrowed money from his father-in-law to buy the college and had made no progress toward repaying that debt. He very likely did brag to Susan Tarrant, back when they were friends, that he was so broke, no one could make him pay.[20]

She then brought up his alcoholism, which she had been too polite to mention until now. His "card" to the *Paris Kentuckian* was so bombastic and ludicrous, she wrote, that he must have taken a double dose of "medicine" before writing it. Everyone knew he had claimed that his whiskey consumption was only for medicinal purposes when he had been brought before a church trial for drunkenness, an episode she did not neglect to mention as well. In response to his assertion that the faculty had no role to play in running the school, she suggested that in his case perhaps they should. "When the President of a college has no control over his temper nor his language, and when he has to take 'medicine' as strong as whiskey if he has no guardian, he ought to consult with his Faculty, on momentous questions."[21]

She asserted that his discipline of the students was not always uniform: "If he is angry or has taken too much 'medicine,' he pursues one course; if not, another." One student was dismissed for bringing a note from a young man in town to a young lady in the college, while of others who had brought several notes he said not a word. Nor did he send home the girl who received the notes. "I question whether he, at some time, would order a girl to leave when he knew she had stolen money from other girls."[22]

The check he claimed was in the mail was not. Mattie Couts left Millersburg on November 1 but had not received it by November 12, when she wrote Tarrant to say she might have to hire a lawyer to make him pay. As late as November 23, Mr. Couts wrote to Mrs. Tarrant that "Mattie has applied to him [Mr. Gould] twice for the money, but he has not refunded it, and as he is almost a bankrupt I guess he is sure to keep it."[23]

Gould did not publish a reply to Mrs. Tarrant's second "card" to the *Paris Kentuckian*. He had sent his rebuttal of Tarrant's first "card" from Waxahachie, Texas, in early December and did not return to Millersburg until December 31.

Tarrant's new position was at the Lexington Female College, a defunct institution that she reopened. Her creditors may not have been rejoicing yet, for to make any salary at all she would have to find some paying students. The school had "very flattering prospects," however, according to the *Interior Journal* on February 7, 1882, which had followed her career since her years at Crab Orchard. A few months later, the editor of the *Bourbon News* visited Mrs. Tarrant in Lexington and found her "very happily situated, with a nice little school at present and a bright prospect for the fall term." He met some of the teachers, one of whom was Mrs. Meininger. At the college's graduation exercises a few weeks later, Mr. and Mrs. Meininger performed on the piano. The couple, both of whom used to teach at Millersburg, had evidently transferred their allegiance. Had Gould fired them too?[24]

Apparently so. On January 25, 1882, the *Paris Kentuckian* had reported on "the reorganization" of the Millersburg Female College faculty for the spring term. "Prof. J. C Meininger and wife go out of the Music Department, and Prof. F. L. Bristow comes in." Meininger "and his wife have made a fine reputation in their line while in our community." Could Gould have been angry at Meininger for his role in the Mattie Couts business? Susan Tarrant recalled that the trouble began when Mattie "ordered a piece of music through Mr. M[eininger] at the bookstore." But it is very possible that Gould simply wanted to replace Meininger with Bristow because of the latter's expertise in two areas Meininger lacked: orchestral music and calisthenics. In a sermon Gould had given on February 14, 1880, he had happened to mention that "I once had in my school a professor of music who organized a band among the girls, consisting of some 36 pieces and about 20 different kinds of instruments." By hiring Bristow, he could bring back that orchestra.[25]

10

Copperheads and Pearly Gates

Frank Leslie Bristow was born on April 15, 1845, in Bethel, Illinois. His parents were transplanted southerners, his mother coming from South Carolina and his father from Kentucky. Frank Bristow and Benjamin Helm Bristow (1832–1896), the presidential candidate for whom Elisha Green voted at the Kentucky Republican Convention in 1876, were first cousins, their fathers being brothers. Benjamin Helm Bristow's father was Francis Marion Bristow (1804–1864), a US representative from Kentucky in 1854–1855 and 1859–1861. Frank's father, Benjamin Franklin Bristow (1815–1888), was a merchant and part-time Methodist preacher, having obtained his license in 1837. He had a pleasant singing voice and typically concluded his sermons with a song. It was said that he had preached and prayed "on every hilltop and in every valley of Morgan county." In 1843, for example, there being no church in the village of Meredosia, Illinois, he held forth for several days in a whiskey saloon while drunks caroused in the back room but succeeded in starting a religious revival that led to the building of a church. By 1850, the Bristows had relocated to the larger town of Jacksonville, Illinois, the county seat, thirty-five miles west of Springfield.[1]

Jacksonville, as Charles H. Rammelkamp observed in 1928, "is located in that region of Illinois where the streams of migration from the South and New England mingled, the larger element coming from the South." Illinois College, founded there in 1829 by New Englanders, was the first college in the state to grant a degree. Edward Beecher, brother to Harriet Beecher Stowe, was its first president. It had always had abolitionist tendencies that put it at odds with some of its neighbors. "The faculty, therefore, had great difficulty in trying to maintain the College, and at the same time stand for what they believed to be right." The students were divided in their loyalties, though by 1862 many coming from the South had already left the school to join the Confederate army.[2]

Frank's two older brothers, Benjamin (1838–1896) and Edmund (1841–1900), enlisted with the Confederates in 1861. But when Frank answered the call of battle, it was to join the other side. In the spring of 1862, he and five other Illinois College students marched up to the recruiting officer's table to sign their names, "encouraged," as he told a newspaper reporter in 1906, "to this patriotic duty by the stirring strains of 'Barbara Allen,' beautifully rendered upon the fife and drums." According to army records, Frank was five foot seven inches and had light hair and blue eyes.[3]

Strangely, Frank Leslie Bristow enlisted in the Union army under a different name than his own, that of his uncle Francis Marion Bristow. In the US Census of 1850, his first name appears as "Franklin" but in 1860 as "Frank"; in neither instance did a middle name appear. His first name came from "Franklin," his father's middle name, not from "Francis." We can only speculate as to why he made the double change, from "Frank" to "Francis" and from "Leslie" to "Marion." Was he patterning himself after his uncle and rejecting his father? If so, was it because his father was a rabid apologist for the Confederacy and slavery, whereas his uncle freed his slaves and was so vocal in opposing the Confederacy that he had to flee Kentucky and take refuge behind Union lines?[4]

Had Bristow been less certain whether to go north or south than his change of name would indicate, music might have helped him decide. The fife and drums playing those "stirring strains" drew him in, and he indeed joined the drum corps, became a fifer, and was eventually made bandleader of Company D of the 101st Illinois Infantry Volunteers. Another inducement was the bounty of $50 for each new recruit that Morgan County provided in the hope of avoiding the use of conscription. "As the bounties piled higher, young men streamed into the

Union Army; by the end of March 1862, nearly 650 brave sons of Jacksonville had enlisted." For whatever reason, Bristow was one.[5]

The 101st Regiment formed at nearby Camp Duncan near the end of August, drilled until October 6, took the train for Cairo, Illinois, and drilled again until the end of November. They proceeded by boat to Columbus, Kentucky, then by rail to Davis's Mill, Mississippi, where they joined the Army of the Tennessee. They marched to Holly Springs, Mississippi, where they were assigned provost and garrison duty.[6]

One of the other company musicians, Bristow remembered, was a "peculiar looking and acting fellow" named John Ham, a bugler who constantly expressed his hatred of the rebels. He was also a talented fiddler who never failed to attract a crowd as he struck up "Devil's Dream" or "Sugar in the Gourd," delighting "the lovely and lovable listening young ladies" of Jacksonville before the regiment left that town and again later in Holly Springs.[7]

As musicians, Bristow and company did not usually have to fight. In December 1862, they were assigned to play reveille, taps, and other calls for troops guarding the Union supply store at Holly Springs. They were invited to perform at the home of a Mrs. Long, which their commanding officer had commandeered for his headquarters. An official report on the disaster that ensued would take the officers to task for sleeping at rebel homes instead of with their troops. To mollify Mrs. Long, the major invited his musicians in to play. She invited them back, and they took pleasure in her company and that of her pretty niece. Vocal in her support of the southern cause, Mrs. Long would frequently joke with the major, predicting Union defeat. "And then all of us would laugh together," Bristow recalled. "Mrs. Long and her niece in full confidence of the fulfillment of her prophecy, and we Yanks at the seeming absurdity of such a prediction ever coming true."[8]

One day Ham the bugler was missing from mess. When asked why, he said he had been at the widow's, wooing her niece with his fiddle and trying to make her into "a good Union girl." That seemed a project unlikely to succeed.[9]

On the night of December 20, Bristow and his fellow musicians were awakened by rapid and continuous musket fire and heard the rebel yell. He ventured outside and saw what seemed to be a herd of mad buffalos headed in his direction. Bullets whistled by his head. He ran back into the law office where the musicians had been housed, locked the door, and announced: "By George, boys, the Rebs have got us sure and certain this time.'"[10]

They surrendered to a Confederate officer, who told them to hurry down the street before the arsenal blew up. Bristow was about to do that when he heard the officer say, "Why John Ham, how on earth did you come to be here?" Ham went up to the officer's horse, put his hand on the stirrup, and as the Confederate bent down, the bugler whispered something in his ear. The officer smiled and told him to follow the other prisoners down the street. The bugler told Bristow, "I knew that fellow out in Missouri, Frank."[11]

When the prisoners were issued paroles, Ham was nowhere to be found. Then he came up on a horse and cheerfully bid farewell, telling Bristow that from then on Bristow would have to find someone else to play the bugle. Bristow later learned that Ham had been a Confederate officer in Missouri who had been cut off from his unit but then slipped into Illinois and joined the 101st Illinois as the shortest path to rejoining his comrades in gray. It appears he had not gone to woo the niece but to tell her aunt there would be no pickets on guard that morning and Holly Springs was ripe for attack. She sent word to the rebels, and the Yankees were taken by surprise. A Confederate recalled: "As we dashed down one of the main streets by a two-story residence on the right, there were on the little front portico upstairs two ladies, mother and daughter doubtless, in their night dresses, both jumping up and down and clapping their hands, one of them crying at the top of her voice: 'I told the Yankees our boys would come in here and catch them. I told them so.'" Those two ladies were Mrs. Long and her niece.[12]

Bristow and his regiment returned to the fighting, and he and his musicians eventually serenaded General William Sherman's men on their march to the sea beginning November 15, 1864.[13]

While Frank Bristow was fighting the war, his father back in Illinois was trying to end it. He was active among the Copperheads of the Democratic Party, who criticized Lincoln for pursuing the war and wanted it stopped. From January 1863 on, opponents of the war attacked supporters with increasing violence. Farmers found their orchards destroyed and horses poisoned; Union soldiers home on furlough were attacked and in at least one case murdered. The Knights of the Golden

Circle, an extremist group that sympathized with the Confederacy, met at night for military drills. In September, Jacksonville, Illinois, came close to having a pitched battle between the Knights and the town's defenders. Three hundred armed men rode in with the aim of rescuing one of the Knights' number from jail. "Bank clerks on the square strapped on pistols," the newspaper office barricaded its doors, and repeating rifles were issued. Seeing how well the town was defended, the invaders "turned tail and left," according to the *Chicago Tribune*—which editorialized: "This is the legitimate fruit of the teachings of such men as Benjamin Bristow," showing how prominent Frank's father was in promoting what the *Jacksonville Journal* called "a sort of semi-reign of terror."[14]

Benjamin F. Bristow at this time was running for the office of circuit clerk of Morgan County on the Democratic-Copperhead ticket. He was prominently featured in the *Chicago Tribune*'s reporting on the politics of Morgan County, which noted: "This fellow Bristow declared, at the commencement of the war, that he was ready and willing to be one of 140,000 Illinois men over whose dead bodies the Union soldiers would have to pass before they could subjugate the State of South Carolina. He has also two sons in the Southern army." Bristow subscribed to the doctrine of the Knights of the Golden Circle, "that all men are *not* created equal." He was "an acknowledged fire-in-the-rear man," an allusion to Lincoln's having said that he feared "the fire in the rear" fanned by Copperheads in the North more than he feared the Confederate army.[15]

On September 24, 1863, the *Chicago Tribune* reported that Benjamin Bristow began his campaign by suing for libel and slander a certain James Dangerfield, who had charged him with "running off" two black servants and selling them in Tennessee. "The general impression is that he [Bristow] has brought the suit to help in his election, and that it most likely will not be tried this term of court, which sits on the 4th Monday in September, and that before next term he hopes to be elected." In other words, to be seen as a man who kidnaps black citizens and sells them into slavery was considered just the thing to attract votes.[16]

Bristow was the only Copperhead to win his race, though some doubt was cast on whether he won it fairly. Losing Jacksonville by more than four hundred votes, he nevertheless won the county by thirteen votes with the help of a big turnout in Meredosia, the strongest Copperhead precinct, where more people voted than in any previous election, "and there are strong presumptions of fraud." Bristow had famously preached in a saloon in Meredosia several years earlier.[17]

Bristow was sworn in as circuit clerk on November 18, 1863, "to fill a vacancy"—which suggests he was appointed, not elected. Was his election overturned, and was he appointed anyway because everyone else was off to war? In any event, he did not serve the customary four-year term because he was succeeded in that office by Stephen Sutton on December 1, 1864. He left Jacksonville that year to begin a career as a Southern Methodist preacher in Owen County, Kentucky. When he had first received a Methodist license to preach in 1837, the Southern Methodist Church did not yet exist, the split occurring in 1844–1845. But now in 1864 he found the Southern Methodist Church more congenial to his racist southern sympathies than the original church, which still had some congregations in Kentucky, including in Lexington, Nicholasville, Shelbyville, Newport, and Flemingsburg.[18]

Frank Leslie Bristow, alias "Francis Marion Bristow," was mustered out of the Union army on June 7, 1865, and resumed his musical studies at Illinois College, graduating with a bachelor of arts degree in 1866. He began his teaching career at the Patterson Institute in North Middletown, Kentucky. A visitor to the school in July 1867, when Bristow was likely there, commented: "I have nowhere heard finer singing than the girls are here taught to do."[19]

Frank Bristow taught at Warsaw Female College in the Kentucky town of that name before going with his wife—Linnie Frank of Carroll County, whom he married in 1870—to Tuscaloosa, Alabama, where the Bristows would spend most of that decade. He began as director of music at Tuscaloosa Female College in the fall of 1871. Their daughter, Daisy Dell, was born in Tuscaloosa on December 8, 1873. He soon composed a song in her honor, praising her "cheek lily-white." The *Tuscaloosa Weekly Times* applauded his song "The Spelling Match" as "irresistibly humorous" and called him "a Southern gentleman, with Southern tastes, and in every respect a suitable instructor for Southern young ladies." Perhaps the reporter was unaware of Bristow's Illinois birth and his serenading of Sherman on the general's march to the sea. Bristow had become so acclimated to Alabama that he had erased all trace of his Yankee–Union roots.[20]

Probably worried about the future of the Warsaw Female College, then in financial difficulty, Bristow in the summer of 1875 accepted an offer from Arkansas Female College in Little Rock. There he taught calisthenics as well as music, combining Haydn with gymnastics in a concert given June 5, 1876. But by that date he had already accepted an offer to return to Tuscaloosa Female College in the fall.[21]

In the spring of 1877, however, a new owner took over the school. In the fall of that year, an announcement appeared in several places that Bristow had accepted the position of head of the music department at the Judson Institute in Marion, Alabama, but when the new semester began, a conservatory graduate from Germany held the post instead. With no academic post, Bristow set up his own music school in Tuscaloosa. His students gave a grand concert on February 28, 1878, that featured his own daughter as well. When "little Daisy Bristow, about five years of age. . . stepped to the front of the stage the silence was profound, while she sang in a sweet, childish voice a little song, the very words of which would be heard in the back of the house. She was showered with bouquets and applause, and was encored until she favored us with another." That summer Bristow started a band and soon raised money for a two-story octagonal bandstand in Tuscaloosa.[22]

By the fall of 1878, he was teaching both music and calisthenics at another Tuscaloosa school, Central Alabama Female College. But there, too, came a change in administration, and Bristow was not on the roster in the fall of 1879. He returned to private teaching, adding to his skills the tuning and repair of pianos and organs and proposing that he would teach vocal and instrumental music for the same fees as the two female colleges in town, indicating he was in direct competition with both of his former employers. He directed Gilbert and Sullivan's *H. M. S. Pinafore,* as earlier he had *Esther* and *Belshazzar.*[23]

But the week before Christmas of 1879, he gave his "Farewell Concert," having received an offer from Southwestern University in Georgetown, Texas. He explained to the Tuscaloosa audience the reason for his departure but spoke as well of "a little green mound in our graveyard which would always keep memory of Tuscaloosa fresh"—an allusion to the death of his second child there in 1875. He made an intriguing reference to a problem with anger management: "For occasional slips of temper he asked pardon; twenty-one years of music teaching may look as if it would improve temper but it does not."[24]

Soon after their arrival in Texas, the Bristows were again entertaining the public, Frank and Linnie playing a piano duet and Daisy singing. She brought down the house with "The Little Cadet," one of her father's songs. But at the commencement concert in June 1880, he announced that he was returning to Kentucky, after just one semester in Georgetown.[25]

In September 1880, he was teaching in Missouri at Plattsburgh Female College. That engagement lasted but one academic year, and by the summer of 1881 he was back in Covington, Kentucky, where his parents lived, directing the music at camp meetings where his father preached. He played the organ, Linnie the piano. He was hired as music director at the State Female College in Memphis, Tennessee, which announced his imminent arrival with some fanfare on September 8 but on September 22 stated that "unforeseen circumstances" had prevented him from keeping the engagement. He may have backed out upon learning that the school was about to go bankrupt: in April 1881, the owners had tried to sell it to the city to house the local insane asylum, and the college appears to have folded before the end of the year.[26]

George T. Gould came to his rescue, terminating Julius C. Meininger, as we have seen, and hiring Bristow to replace him in January 1882. The Bristow family trio performed at the Millersburg Female College chapel on January 28, and Frank took over the local Methodist church choir in addition to his duties as teacher of music and calisthenics at the college.[27]

Not all the reviews were positive. The Millersburg correspondent for the rival Paris paper, the *Bourbon News,* attended a revival at the Methodist church and found Frank's comportment not very worshipful. His voice was splendid, but his performance sounded more like "a seductive waltz than heartfelt praise to a Deity." The correspondent recommended that Bristow keep his head and hands still and not drown out the choir. He also objected to setting religious texts to popular tunes, such as the Doxology to "The Blue Danube."[28]

A reporter from Carlisle, Kentucky, took a kinder view: "The Bristow music has captivated us all." And so too did a different Millersburg correspondent for the *Bourbon News:* "The Bristow family entertained a large audience at the Methodist church Wednesday night. Mr. Bristow,

Sr., preached an old time sermon, full of heaven, golden harps, pearly gates, jasper walls, and departed loved ones. Mr. Bristow, Jr., and sister [Pauline] furnished the singing and very sweet it was too."[29]

Frank had probably inherited his musicality from his father, who moved more souls by his singing than by his sermons. One day the elder Bristow was traveling to a church where he was to hold a revival. He met another horseman on the road and asked him where he was going. "To the revival." Bristow asked who was preaching. "An old fellow named Bristow," the stranger replied. Fishing for compliments, Bristow asked, "Is he much of a preacher?" The traveler didn't know but reported, "They say he can sing like an angel but can't preach worth a damn."[30]

Perhaps for lack of instruments, Frank did not form a student orchestra at Millersburg until March 1883, but he began the calisthenics right away, assembling a creditable team of students after little more than a month of practice. "The entertainment given by the Calisthenic Class of Millersburg Female College . . . was largely attended and all present were highly pleased," the *Paris Kentuckian* reported in early March. "The class is well-trained, and in its workings is almost perfect. By engaging in such exercises the young ladies become more graceful and acquire strength and health."[31]

Bristow left a detailed account of his methods in *Calisthenic Exercises and Marches,* published in 1891. Three characteristics stand out: (1) these exercises were designed for public display; (2) the drills involved remarkably complex patterns of movement as the students marched up, down, diagonally, and even in spirals across the floor; and (3) music was not just an accompaniment, but at times the students themselves produced it. For instance, in the preliminary exercises the pupils had to sing the solfège scale up and down. Bristow composed the music for this book, starting with a march to accompany the students' getting into their initial positions, going on to include music for the finger, foot, dumbbell, and ring exercises, specifying certain passages for certain parts of each exercise, and then including some more marches.[32]

His book had a number of predecessors. A good one for comparison might be *Watson's Manual of Calisthenics* (1864). Jan Todd writes that Watson's exercises copied those in Dio Lewis's *New Gymnastics for Men, Women, and Children* (1862). Watson's exercises were for both sexes, as were Bristow's. Although not dangerous or difficult, Watson's

Frank L. Bristow, from Frank Leslie Bristow, *Calisthenic Exercises and Marches with Pleasing Drill Songs and Music Suitable for Schools, Colleges, Private Entertainments, and Public Exhibitions* (Cincinnati, 1891). (Library of Congress)

required the use of many more muscles and provided a fuller workout. Bristow's exercises, for instance, did not include knee bends. Both used wands, rings, and dumbbells. Watson also used Indian clubs (bowling-pin-shaped wood clubs of various weights that were swung to strengthen the user), which Bristow omitted, for he found them potentially dangerous, especially in public exhibitions.[33]

Watson provided musical selections from classical composers such as Giuseppe Verdi, Gaetano Donizetti, and the waltz king Johann Strauss, and his musical accompaniment to the exercises was therefore more pleasant to listen to than Bristow's yet lacked the advantage of having sections keyed to specific parts of each exercise. Although Watson gave passing reference to the possibility of public exhibitions, his exercises were uniquely designed to strengthen the body and not, as in Bristow's case, to delight the eye of the observer.

In 1882, Bristow published "Marche Calisthenique" for piano, which is surprisingly good. Its stirring strains were doubtless heard during his students' performances that year. The cover design features the traditional accoutrements: dumbbells, wands, rings, and Indian clubs—even though, as we know, he declined to use the latter. His calisthenics troupe performed to a crowded and appreciative audience during graduation week in June. A reviewer enthused: "The workings of the class were perfect, and the most difficult parts were perfectly acted by the youngest members."[34]

Soon after commencement, Bristow traveled with his wife and daughter to Tuscaloosa, renewing old acquaintances. He sang some comic songs at a minstrel show, likely ones he had composed, such as "Ain't I Glad," with its cakewalk harmonies and racist content. Returning to Kentucky in mid-July, he played the organ at Methodist camp meetings at High Bridge (in Jessamine County), Kavanaugh (near Crestwood, in Oldham County), and Stevenson (near Corinth, in Grant County).[35]

All three towns were accessible by rail, which made large crowds possible, especially at High Bridge, a park that overlooks the Kentucky River from the top of a cliff nearly three hundred feet in height. Special trains arrived every hour from 7:00 a.m. until noon on Sunday, bringing an estimated 8,000 visitors. One reporter conjectured that nine out of ten came for the scenery and to see who else would be there. The stock company that owned the grounds charged ten cents admission and reaped a handsome profit. Liquor sales were banned within a two-mile radius, but many visitors brought their own. "Whenever a fellow was seen to wink as he started towards a grove he was followed by a dozen friends. They took it straight."[36]

Gould promoted Bristow to principal at the college, and by early September Bristow was back at his post, having been entrusted with running the school in the absence of its president, who would not return until a week or so later.[37] He played the organ and sang for the Carlisle meeting of the Kentucky Conference of the Southern Methodists, and a correspondent for a Maysville paper found one song "especially beautiful," noting that the words were by Gould and the musical arrangement by Bristow. It was entitled "Beautiful Rest" and was undoubtedly "Sweet Rest at Home," which Bristow would publish the following year, precisely the kind of thing the Millersburg critic complained of when he thought Bristow capable of singing the Doxology to the tune of "The Blue Danube." Gould, with Bristow's assistance, took Stephen Collins Foster's "Old Folks at Home," popularly known as "Swanee River," and gave it these words:

> O'er Jordan's dark and stormy river lies heaven's fair shore;
> There joy shall fill the soul forever, sorrow shall come no more.
> There, streets of gold and walls of Jasper, within the gates;
> There, homes prepared by our dear Master, each ransomed soul
> awaits.
> Safe at home, at home with Jesus, never more to roam;
> O! brothers, how my heart grows happy thinking of sweet rest
> at home.

If Bristow performed the song when his father preached on April 21, 1883, then it supported the sermon well, giving the same depiction of heaven with streets of gold and jasper walls.[38]

11

Delicacy, Refinement, Propriety

In 1882, George T. Gould was at the high-water mark of his career as college administrator, enjoying near unanimous support both from the local citizens, whose two colleges were a source of local pride, and from his fellow Southern Methodist pastors, who considered the Female College a jewel in the crown of the Kentucky Conference. He reflected on his success in an autobiographical sketch (written in the third person) for William Henry Perrin's *History of Bourbon, Scott, Harrison, and Nicholas Counties, Kentucky,* published that year. The sketch appeared along with other such sketches in an appendix at the end of what was otherwise a detailed and valuable history of the region. The *Bourbon News* pointed out that the book was sold by subscription and complained that "it ignores the merit of nonsubscribers and applauds the subscriber in his own terms, according to his vanity, egotism, and money." The subscription price was $12, perhaps the equivalent of $275 today. But Gould got his money's worth as his sketch contained lots of self-praise: "Though somewhat known as a controversial writer, a reviewer and a platform speaker," he "has thus far led too active and busy a life in the ministry, and more especially in the school room, to produce any thing of a permanent and extended character. His greatest distinction is having under adverse circumstances built up the Millersburg Female College from a mere local school . . . to one of the largest and most celebrated Institutions in the South and West." He was candid, though, about his physical attributes: "Dr. Gould is small of stature, but fleshy, weighing 160 pounds, though less than five feet, six inches in height." Such frankness might have led readers to believe he was not in fact the author of these words. The rest of his assessment was more self-serving: "Vim, enterprise, determination, self-reliance, untiring energy, rapidly formed conclusions, and willingness to assume risks from which the more timid or less reliant shrink, seem to be the main ingredients in his character."[1]

Millersburg Female College faced some competition for female students. In Paris, just eight miles away, could be found the Garth Female Institute, Miss Tipton's School for Girls, Mrs. Clay's School, and Bourbon Female College. Other female-only schools in Kentucky included Mrs. Tarrant's Lexington Female College; Science Hill in Shelbyville; Hampton College, the Kentucky Home School, and the Collegiate Institute in Louisville; the Jessamine Female Institute in Nicholasville; Miss Sevier's School in Russellville; and Bethlehem Literary Institution in St. John.[2]

To distinguish itself from its rivals, Millersburg marketed itself as quintessentially southern. Its prospectus declared: "The President is Southern by birth, by rearing, by education, and by sentiment; the teachers are all Southern in sentiment, and, with the exception of those born in Europe, were born and raised in the South. Believing the Southern to be the highest type of civilization this continent has seen, the young ladies are trained according to the Southern ideas of delicacy, refinement, womanhood, religion, and propriety; hence we offer a first-class female college for the South and elicit a liberal Southern patronage." It almost sounds as if one had to take an oath of allegiance to the Lost Cause to teach there.[3]

Its catalog boasted of its prominence among southern schools and the advantages of its geographic location: "This is, we believe, the largest female college in the South. It is located in one of the brightest spots of the lovely blue grass region of Kentucky, which is noted for health, refinement, and all those advantages that go to develop the higher and better nature, together with physical force and strength—necessary conditions to a high order of scholarship as well as usefulness in society."[4]

Among the new students arriving in September 1882 was Miss Texie Head of Roanoke, Missouri. Ella Gould had spent several weeks in Missouri in July and August with her sister, Aurelia. The latter's husband, James W. Wight, an orphan, had been raised by a stepmother, whose brother was Texie's father. Aurelia brought Texie to Millersburg in September. Blond and "famed for her beauty," Texie "attracted admiration and attention." She would eventually attract Gould's.[5]

As we know, Gould often left town to get away from his wife. In September, having just returned from Texas, he went to Atlanta, Georgia, ostensibly recruiting for the school. Then he traveled to Virginia to attend a Southern Methodist conference. In January, he was off again to Texas.[6]

Millersburg Female College, with sixty-five boarding pupils from ten states, was prospering, but the town was going through a rough patch. The post of marshal was momentarily vacant, and consequently "the howl of the drunken rabble and the firing of pistols on the streets at night" were too often heard, even disturbing peaceable citizens returning from church on a Sunday night. A wooden cigar-store Indian was kidnapped, hung up in the public square and later in front of the Female College. Christmas brought even more destructive revelry; fences were built across streets, gates stolen, and street lamps broken.[7]

In late January 1883, Gould returned from Texas with six new students, but he arrived two days too late for the birth of his daughter. Jane was the Goulds' fourth child, joining George H., fourteen; Mamie, eleven; and Kenneth, four. Mrs. Gould resented her husband's tardy arrival, for which he would later try to spread the blame by saying not "I" but "we" had missed the due date in "our" calculations.[8]

Within four days of his return to the college, he expelled seven students for carrying notes to the boarders. But then he relented and received them back into the fold.[9]

It was the custom of the Millersburg Methodists to enliven the winter doldrums by holding a February revival. The students from the Female College found there an outlet for their emotions, while others found it amusing to watch them. There is so little social life in Millersburg, the *Bourbon News* observed, that "everybody is forced to fall back on religion for both fun and consolation." At least a score of onlookers came for the "show," as they called it; among those seeking consolation one evening, three girls said they had found Jesus, and one of them claimed to have actually seen him. This caused twenty others to crowd around the altar, seeking a glimpse of their Saviour.[10]

Benjamin Franklin Bristow was doing the preaching, and his son Frank was in charge of the music. The religious enthusiasm was so contagious that even Frank Bristow succumbed and had to abandon the organ bench for his bed.[11]

But he recovered by the time he had to lead his calisthenics class in their "tip-topical and skiptical evolutions," as the *Bourbon News* put it, in a grand musicale at the Paris Opera House on April 27. The event also featured the newly formed college orchestra, who at last had their instruments, though only eight weeks to rehearse. The evening included as well pianists, vocalists, and *The Little Shaking Quakers,* a Bristow musical comedy sketch. The actual Shakers were still living in their utopia at Pleasant Hill, twenty-five miles southwest of Lexington, though by then their numbers had declined. They led a celibate life, with separate rooms and stairways for males and females, but it was their vigorous dancing and whirling as they worshipped that gave rise to their name and to Bristow's piece. It called for seven girls and a boy, dressed in Shaker garb, to perform a complicated choreography involving clapping, knee slapping, head bobbing, sitting, standing, and bowing. It was as much a calisthenics display as a piece of music, but that was Bristow's intention.[12]

On May 19, two omnibuses and a wagon transported sixty-five Female College students on an excursion to the Blue Licks Hotel. Located fourteen miles north of Millersburg, the three-hundred-room establishment had been a popular summer resort since 1850. Some of the other guests thought the girls were singing and laughing with too much exuberance, but an eyewitness wrote a letter to the *Paris Kentuckian* in the students' defense: "They were all full of life and fun," he wrote, but "they ought to have their fun after being at school so long."[13]

Strangely, Gould was enraged by the references to this occasion in the paper. On June 6, he dashed off an angry note to the *Paris Kentuckian:* "I do wish the next time some fool undertakes to write about my school you would have discretion enough not to publish it. I and all the young ladies are indignant at the piece in your last issue about our trip to the Blue Licks. It seems to me very strange that you did not put it into the waste-basket, the whole piece showing itself to be from some ass who did not know what he was about." Editor John G. Craddock found Gould's anger incomprehensible. The letter, he wrote, had been "intended by the writer to be a complimentary notice" of the school outing and the students' commendable (or at worst excusable) behavior.[14]

It is difficult to believe, as Gould contended, that "all the young ladies" were indignant at being described as "full of life and fun." At most, they might have objected to the letter writer's saying, "We could hear many people say on the occasion alluded to, 'Oh, those girls are so bad, listen to how they are singing and going on.'" But it is highly unlikely the writer would have invented that detail, given his heartfelt defense of their conduct, so he was simply reporting the truth.

Perhaps Gould was hypersensitive because he was developing a romantic interest in one of the students, Texie Head. She had injured herself at the outing in climbing a steep ravine and strained her abdominal muscles. She suffered acute pain and could hardly walk. The doctor ordered bed rest, and all the teachers paid frequent visits to her room because she was a favorite of the school. "It often happened," Gould would recall a year later, "that four or five teachers and pupils might be in the room at the same time, and chairs being scarce some of us would sit upon the side of the bed." Mrs. Gould, however, found that he was paying Texie too much attention and accused him of sitting on her bed when the two were alone. Gould denied it but did say he paid Texie "considerable" attention because she was the first student ever to suffer a serious accident at the school; he added that she was one of only two students ever to come from Missouri, and he wanted their assistance in recruiting more from that state.[15]

On the evening of June 7, George Gould invited his wife to accompany him the next day as he and Bristow took the music and calisthenics classes to Versailles on the train for an evening performance. She declined, saying their daughter Jane, born in January, was too young. "The next noon just before we were ready to start," Gould would later recall, "I repeated my regrets" to Ella that she was not coming along. "Going out on the porch she saw Jennie Trainer, who did not belong to the music class, dressed and ready to go with us. She came back blazing with rage and said, 'I thought last night you were lying when you asked me to go to Versailles, and now I know you are, since I see you are going to take your wall-eyed hussy along.'" Had Ella been more perceptive, she might have worried less about Jennie Trainer and more about Texie Head.[16]

Given Gould's precision regarding the time of this conversation, saying it took place at noon, we can conclude that at the very moment Elisha Green was preparing to board the train in Maysville, Gould was being provoked to anger by his wife. The train Elisha boarded was scheduled to leave Maysville at 12:30 p.m., arrive at Millersburg at 2:18, and reach Paris at 2:40.[17]

12

June 8, 1883, and Its Aftermath

If Gould was angry at his wife for her accusation that he was taking "his wall-eyed hussy along" to Versailles, he found someone to vent it on soon after he and his entourage boarded the train in Millersburg: the sixty-five-year-old Elisha Green. Reverend John Barbour (1849–1929) was well placed to see what transpired. He knew Green personally and Gould by sight. Green was seated two seats in front of Barbour, who saw Gould come in with about twenty students, all talking and milling about. There were twenty-eight students and seven adults in the entourage in total, but they all did not enter the same car.

Barbour saw Gould standing in the aisle next to where Green was seated and talking to him. Because the train was in motion, Barbour could not hear what was said. He first thought it was a friendly chat, but when he saw the expression on Gould's face, he realized it wasn't. Gould grabbed Green by the arm and shoulder and tried to pull him out of his seat. Green resisted and pushed back. Then a young man with Gould, Joe Corrington, threw back his right coattail, and Barbour thought he saw the handle of a pistol sticking out of his pants pocket. Corrington placed his hand on the gun as he addressed Green in a threatening manner. Barbour must have thought he was about to fire at Green, for he got up immediately and went up to them, accompanied by the stranger sitting next to him. Both men offered their seats, but Gould and Corrington declined. Then Barbour saw Bristow, who was standing two seats in front of Green, swing his brass-bound valise at Green several times, hitting him on the head and drawing blood.[1]

According to other reports, Gould joined Bristow in the attack, pummeling Green with his fists and holding him down while Bristow struck him repeatedly with the valise. The man seated next to Barbour and who had gone with him up to Gould was Colonel Bob Morrow, a government storekeeper in Paris and, as Green later recalled, "an intimate friend of mine." When Barbour and Morrow offered their seats, Barbour heard Gould say, "No, I'll make this nigger get up." When Bristow and Gould took hold of Green to try to pull him out of his seat, Green objected: "I paid for this seat in Maysville. I will hold it to Paris or die in my tracks. If you had asked me like a gentleman I would have come out, but I will die before I will be pulled out like a dog."[2]

Green was perfectly aware that when Barbour and Morrow offered their seats, there was no reason for him to give up his, for the two students who had been seatless were now accommodated—or would have been had Gould accepted the offer.[3]

As Gould and Bristow attacked Green, conductor Johnnie Martin came up and told them to stop it, or he would throw them off the train. Before the attack began, Gould had asked Martin to make Green leave his seat, but Martin had refused, "stating that he [Green] was a quiet and inoffensive old preacher who had paid for his seat, and that he [Martin] had no right to force him to give it up."[4]

Barbour and Morrow remained standing for the rest of the twenty minutes to Paris. When the train pulled into the station, as Barbour was approaching the door, he noticed Bristow standing there and feared he might attack Green again. The music professor must have looked as if he had that intention, for two or three of the girl students spoke up, saying, "Oh, don't whip him. Let him alone." As they all filed out, Gould was directly behind Green and in front of Barbour and seemed to nod to Bristow as if to say, "Don't molest him." At the train station, Bristow approached Barbour in a threatening way and said, "Do I understand that you sympathize with this man, because if you do you can get what the nigger got." Barbour, who at that point was waiting for the train to Cincinnati, replied, "I am traveling on, sir," and Bristow walked away.[5]

Paris train depot, date unknown (Hopewell Museum, Paris, KY)

Bristow could tell Barbour was a friend of Green's because he had seen them conversing after leaving the train. "Uncle Elisha," Barbour said, "are you going to do anything about this?" "Yes, I am," Green replied. He was seconded in that intention by Charlton Alexander, who caught up with him as he was walking into downtown Paris. Alexander said he had heard what had happened on the train and asked Green what he planned to do. Green said he would consult with some Maysville friends. Alexander replied that he had friends in Paris, too. "Go up to Mr. Lockhart's and get out a warrant for assault and battery." Together they did so and also went looking for Colonel Morrow because he knew the names of all the Millersburg assailants.[6]

Born in Maysville in 1817, Charlton Alexander was now a Paris banker and a major stockholder in the Kentucky Central Railroad. In the latter capacity, he was worried about losing passengers if Gould and Bristow's assault went unpunished. In addition, the railroad was dependent on black votes to win county referendums to authorize stock subscriptions for rail expansion, for the Kentucky Constitution of 1850 forbade state funding. George C. Lockhart, born in 1848, was a lawyer for the railroad. He had married a teacher at Millersburg Female College in 1882; Gould had taken part in the ceremony, for which Bristow had played the organ.[7]

In recounting the events of that day in his autobiography, Green generously gives space to both Gould and Bristow's attempts at self-justification. He quotes in its entirety the statement Gould published in the Paris and Maysville papers, in which his primary defense was to play the race card, apparently confident it would resonate with readers. Gould wrote that when he entered the car, passengers were excitedly complaining about "a big black negro man complacently occupying a seat to himself," while two of Gould's young ladies were left standing in the aisle. Gould claimed he heard such exclamations as "It is a shame!" and "He ought to be put out!" and "If he does not get up he ought to be made to." Barbour made no mention in his deposition of passengers complaining, nor have I been able to find any indication of it in other witnesses' accounts. But Bristow may well have made such a complaint, for these musicians and calisthenics performers were his students; Corrington and other members of the Millersburg group may have seconded it. That does not mean, however, that passengers with no relation to the college were complaining.[8]

Gould wrote that he went up to Green and found that the only vacant seat in the car was the one next to him. That was true because Morrow and Barbour had not yet offered their seats. Gould claimed that he then said to Green, "I wish you would give your seat to these young ladies, because if you do not there will be a disturbance." If he said that, it was a threat couched as a polite request. Green refused. Gould sent for the conductor, who was in another coach taking tickets. Gould wrote that while he was waiting, Green told him that if the conductor made him give up his seat, he would make the railroad company suffer for it. We have no way of knowing if this is true.[9]

When the conductor came, Gould wrote, "I appealed to him whether the young ladies must stand and let the negro sit." Martin said there was nothing he could do. "All right," said Gould, "then I will see what I can do." He grabbed Green's arm, saying, "Come, get out of here." Gould claimed that Green then hit him and admitted that Bristow, in defense of Gould, hit Green with his small handbag but claimed he did so only once. In his deposition, Barbour clearly contradicted Gould on this point, saying that Bristow struck Green "more than once." Gould concluded with a fully racist peroration:

> I did not know who the fellow was. I did know, however, that he was a big black negro and that two young ladies were stand-

> ing while he sat. Having never been accustomed to see such an indignity as that put upon a lady, that she must stand through a ride of eight miles while a negro man lolls at his ease, I could not bring myself tamely to submit to it. I do not believe that there is a gentleman in Kentucky who would stand idly by and see his wife and daughters thus insulted. These young ladies came from the extreme south, hundreds of miles from their homes, with neither father nor mother near, but depending upon me for protection from insult and injury. I had been recreant to my trust and unworthy the position which I occupy had I not, after exhausting appeal to the negro and conductor, myself attempted his ejection from the seat. If any man has fallen so low as to think white women should stand while negro men keep their seats then him I have insulted, and really I do not care if I have.[10]

He totally left out the fact that the two young ladies had no need to stand, having been offered seats by Morrow and Barbour. Gould apparently refused that offer in order to stage his "white defender of southern womanhood" act.

Green quotes Gould's statement in its entirety, then comments: "I take the liberty to say that there is not an ounce of truth in the thing. I am a negro, as Mr. Gould says, but I would rather be a big black negro with the character and reputation I have, and one that tells the truth, than an educated dude of a white man that can lie faster than the Recording Angel in heaven would have patience to write. There is an expression which says: 'A lie can go a mile while truth is putting his boots on.'"[11]

Among the lies he may have noticed were that, according to Gould, several passengers were exclaiming that Green should be put off the train (unless the complainers were Bristow, Corrington, and other Millersburg friends of Gould), that Gould asked him in a civil tone to give up his seat (though even then he accompanied it with a threat), that Green said he would make the railroad pay if he had to give up his seat, that Green viciously struck Gould, that Bristow struck Green only once, and that Bristow struck him only because Green first struck Gould.

Gould made no attempt to deny his racism; instead, he seemed to think it would play well with his audience. Millersburg Female College, as we have seen, marketed itself as a deeply southern school that just happened to be located in Kentucky. Apparently, the "Southern ideas of delicacy, refinement" and "womanhood" to which the school's prospectus in 1882 referred meant that a black man was forbidden to sit while white women were standing (even when the latter had no reason to stand, seats already having been offered to the women).

In his autobiography, Green then turns to Bristow, who did not submit a written statement to the press, as Gould had done, but was interviewed by the *Paris Kentuckian* on Saturday, June 16. The reporter, probably editor Craddock, encountered Bristow on a train, surrounded by female students. He asked Bristow to write down everyone's name and where they were from. Bristow wrote that he was from Tuscaloosa, Alabama. We know that he had lived there from 1871 to 1879 but that it was neither his place of birth nor his most recent address before coming to Millersburg. To have admitted he was born in Illinois might have marred his southern allure. The students were Charlotte Kirkpatrick of Cartersville, Georgia; Lutie Peterson of Tuscaloosa; and Jennie Saunders of Parkersburg, West Virginia. "All seated, and no Reverend African molested," said Bristow, treating the whole thing as a joke. Charlotte Kirkpatrick's presence is intriguing. Ella Gould was convinced that Bristow was courting her. That summer of 1883, Professor J. C. C. Newton would urge Gould not to rehire Bristow in the fall for that very reason. That year saw the publication of a love song by Bristow dedicated to "Little Lottie of Cartersville, Ga." The lyrics allude to the singer's "longing" for her "gentle look of love." By this time, Bristow had separated from his wife. However ardent his feelings were, Lottie probably did not share them; the following year she married a more age-appropriate suitor. We may interpret Bristow's bravado in this interview for the *Paris Kentuckian* (and maybe even in the attack on Green on the train) as an attempt to impress Miss Kirkpatrick.[12]

Bristow's account of what happened is identical to Gould's (they might have conferred on getting their stories straight). Bristow had the valise with him and displayed it to show how light it was. "I knew nothing of his being a preacher or crippled, as he is a very large, robust looking darkey, and I notice gets about very well. I think any man, white or black, that won't readily accommodate ladies, ought to be made to do so. I knocked a darkey down once in Little Rock, Arkansas, who wouldn't give way to ladies in the street. I did tell a man," alluding to Barbour, "who sided with Green, that I could accommodate him." In saying he didn't know Green had difficulty walking, Bristow may have had in mind what the *Maysville Evening Bulletin* reported on June 15: "[Reverend Green] was injured several years ago in a railroad accident and has since been a cripple." That accident was the derailment over Hinkston Creek on May 19, 1876, that broke his leg in two places. Gould justified his behavior by making it a defense of southern values; Bristow did the same but also boasted of his propensity for violence, gleefully citing three instances here: hitting Green with his valise, knocking a man down in Arkansas, and threatening Barbour for sympathizing with Green.[13]

His vaunted violent tendencies might have played well with Lottie and the other girls, but not with public opinion. Green quotes some press reaction, beginning with the *Lexington Transcript:* "There is a deep-seated sense of justice to the black man in the breast of our best white men that arouses their indignation in this community." Gould "has in the public estimation so proclaimed himself a bad citizen" that the Female College "cannot flourish until that man and the other two associated with him are dismissed from its employ." This barb must have hit home, for Gould threatened to sue the *Transcript* for libel but later apparently thought better of it.[14]

Green then quotes from a letter to the editor of the *Maysville Eagle* evoking Gould's alcoholism. When Gould was the pastor of Maysville's Southern Methodist church in 1871–1872, he was well thought of by all. "But since he has been teaching the Female Seminary in Millersburg various reports prejudicial to his reputation have obtained circulation and among many persons credence. Whether the charges of intemperance have been true or false," what he did on the train was an outrage. By contrast, Green, both as a slave and as a free man, had a reputation for honesty and religiosity that many white ministers might envy. The writer of the letter added that Conductor Martin said if Gould or Bristow had desired the other half of the double seat for one of the students, he (Martin) would have seen that Green yielded it. The conductor, in other words, saw no problem in one of the college girls sitting next to a black man.[15]

Conductor Martin was quoted by yet another Maysville paper saying that when Gould said, "If you don't put him out we will," he began removing his gloves, as if getting ready to fight. More details emerged of what Martin saw when he returned to the car where the assault was taking place: "Professor Corrington was mounted on the seat holding Rev. Green, Rev. Gould pinioning him from behind and Professor Bristow raining blows with a brass-bound valise upon his head." Green could hardly comply with their demand that he leave his seat if he was being held in place by both Corrington and Gould. They had now passed from coercion to punishment, all three conspiring to injure and humiliate the beloved pastor of two Baptist churches. Then the writer for the *Maysville New Republican* made an essential point: "It is a shocking and disgusting outrage when we consider that the attack was made upon a colored man, and we are of the firm belief that it never would have been attempted if he [Green] had been white."[16]

Abraham L. McKay, editor of the *Vanceburg Courier*, joined the *Maysville Eagle* in bringing out some of the dirty laundry of Gould's Millersburg past. "If the walls of his College could talk," the evidence would be overwhelming. "Only a few years ago this ogre was a bloated drunkard, but when the charge was brought against him a gang of partial if not perjured preachers returned a verdict of not guilty." That charge, of course, was Professor Joseph Young's failed attempt to get the Kentucky Conference to convict Gould of drunkenness in 1880. Despite the whitewash of a church trial, Gould soon again "stood before an outraged community with whiskey streaming from every pore and vulgarity and brutality oozing out at every joint." Thankfully, now that Green was taking Gould to court, "this animated clod will at last appear before a tribunal where the judicial ermine will take the place of the tainted broadcloth of the clergy."[17]

McKay went on to say, "We personally know of instances in which this man has violated all sense of duty toward students placed under his care, and only last year" some young ladies "were forced to leave his school on account of his tyranny." How could McKay have been privy to this knowledge? Writing a few days later, McKay responded to rumors circulated by Gould's friends to the effect that McKay's attack on the college's president was not written by him but by Professor H. K. Taylor: "I deem it but justice to [Taylor] to state that he was not at or near Vanceburg at the time the article was written or printed, and did not have any connection in any manner with the wording." But that Taylor had nothing to do with the wording did not preclude his having had a great deal to do with its substance. Taylor was a Vanceburg native, born there in 1858. In 1879, the Riverside Male and Female Seminary in Vanceburg was incorporated, with Taylor as its principal and Abraham L. McKay among its trustees. Through this association, we may presume they were acquainted, and as it turns out, Taylor would have been an impeccable source for McKay regarding Gould's personal and administrative shortcomings. In the fall of 1879, Taylor became professor of natural sciences at the other Millersburg college, Kentucky Wesleyan, from which he had graduated in 1878. Taylor continued to teach there until 1881. In the spring of that year, he announced that he was leaving Millersburg to return to Vanceburg as principal of the Riverside Academy. Illness prevented him from doing so, but the 1882–1883 school year found him again teaching in Vanceburg. The church trial to which McKay referred when he complained of the "partial if not perjured preachers" who found Gould not guilty had taken place in March 1880, during Taylor's Kentucky Wesleyan tenure. Taylor must have either been present at the proceedings or known someone who was.[18]

The *Carlisle Mercury,* Green notes, said that Gould and company "have made a serious mistake and placed themselves in an ugly attitude before the public," but it nevertheless published a letter from a Millersburg resident who clearly felt otherwise. The writer maintained that what Bristow had done was simply "a muscular lecture on the subject of politeness" and poked fun at Colonel Craddock of the *Paris Kentuckian* and other editors sympathetic to Green as filling the land "with lamentations diresome." He then proceeded to state what he called the facts of the case as Gould presented them, repeating the lie that Gould had politely asked, as opposed to ordered, Green to give up his seat. Corrington, the writer for the *Carlisle Mercury* asserted, did not attempt to draw his pistol. True, but no one said he had; several witnesses instead reported that he showed he had a gun by pulling back his coat. According to this writer, "The three gentlemen, so it is said, will be arrested for insisting upon women being respected, but that it will amount to anything no one believes."[19]

The *Cynthiana News,* in contrast, came out against Green, Maysville Yankeeness, and racial equality. Green "doubtless entertains a terrible hatred for the white people. He lives in Maysville, a city filled with bad Northern men, who are worse, perhaps, than the negroes, and who have doubtless placed such old fellows as Green, in the scale far above their station." Then came the imputation of guilt by association: "Since the newspaper gush has appeared over the old man, making him a persecuted martyr from Maysville, another of his race caught a little girl in an unfrequented place in Mason county, and outraged her." This was an allusion to Samuel Bulger, who had attempted to rape Hannah Bell McAuliffe on June 21, 1883. Bulger was arrested, tried, and sentenced to hang.[20]

Despite the attempt by the *Cynthiana News* to tar Green, Craddock of the *Paris Kentuckian* pointed out that "even with President Gould's statement of the Green affair, the papers generally condemn the attempt to remove Green by force" and added that contrary to the *Cynthiana News*'s assertion that blacks must be taught to be "more respectful," the Baptist preacher needed no lessons in that regard: "It was the general good character of the old man Green that won for him the sympathy he has received."[21]

The unpleasantness on the train did not prevent the Millersburg Female College students from reaching Versailles and giving their performance that day. In addition to the members of the orchestra and the calisthenics class, Gould had brought along some graduating seniors (including, as his wife pointed out, Jennie Trainer). He said he "wanted them to see the Bluegrass region to advantage" before departing for their distant homes. As it happened, they saw a lot more than that.[22]

Green's lawyer, George C. Lockhart, initially had Gould and Bristow arrested for assault and battery, and their bail was set at $100 each. But lawyer and client subsequently concluded they could not get a jury to convict in a criminal case, so they instead filed a civil suit. A hearing was set for July 4.[23]

The events of June 8 and the resultant controversy put a damper on the college's commencement activities the following week. The dance was not as largely attended as in past years, nor were the graduation exercises. Many in the Wednesday-night audience for the entertainment by Bristow's orchestra and calisthenics class thought it went on too long to be interesting. When Gould announced that there were only three more performances on the program, the news was loudly applauded. "This riled the Dr., who threatened to quit there, but he didn't." Gould, to his surprise, could no longer dominate his audience and almost had a public meltdown.[24]

Texie Head was not among those who took the train for Versailles on June 8. Had she not been recovering in bed from the injury suffered in climbing a ravine at Blue Licks, she probably would have gone with the group, for, like Jenny Trainer, she was a graduating senior and a favorite of Gould's. But she was practically unable to walk, and when she was to board the train home on June 18, she had to be carried to the buggy that would take her to the station. Gould did the honors. His wife told Texie to put her arms around his neck so she would be easier to lift. She did as told, saying, "Mrs. Gould, you will just have to be jealous." Ella Gould said she would have to be "a very wicked woman to be jealous of a poor sick girl." Later, she would change her mind on that score.[25]

On the way to the station, Gould reflected on what he took to be the probability he would be offered a position in Arkansas for which he was applying. "I was very loath to part with my girls, expecting to go to Little Rock and never again to see most of them," so on the spur of the moment he decided to accompany his students as far as Lexington and then to Cincinnati. When he returned to Millersburg, he jokingly told his wife that if he had had his good clothes on, he might have followed them all the way to their homes. He later claimed that he was not thinking of Texie any more than of the others.[26]

But after he wrote to several of them, as was his habit, Texie wrote back, and Ella read her letter. She was troubled when she came upon Miss Head saying, according to Gould's later statement, "that after leaving me [Gould] [in Cincinnati] she had other long dark tunnels to pass through, but there was no dear Doctor Gould with her." Ella demanded to know what she meant about the tunnels and in calling him her "dear Doctor Gould." He explained that there was a tunnel on the rail line between Paris and Covington, the city across the Ohio River from Cincinnati. As the train passed into the tunnel and the coach was plunged into darkness, he happened to be standing next to her. He asked if she was afraid, "and she said no, not when I was with her."[27]

He soon went to Little Rock to see about the position there, but it did not materialize. He decided to stop on the way home to see Texie. He had to pass through St. Louis, anyway, and claimed he had wanted to visit his wife's Missouri relatives. He first visited the other Missouri student, Shirley Horner, and together they went to see Miss Head and her family.[28]

This extracurricular leg to his journey caused him to miss his trial date with Elisha Green, which was scheduled for July 4 and had been announced as such on June 19. The *Paris Kentuckian* on July 7 reported that "the suit for damages brought by Rev. Elisha Green against Rev. Gould and Professors Bristow and Corrington was called Wednesday [July 4, 1883] and continued until March [1884] on account of Rev. Gould not returning from Arkansas on the morning train instead of the afternoon train." Eight months is a long time to have to wait for justice because the defendant was dallying with his paramour.[29]

The incident on the train continued to reverberate in the press. A group of Millersburg citizens published a statement in the *Paris Kentuckian* praising Gould for the success of his college, as if that could counter the damage he had done to his reputation by his behavior on the train. The *Vanceburg Courier* replied, however, that the statement did not represent the people of Millersburg but only the merchants, whose personal prosperity depended on the two colleges, and that these very signers had no love for Gould, having bitterly opposed him in the past. The *Bourbon News* confirmed this assessment by reporting that some of the signers said that they were "for Gould right or wrong, that his college is the life of the town and it must not go down." In this, as in earlier disputes such as the Tarrant case, "Gould could count on the continuing support of community and church leaders," according to Charles L. Davis, "because the local economy depended so much on his successful management of the school."[30]

The *Bourbon News* taunted Gould by showing the proper way to deal with a shortage of seats:

> Didn't Get Struck with a Valise.
>
> On the train coming down from Lexington on the 4th of July, every seat was occupied by two passengers but two, and they were each occupied by a large black woman and a basket. Wm. Tarr, of this county, and Judge Ross, of Carlisle, came in the train together, and politely asked one of them to double up with the other. The request was readily acceded to, and the men took a seat in the rear of them, and the train moved off without trouble. We give this as an illustration of the fact that kind words won where coercive measures would have probably caused big trouble.[31]

The story reminds us that in 1883 trains were not segregated by race and that it was completely normal for Elisha Green to be sitting where he was. As Charles L. Davis points out, "The right of Green to a seat in an integrated coach was never in dispute."[32]

Gould left Millersburg on July 9 for Texas on a recruiting trip. He wrote Ella from there to protest once more that she showed him no affection and added that it was the last protest he would make, as if he were declaring his intention to leave her. Then, as he reported later, he went on to say "that if she did not love me, all right thank you God, there was one person who did (meaning my mother). I found out afterwards that she thought I meant Miss Texie Head." It was an unwise thing to say unless he wanted to provoke her still further.[33]

On his return, Ella informed him that "she did not want any of my embraces, that she would thank me to stay in my own bed, that when she wanted me she would call for me, and if I wanted any sexual gratification to go downstairs and kiss Texie Head's rotten backside." The Goulds' apartment and Texie's room were in the same building.[34]

Gould had his Texie, and Bristow his Lottie. As we have seen, Professor J. C. C. Newton had written to Gould over the summer to complain about the music professor's amours and to urge he not be rehired for the fall semester. "Knowing as I did that Prof. Bristow was innocent of the charge made against him and that my wife was principally responsible for starting and circulating the reports against him," Gould paid no attention, as he explained later.[35]

Newton's accusation was highly displeasing to Gould. Instead of firing Bristow, he decided to fire Newton, writing a letter of dismissal from Texas and urging Newton to seek another position at the September meeting of the Kentucky Conference. The conference's annual meeting had always been a sort of job fair for Methodist clergy, and there were other colleges under its aegis. Not knowing Newton's summer address, Gould sent the letter to Joe Corrington, his own secretary, with instructions to send it on. He also wrote to a recent graduate of the college to offer her Newton's job.[36]

When Gould returned to Millersburg in September, he naturally expected to find the new teacher there and Newton gone. But Corrington had never forwarded the letter of dismissal, and Ella Gould had told his replacement not to come. Gould was angry but said nothing to

Newton, who remained at his post. Their relationship had been friendly in the past and appeared to remain so, at least on the surface as the school year progressed.[37]

The new school year did not begin any better for Bristow than it had for Gould. About the same time Ella exiled George from her bed, suggesting he seek succor from Miss Head, Bristow met with a painful accident. Returning to Millersburg on the train from a visit to his father in Covington, he stuck his arm a little too far out the car window to point out some object just as the train was entering a ravine, and the rocks smashed his hand. It may have been the same hand that swung the valise at Elisha Green.[38]

Just before Thanksgiving, the *Bourbon News* reported that "Dr. Gould is in trouble again." This time it was over eight barrels of whiskey that he had received in payment for the board and tuition of two students. He gave it to a local druggist to credit his account there, which suggests he was consuming an inordinate amount of bourbon. The problem was that the government revenuers were now accusing him of being a wholesale dealer because of this transaction and saying he would have to purchase a license. However, the case was later dismissed on account of his ignorance of the law.[39]

On a Saturday morning in early January 1884, Gould and Professor Newton were working together in the former's study on their respective scholarly articles (Newton unaware that Gould had tried to fire him the previous summer) when Ella barged in, "her eyes flashing with rage." Despite his colleague's presence, she began to berate her husband for not having sent a sick student home. George replied that he was simply waiting for the doctor to say she was well enough to travel. Newton made his exit, and the rebuking continued. Gould later described how she said he was "a liar, a thief, a whore-monger, a seducer of young girls, a drunkard, hypocrite and a house-burner." The last of these accusations was a new one to Gould. She was charging him with starting the disastrous fire that destroyed the college building in December 1878 and doing it to get the insurance money. She may have been right, for he was in debt, unable pay back one penny of the money he had borrowed from her father. And because he was the owner of the college and its buildings, he could have pocketed the insurance money and left town to start a new life—without her. According to Gould's later statement, she added that "if Dr. Best would tell what he knew, I [Gould] would be in the Penitentiary in less than a month." It never became clear what I. R. Best, a Millersburg banker and physician who was acquainted with both Gould and his wife, knew, but as time went on, he would reveal himself to be Gould's inveterate enemy and a faithful friend to Gould's wife.[40]

Gould made no reply to her accusations but left his study and started walking down to the drugstore to buy a fatal dose of morphine with the intention of taking it. On his way there, however, "the thought came suddenly into my mind why rush from a hell here to a hell to come. Get out of your troubles not by going into eternity, but by living separate and apart from this woman." So he went back and told Ella that what she had just said "settled the matter" and proposed that after the school year ended in June, they separate. She replied, he later claimed, that this suited her fine and would be best for both.[41]

Despite her having, according to Gould at least, agreed to a separation, she was still jealous of Texie Head. One night a week or two later that January, near the end of the fall–winter semester, she became convinced George was in Texie Head's room. She stood for a while outside the door listening, then burst in. She told Texie to pack her trunk and go home, which Texie did the next morning, taking the early train. Gould accompanied her as far as St. Louis; he was going to be on the train in any event because he was taking two other students to Arkansas. Before he left, Ella asked him if he was going to tell her good-bye. He said he would only if she took back the charges she had made of his burning down the school in 1878 and seducing Miss Head. She refused, and consequently his parting words to her were that he would be damned if he would ever again live with such a woman.[42]

The civil suit that Green brought against his three assailants was held at the Court of Common Pleas in Paris, Kentucky, on March 5–7, 1884. George C. Lockhart appeared for Green, and Harry Ward represented Gould, Bristow, and Corrington. Gould and Bristow were not unknown to Lockhart, for, as noted, they had participated in the ceremony when Lockhart married Florence L. Kelly on January 31, 1882, Bristow providing the music and Gould assisting as a minister, although the officiant was Miss Kelly's brother, Gilby C. Kelly. Until her wedding, Miss Kelly had been an English instructor at Gould's college. But such ties in no way prevented Lockhart from making a spirited and

Paris Courthouse, date unknown (Hopewell Museum, Paris, KY)

effective case, as Craddock of the *Paris Kentuckian* observed: "G. C. Lockhart, as counsel for Green, had rather an undesirable position, as Mrs. Lockhart, as assistant teacher for Mr. Gould, had been a great favorite, but he did his duty fully to his client."[43]

Bristow had successfully petitioned the court on July 4, 1883, to postpone the trial until eleven students of the college, none of them

Kentucky residents, could be present to testify. He argued that they were the only witnesses "by whom he can prove all the said facts." As Davis notes, "One wonders why eyewitnesses could not have been found among the other train passengers if the accounts of Gould and Bristow about this incident were true." It was precisely among those passengers not connected with the college that Lockhart found three who testified that Gould and Bristow's version of events was false: John Barbour, who though not present at the trial gave a lengthy deposition in February; Conductor John Martin; and Colonel Robert Morrow. No record exists of what the witnesses said at the trial, but Martin and Morrow's testimony was doubtless consistent with what they had said in newspaper interviews in 1883.[44]

According to the *Paris Kentuckian,* "The bevy of beauties from Millersburg Female College that were in attendance attracted great admiration not only by their good looks, but by the bright and interesting manner in which they gave their testimony. Harry Ward, in his speech, called them a bouquet of beauties, saying he couldn't particularise, but he did afterwards speak of one as a Goddess. She testified to going up to Green's seat, expecting to get it, but when she heard his tart reply to Gould she at once crowded in with two other girls."[45]

We learn more of Ward's approach from Green's recollection:

> "Judge, Your Honor, Gentlemen of the Jury: Here is Bishop Green, Elder Green, Rev. Green, and I believe the conductor calls him 'Uncle 'Lisha.' Don't you know that it is wrong for you to go to law? And here you sit in the Courthouse attending a law suit and I look up to you for instruction. Brother 'Lisha, you don't like to be called a negro."

Said I [Green, referring to himself]: "So far as nigger is concerned I do not like that; but negro, I am proud of it."[46]

Given the weakness of his case, Ward thought he had to belittle the plaintiff with racist remarks and make a mockery of Green's going to court at all. But for twelve years now blacks had been permitted to testify in criminal cases against whites, and in Kentucky and other southern states they had been suing whites in civil cases since 1865. "African Americans," writes Melissa Milewski in a study of eight states, including Kentucky, "not only litigated civil cases against whites in the highest level of Southern courts; they often won these cases." So there was no legal justification for Ward's telling Green it was wrong for him to go to law, though there was perhaps a social one. Lockhart, Green recalled, countered: "Judge, Your Honor, Gentlemen of the Jury: I am a lawyer and sworn to enforce the law. I intend to do it irrespective of race, color or previous condition of servitude. My opponent, all he has done is to make fun of Uncle Elisha, but he can't laugh this thing out of court."[47]

The defense won a small victory when Green was caught in a mistake about which hat he had been wearing on the train. He brought a black slouch hat to court, but several witnesses testified that he had been wearing a brown straw hat at the time. Lockhart in his address to the jury acknowledged the error, which in the end did not jeopardize Green's case.

The jurymen were not so dazzled by the beauty of Gould's young ladies or moved by Ward's appeal to white supremacy as to deny Green any semblance of justice. They ruled in his favor, finding Gould and Bristow guilty, while absolving Corrington. But actual damages were another matter. Green had asked for $1,000 but in the end was awarded only $12.50 each from Gould and Bristow. The *Paris Kentuckian* printed the names of the jurors, whether they were from the town or the county, and how they initially voted before the compromise figure was reached. The ten from the county had voted for only one cent in damages; of the two from Paris, one was for $25, and the other for $500.[48]

In addition to damages, Gould and Bristow had to pay $15 each for Green's court costs. The combined sum of $27.50 from each would be the equivalent of about $800 today, a not insignificant figure.[49]

Bristow threatened to sue Green for perjury for swearing to the wrong hat but does not appear to have done so.[50]

Elisha Green did not have much time to savor his victory before he was devastated by terrible news. On March 29, 1884, his son Thomas was killed by a stray bullet during a civil disturbance in Cincinnati. A mob of 10,000 people, enraged that a murderer had been convicted only of manslaughter, had resolved to lynch him. They attacked the city jail, unaware that their intended victim had already been removed to a safe location out of the city. The next day, fueled by alcohol consumed in the city's many bars, the mob turned its attention to the courthouse and succeeded in burning it down, to no purpose. Some of the rioters had gathered in front of William F. Powell's gun store on Main Street to demand arms and ammunition; Powell told them they could have all they wanted, but they decided to set fire to the store anyway, perhaps because they thought someone inside had shot in their direction. Powell armed four of his clerks and himself with 10-gauge shotguns and fired at those in the crowd carrying torches and fuel oil and in particular at a man at the side of the building trying to pry off an iron screen from an upper window to the store. Fired upward and at an angle, those shots traveled far down the street, and one of them struck Thomas Green in the chest. He was not among those assaulting the store, was not even in front of the store, but was simply walking to a streetcar some distance away to take him home to 524 West Court Street.[51]

Police patrol number 1 took his body to a makeshift morgue. He was neatly dressed, with a silver watch and an appointment book. Born about 1853, Thomas was one of the two children Green had bought out of slavery, together with his wife, in 1858. Employed as a coachman, he was well liked in Cincinnati, was a member in good standing of the International Order of Odd Fellows, and was described by his employer as "a most exemplary young man."[52]

Soon after losing his court case to Green, Gould left for Alabama, Tennessee, and Texas. This time he was not recruiting students but looking for a job. But he found no takers, and by April 28 was back in Millersburg, for, after all, he had a school to run, even if not for long.[53]

On April 29, the rumor surfaced that the college would be moved to Maysville. By coincidence or not, on May 4 Gould gave a morning sermon and an evening lecture at the Southern Methodist church in Maysville. A reporter found the sermon "truly eloquent, fascinating and sublime," the lecture "scientific and metaphysical," and expressed the hope that Gould would return to Maysville. Perhaps Gould had hinted that he would and bring the college with him.[54]

On May 27, another rumor held that Gould was thinking of joining the Northern Methodist Conference, which might allow him to avoid being kicked out of the southern one because news of his marital and other troubles had surely reached the ears of the hierarchy. Perhaps the Northern Methodists would be more tolerant of his behavior.

The *Bourbon News* said this rumor was not true but did affirm that it was widely thought that Gould would sell the Millersburg campus and open the school somewhere else. The same article reported that Newton and several other professors were leaving the college.[55]

Newton, who the previous summer had urged Gould to fire Bristow for his dalliance with Charlotte Kirkpatrick, was not himself free of taint. That same month, May 1884, clad only in his nightshirt, he had pounded on the door of some girls' room demanding they let him in and saying if they did not, he would assign them a history composition as punishment. This caused a lot of talk in the school. On earlier occasions, he had just walked in when he could and found students undressing or in bed. To keep the young ladies from complaining to their parents, Gould gave them keys so they could lock themselves in. He confronted Newton, reminding him that he (Newton) had engaged in inappropriate behavior with Texie Head the previous year. When she had been confined to her bed in the spring of 1883, she told Gould that she wished he would tell Professor Newton not to come to her room, "that he talked to her as no one ought to but a woman. At this he [Newton] became quite heated and said he had heard that I [Gould] was too intimate with that girl anyway, and that she said I had promised to marry her." Newton said he had heard it from Ella. Gould chose this occasion to tell Newton he had tried to fire him the previous summer. "We parted in high temper," Gould recalled in October 1884, "and he has been unfriendly with me ever since."[56]

On June 3, the *Bourbon News* reported that one way or another the end was near, that Gould was going to wash his hands of the college after the close of school, thus ridding himself of about $10,000 in debt on the building, "and go to Texas on the proceeds, if there are any." As we know, over the years he had made frequent visits to the Lone Star State, where it would later emerge that he owned $1,750 of real estate. Back in 1881, he had written to Colonel Craddock of the *Paris Kentuckian* a letter full of praise for Texas's fine climate, cheap and plentiful land, rich soil, magnificent resources, and unlimited possibilities. It was a mystery, he wrote, why any poor man would not go there to make his fortune. But Gould was no farmer; he needed a salaried position in a school or church.[57]

The *Bourbon News* could not resist taunting Gould by throwing back at him what he had said about his predecessor and former partner at Millersburg Female College, Judge W. H. Savage. Some three years earlier, Gould had written in the *Central Methodist* that he had happened to run into Judge Savage in Dallas, "wandering disconsolately up and down the streets with nothing to do." Gould might now confront the same fate.[58]

On June 4, the *Paris Kentuckian* asked the question on everyone's lips: "Shall we have a Female College here next year? Who knows?" The following day, graduation exercises began under this cloud, with Bristow's calisthenics class and orchestra doing their usual thing, followed by the elocution contest and the awarding of diplomas on June 6, culminating in Gould's announcing his departure. Reverend Morris Evans reassured students and parents that as the school's new head he would continue its fine traditions. On June 8—exactly one year after the incident on the train—the Millersburg Southern Methodist church was filled to the rafters in anticipation of Gould's commencement sermon. His announced topic: "'She Hath Done What she Could,' Treating of the Usefulness and Responsibility of Woman."[59]

The title alludes to the anointing at Bethany in Mark 14, in which a woman pours expensive perfume on Jesus's head a few days before his crucifixion. When Judas complains that the perfume could instead have been sold and the money given to the poor, "Jesus replies, Let her alone; why trouble ye her? she hath wrought a good work on me. For ye have the poor with you always, and whensoever ye will ye may do them good: but me ye have not always. She hath done what she could" (Mark 14:6–8). Gould's theme was women's work and responsibility, appropriate for the graduating seniors going out into the world.

After remarking on the wider range of professions now available to women and inviting his young listeners to pursue them, Gould began to speak of the institution of matrimony, in which he encouraged the graduates to imitate the woman at Bethany and do what they can, for a wife can make of her marriage a heaven or a hell. "Many a woman has passed through life as pious and chaste in thought and deed as the snow itself, and yet she has driven her husband to distraction, has made him willing to curse God and die, has almost tempted him to lay violent hands upon his own life, and end his torment here by rushing into the torment which is to come." He was speaking from experience, as we know.

Such a woman could drive a husband if not to suicide, as Gould claimed Ella almost did, then at least to drink, an expedient to which he never confessed but certainly hinted at here. "Let her"—an insufferable wife—"cultivate a censorious, fault-finding spirit; let everything her husband does be wrong . . . contravene every plan he may propose . . . and the husband will gradually lose hope . . . bury away his ambition . . . or seek in intoxication's forgetful bowl oblivion of his loss." It is hard to read these words and not think back to the Christmas of 1874, when an inebriated Gould was sleeping off a bender on a bench in the college chapel and his wife knelt down in his vomit, put her arms around his neck, and exclaimed, "Oh my God, has it come to this?"[60]

It is reasonable to assume that Ella was in the audience when he gave his farewell address and was humiliated by his allusions to their marital secrets. But they had long ceased to be secrets. Newton would recall in the church trial of Gould later that year that "to me as to all who dwelt at the College, both teachers and pupils, it has for some time been evident that the relations between Rev. G. T. Gould and wife were far from being harmonious. There were frequent discords, and sometimes angry words in presence of company. On more than one occasion I remember leaving their presence because of the embarrassment which I felt."[61]

Millersburg Methodist pastor D. A. Beardsley said, "Gould told me that it appeared or seemed to him that his wife always was on the opposite side of a question to himself. This I think was with reference to the trouble with the negro on the cars." Ella had thus sided with Elisha Green, which contributed in at least some small way to the breakup of their marriage—though it was but the latest chapter in a dissolution long in progress, for Beardsley testified as well that Gould was angry that Ella had "opposed his discharging the lady teachers after his trial for drinking," referring to his firing of Platte, Stillman, and Crouch four years earlier.[62]

Nearing the conclusion of his sermon on June 8, 1884, Gould returned to the anointing at Bethany. "The woman in my text could not preach like Peter, she could not travel and found churches like Paul, she could not write epistles and gospels like John, she had not even the learning of Luke; but oh! she could break the alabaster box of precious ointment upon the Savior's head, she could anoint him for his burial. And because of that act of loving sympathy with his sorrow, wheresoever the gospel is preached throughout the whole world this which she did is spoken of for a memorial of her." But the passage does not speak of Jesus being sorrowful, nor do the versions of this incident given in Matthew, Luke, and John. It does speak of his awareness that he would soon leave this earth. Gould had likewise told his audience that he would soon be leaving them. In saying that Jesus was sorrowful, he may have been projecting onto him his own grief at abandoning his life's work, the college to which he had devoted the past twelve years.

"Young ladies, the world is so full of sorrow. . . . And many there be who pass us in the way, with quivering life, pallid cheek, and haggard eye; hiding in their hearts a greater sorrow than even death can bring. Go, then, Young Ladies . . . and upon these sorrowing souls pour the precious ointment of a Christian sympathy." He probably wanted some of that sympathy for himself. "Thus it may be said of you in the presence of God and all his holy angels, 'She hath done what she could.'" And at these final words, the *Paris Kentuckian* commented, the "Young Ladies" did weep, for his "eloquence . . . drew forth the sympathetic tears of his hearers."[63]

13

Go West

On the day after his farewell address at the close of school in June 1884, Gould boarded the train with his southern students to escort them home. In his absence, Ella went through his coat pockets and his desk and did not come up empty-handed. On June 11, she began an angry letter to Texie Head, writing that she had discovered that her husband had been corresponding with divorce lawyers in Chicago and other cities. "It is evident from what I can find out that Dr. Gould is trying to be divorced from me in order to marry you."[1]

But if George is to be believed, Ella already knew about his lawyer inquiries and was herself in favor of divorcing, though out of mutual incompatibility, not so that he could marry Texie Head. "I talked it over with Mrs. Gould and she thought it worth looking into," he later said. One lawyer claimed he could get a divorce in two weeks if Ella joined George in the petition. She supposedly consented but said he should go to Chicago to find out exactly what was involved before paying any money. He did and learned that the scheme was that she would have to charge him with committing adultery in Colorado, where he could get a certain county judge to grant the divorce, but he decided not to pursue that route.[2]

In her letter, Ella told Texie that she (Ella) was "crazy with anguish and shame" and, having lost all respect for her husband, no longer loved him, and she predicted that if Texie married him, Texie would become just as unhappy. She begged her to break off "this infatuation" for the sake of the children. She added that several weeks earlier she had seen a letter written to Texie by a friend who had alluded to Texie meeting George on his travels. It is not at all clear how Ella could have seen the letter, but Gould later acknowledged its existence. Professor Newton also saw it and said that it contained a warning to Texie about the danger of meeting Gould in private places and the hope that he would succeed in getting a divorce. It was unsigned but apparently was from a woman in St. Louis. Newton mentioned it to Gould, who said it was probably from a Mrs. Terry, with whom he had left Texie in that city back in January that year when he accompanied her there on the train. As we know, he saw Miss Head again on his return from Arkansas. He spent a Saturday night at the house where she had been living with her uncle and preached at their church the next day.[3]

Ella did not immediately send the letter she had begun on June 9, which allowed her to add to it on June 24. She was more conciliatory in the second installment, saying Texie was only at fault for not taking her advice to go home and for allowing Gould to visit her so often in her bedroom. Texie did go home in January, though, so Ella must have been alluding to some earlier conversation she had had with Texie. "I don't think that you would have acted as you did had you not been under the influence of Dr. Gould. He is so smart that he manages everything with such skill as to try to lead me to believe that he wants a divorce to marry you." But a divorce at this point was exactly what he did desire. Whether it was to marry Texie is another question.[4]

Ella wrote that she had had a change of heart: "I am willing and anxious for a divorce if he will give me the children." Though she would later deny it, this assertion is consistent with George's claim that she approved of his plans for divorce. Dr. I. R. Best, who was now her "advisor," saw no other way out. "At first I thought maybe it would be best to remain with him [her husband]," she wrote to Texie on June 24, "but my advisor thinks it best for me and my children to leave him. The teachers said that they only blamed me for one thing and that was that I did not long ago gather up my children, spit in Dr. Gould's face and go home." She may have told the teachers what she was about to tell Texie: "I hope that you will excuse me for referring to indelicate matters, but I have *known* him to be intimate with several negro wenches who have had illegitimate children." She makes two more accusations, that he was too

George T. Gould, from Matthew Simpson, ed., *Cyclopaedia of Methodism, Embracing Sketches of Its Rise, Progress, and Present Condition* (Philadelphia, 1881). (HathiTrust Digital Library)

drunk on one occasion to preach the next morning and that he stole a book from her mother. The last charge pales in comparison to the others, and it would later emerge that the alleged theft was simply a misunderstanding. It is strange that Ella would lend it such importance, though. "I could fill volumes with his wickedness, but what good does it do?"[5]

On December 1, 1878, Gould had mortgaged the entire college to I. R. Best for a $1,000 loan but had never been able to pay it back. Owing a total in $10,000 in mortgages to Best and others, on June 19, 1884, Gould "assigned," or transferred, all his assets to Best and John G. Smedley for the benefit of his creditors. An inventory was taken on June 23, showing $2,382.90 worth of school furniture, carpets, kitchen equipment, tables, desks, chairs, and benches, plus an impressive array of musical instruments: one bass viol, one harp, two horns, two reed organs, three violins, and ten pianos. The college building was valued at $12,000.[6]

Gould wrote to the new president of Millersburg Female College, Morris Evans, on July 8 asking that Ella be allowed to teach needlework and embroidery, that their daughter Mamie be enrolled in the college, and how much it would cost to board Ella and the children Mamie, Jane, and Kenneth. Evans later turned down the request for Ella to teach, and she took the children with her to live with her parents in Shelby County, Kentucky.[7]

On Sunday, July 20, Gould took the train for Denver, where he would be offered the job of principal of the Las Vegas Female Seminary in New Mexico. The school was governed by the Colorado Conference of the Southern Methodist Church, which was holding its annual meeting in Denver in late July. He owed the offer to the kindness of George Needham, presiding elder of the New Mexico District, and J. R. A. Vaughan, the school's outgoing principal. Needham was from Kentucky and had first met Gould at the Kentucky Conference in September 1883. Letters had been exchanged among the three of them, and Needham invited Gould to come to the Colorado Conference meeting. There, he heard Gould preach and was impressed enough to urge his appointment to the principalship of the seminary and the pulpit of the Las Vegas Southern Methodist church.[8]

Gould arrived at Las Vegas on July 30 with $30 in his pocket, soon reduced to $10 after he bought a cot, a mattress, a pair of blankets, a mirror, soap, and shoe polish preparatory to moving into the seminary building. His only immediate income was the Sunday offering at the church, which had but twenty members. To save costs, he swept out the church and lit the lamps. His salary from the school would be delayed because the bishop forgot to send in the appropriations request.[9]

Las Vegas lies in the northeastern corner of New Mexico, sixty miles east of Santa Fe, at an elevation of 6,400 feet. To the west rise the Sangre de Cristo Mountains, to the east extend the Great Plains. Its name, Spanish for "the meadows," alludes to the latter. Its location on the Santa Fe Trail brought prosperity; the arrival of the railroad in 1879 improved commercial prospects considerably but also brought in criminals who terrorized the town. Doc Holliday practiced dentistry in an office on Center Street as well as murder, then left for Dodge City. After Pat Garrett captured Billy the Kid in December 1881, the bandit was lodged in the Las Vegas jail.[10]

The more respectable citizens forced the outlaws to leave; many wound up in Tombstone, Arizona. In 1884, Las Vegas had at least 4,000 residents; the Territorial Census conducted in 1885 counted 5,000, although the *Las Vegas Daily Gazette* claimed there were between 8,000 and 9,000. When Gould arrived, the town had two newspapers, an opera house, a music store, three schools, streetcar lines, waterworks, gasworks, a telephone exchange, planing mills, wagon and carriage manufactories, a foundry, a machine shop, a brewery, a fire department, flourishing brass bands, dancing academies, and skating rinks. It also featured a saloon run by Bob Ford, the former bank robber and member of the Jesse James gang who had achieved notoriety for assassinating James on April 3, 1882, and later reenacting it for profit in photographs and on the stage. Ford and his equally criminal partner Dick Liddil arrived in Las Vegas in the summer of 1884 and won over skeptics by their promise to reform. Las Vegas was a place for second chances in life, as George T. Gould would discover.[11]

From the letter Ella wrote to George on August 5, we learn that she and the children would be leaving for Shelbyville, Kentucky, where her parents had already gone. She was in difficult financial circumstances, but the letter, addressed to "My Dear Husband," had nothing approaching a hostile tone. This may be because her father desperately needed George to write out a receipt to show that he had given Gould $7,500 to buy the college years earlier. The letter closes on a touching note: "I showed Jane your picture so that she will not forget you."[12]

Meanwhile in Las Vegas, Gould was getting good reviews from the two local newspapers. The *Las Vegas Daily Optic* called him "a man of great energy and enterprise, besides being a fine instructor and of pleasing address." The *Las Vegas Daily Gazette* enthused: "Rev. Mr. Gould takes hold of his work with a royal good will. We are almost inclined to say that we like the gentleman's methods." A letter to the editor of the *Optic* called him "the right man in the right place," praising him for ordering new desks for the pupils. "With such a live, enterprising man as Doctor Gould in the lead, we predict a bright future" for the school. George Needham joined the chorus of praise, calling Gould "a steam engine," rapidly refurbishing the school with paint brush, hammer, and trowel.[13]

By contrast, back in Kentucky the *Stanford Interior Journal,* noting that Gould had gone to New Mexico, commented on August 15: "He should have gone further still."[14]

In early August, Gould had a seminary brochure printed up. There were still two vacancies in the personnel, with instructors in French and in drawing and painting yet to be named. Gould himself would teach Latin, Greek, and German. There was a native speaker, Señor R. C. Gallegos, for Spanish. A Mrs. Foster would be the intermediate teacher, a Mrs. Whitelaw the primary teacher. Gould's mother would serve as matron of the Boarding Department. Frank L. Bristow would be in charge of vocal and instrumental music. His calisthenics class was not yet announced, but it would eventually materialize.[15]

But by August 15, Gould learned that a key faculty member was not coming after all. He thought of replacing her with Texie Head and so wrote to his former student (and current love interest): "My dear Miss Texie, I am in trouble. Mrs. Whitelaw, my primary teacher, has concluded to go East. I know not where to fill her place. I have had frequent applications; but having declined them all, it is now too late to begin negotiations afresh. Can't you come to my aid? You know my way of teaching, and I know that you want to teach." She wrote a polite refusal, saying that there was no one she would rather teach for but pled poor health. "But the greatest difficulty is I do not think Mrs. Gould would like to have me. You know she did not treat me well upon one or two occasions at Millersburg. Since I left there she has written to me and to my Uncle Patterson. And Uncle and Auntie who have seen this letter, say I must not go to Las Vegas." That letter was, it would appear, the one Ella Gould had written to Texie in June begging her to leave off the affair with George.[16]

In writing that she did not think Mrs. Gould wanted her to come, Texie evidently thought Ella would be joining her husband. So, too, did people in Las Vegas, for the *Gazette* reported that he had leased the Hotel Buckingham to house the students "as soon as the doctor's wife shall have arrived from the east" because she would be managing the makeshift dormitory. She didn't come, of course, but his mother and his son George did, arriving with Bristow on September 5. Two days later Gould preached and Bristow sang at the local Sunday church service.[17]

That afternoon, Gould wrote to Ella, from whom he had just received an unpleasant letter. He replied in kind, complaining about a letter she wrote to him as well as "the letter of slanderous lies you wrote Miss Texie Head concerning me" and clearly stating his intention to divorce. "I don't believe there is a soul on earth who will blame me for refusing to live with a woman who would write to me, and of me, as you have. Not only will I not live with such a woman, but I am determined not to be legally bound to such a woman. I am going to be divorced. You may resist it if you have to, but I shall get it all the same."[18]

She retaliated by bringing charges against him before the Kentucky Conference of the Southern Methodist Church for abandonment, the use of intoxicating liquors, and immorality. Her case would be heard immediately at the annual meeting to be held in Mt. Sterling from September 10 to September 15, 1884. George did not learn of this development until he received a telegram on September 12. He borrowed $10 from Bristow and $5 from Judge Harry Brigham, a friend he had made in Las Vegas, and the next day he took the first train he could to Kentucky. He arrived two hours too late to address the conference before it adjourned. A special committee would hear his case in Millersburg beginning on October 7.

In his absence, his son George, fifteen at the time, wrote to his mother: "Papa left here Saturday for Kentucky. His character is brought up before the conference." Perhaps the boy was unaware of his mother's role in making that happen. "There is a high school here where I can go and keep up my languages. But Papa is trying to get me a place in a store and I will not go to school this year." Gould was so hard up for funds that his son would have to work instead of getting an education. "I have fallen in love with this climate out here for I believe it is curing me of my catarrh." That at least was one good thing about living in Las Vegas; in Millersburg, Gould had taken his son on repeated trips to Cincinnati to see a doctor about the lad's cough. Though the young George could not resume his study of Latin if he didn't go to high school, he could learn a living language in an informal way: "There are a Mexican boy and girl going to board with us and go to school. The boy will room with me and he will teach me Mexican. I already can speak a very little in it. It is very much like Latin." His father had explained the reality of their domestic situation: "I was talking to Papa and he said that you and he could never live together again. But any time that I wanted to go and see you he would pay my way." He told of climbing to a mesa with Bristow, who despite being a calisthenics expert seemed to lack the strength, stamina, and nimbleness of foot to make it on his own: "As we were going up Professor was in a steeper place than I, and he liked to fell. But I got up first and helped him. The wind nearly blew us off." His father had told him of his desire to send for his [the younger George's] brother, though in the end that did not happen: "If Kenneth comes out here he will get a constitution that will last him all his life."[19]

Gould had appointed Judge Brigham as principal of the seminary in his absence; Brigham and Bristow would cover all the classes. Reporters from the town's two newspapers kept visiting the school to report on how things were going. They noted that Bristow's students were progressing well. The music class was large and hardworking, more so than in previous years, displaying great skill in reading music and performing. As were his calisthenic gymnasts, all "dressed in pretty red uniforms that showed off to great advantage."[20]

Gould had assured both school and church that he would be back in just a few days, not realizing how long he would be gone. But he would have to wait three weeks before the special trial, and he did not have the money for a second round trip. The *Gazette* assured Las Vegans that he would be back in time to give his Sunday sermon. The *Optic* on October 11 announced he would preach, but if he could not, a temporary replacement was ready. By October 27, the *Optic* was wondering if he would ever return.[21]

Gould had lied about the reason for his return to Kentucky, saying it was to fetch his wife: "Gould . . . some weeks ago, left for Kentucky, ostensibly to bring his family to New Mexico. The Hotel Buckingham was leased by him as a female boarding school over which his wife would preside." But he had already secretly designated his mother for that task.[22]

14

Rebellious Flocks

Meanwhile, Elisha Green was having difficulties of his own. Both of his congregations were losing members to breakaway factions in the summer of 1884. Members of African Baptist, as the Paris church was then called, unhappy with having services only every other Sunday, asked him to give up either their church or the one in Maysville, which he refused to do. They then asked permission to form a church of their own, which he granted. With the assistance of Lexington pastor M. M. Bell, he even helped them organize it, finding a place for them to meet in Marble Hall on Main Street, home to several fraternal organizations. The new church was at first called Independent Baptist before becoming Zion Baptist.[1]

Green had not been the only black pastor in that part of the state to preach in two different churches on alternate Sundays, for Reverend Reuben Lee did the same thing, traveling between Versailles Second Baptist and Georgetown Second Baptist from 1864 until his death in 1876. Although it is understandable that some in Paris were unhappy with Green's serving two churches, there appear to have been other factors contributing to their wish to form a new church. According to Sharon B. Fields, a prominent member of the Paris black community, a former city commissioner, and currently pastor of the Carlisle Christian Church in Carlisle, Kentucky, the history of Zion has been "a bit sanitized." The reason usually given for the break is that the congregation wanted to have church services every Sunday. "However," according to

Zion Baptist Church, Paris, KY, 2020 (Photograph by Elizabeth Runyon)

Fields, "this is not the whole story. The more pressing and more plausible issue had to do with *internalized racism.* The founding members of Zion Baptist Church were light-skinned blacks; some could pass for white. They no longer wanted to worship with their darker-skinned brethren. I learned of this account," Fields continues, "from Minnie Hitch Mebane, a member of Zion whose family had been associated with the congregation since its early days." Mebane (1906–1999) had taught at

Kentucky State University, Florida A&M University, and Delaware State College. "Those Negroes who formed the church were so white that you could see their blueblood veins," Fields remembers Mebane saying and comments: "Apparently, it was common knowledge . . . that this practice took place within African American churches, clubs, colleges," and other organizations. "As years passed, that little known racist fact was [gradually] left out of the telling and retelling of the church's history."[2]

A third problem for Green was what Reverend E. W. S. Hammond of the black Methodist church had alleged a decade earlier about younger and more progressive members wanting an educated pastor. To the extent that this was a motive, it appears initially borne out in the separators' choice of a first pastor for Zion, for W. R. Davis was more educated than Green. Even if his claim of being a Harvard graduate were untrue, he had indeed been principal of the Kentucky Normal and Theological Institute in its first year of operation, 1879–1880. But his Paris tenure was brief: "a short time afterwards Rev. R. W. Christian was called as the pastor," according to C. H. Parrish. Davis lasted only six months (from February to July 1885) at his next church, Louisville's Zion Baptist, and the reason was that "he did not preach loud enough. Davis is highly educated and preached quiet, logical sermons. This did not suit his flock," the *Louisville Courier-Journal* observed, "who want some loud, noisy fellow who can stir them up to the highest degree of excitement." It is logical to conclude that Davis's sedate approach cut short his Paris pastorate as well. Zion's members were apparently of two minds: some wanted a new-style educated pastor, and some wanted an old-fashioned pulpit banger. This inconsistency suggests something else may have been at work in the founding of Zion Baptist—namely, what Mebane said about skin color.[3]

If this separation in Paris were not bad enough, something similar was afoot in Maysville. Ten members of Bethel Baptist were requesting letters of transfer so that they might form a new church. Green complied on August 5, and they organized their church on August 17. By Sunday, August 31, they had a preacher; the *Maysville Evening Bulletin* for September 1 reported: "Rev. B. A. Franklin, of Louisville, occupied the pulpit of the new colored Baptist Church in this city, yesterday." The name eventually chosen for the church was Plymouth Baptist, a curious choice. "Plymouth" is a New England place-name with no southern or African American resonance and no Kentucky connections but one, that of Louisville's Plymouth Congregational Church. The latter was also a breakaway church, formed in 1877 by members of the Center Street Colored Methodist Episcopal Church. They had been offered financial support by the American Missionary Association, backed by New England Congregational churches, on the condition they call themselves a Congregational church. No record exists of why they named the church after the Massachusetts town where the Pilgrims landed, but it may have been a gesture of thanks to their New England benefactors. Benjamin D. Berry writes that "the later development of the congregation lends credence to the belief, held among some of the older members of the church, that the group left protesting the traditional emotionalism and untutored leadership of the old black churches." The possible allusion to the Louisville church on the part of whoever chose the name of the church in Maysville also suggests a movement in this direction.[4]

The name "Plymouth" was probably chosen by the first pastor at the new Maysville Baptist church, Reverend B. Andrew Franklin, who may well have been the instigator of the Bethel breakup in the first place, for he needed a new pulpit, having been evicted from his own on charges of sexual immorality, and it would not have been the first time or the last that he formed a new church to acquire one. Because he had been in Louisville since at least 1882, he doubtless knew of Plymouth Congregational, but it is unlikely that his first Maysville parishioners did. They almost certainly did not read the Louisville newspapers, for otherwise they would have known of his escapades there, which were so scandalous that they would have prevented any church from hiring him. One headline in the *Louisville Courier-Journal* alone would have set off alarm bells: "Franklin's Follies . . . the Alleged Amorous Capers of the Pastor of Mt. Eagle Baptist Church."[5]

Mt. Eagle was the church Franklin had formed after being kicked out of Centennial Baptist for being "too intimate with several of the female members of the fold." In his defense, he claimed that he visited them only in his capacity as physician. But in fact he only played at being a doctor, for his medical degree was from a phony school in New York City that called itself the Clinton Medical and Surgical College and until 1877 had placed ads for its fake medicines and treatments in newspapers across the country; in 1873, its founder was arrested for forging all the names but his to the certification of incorporation, yet he somehow avoided jail.[6]

A member of the Mt. Eagle congregation explained to a reporter why Franklin left Louisville. "He had to leave the county on account of some charges and now he's married. He had to do this, for the girl was about to give birth to a child." Otherwise, he would not have gone to Maysville, apparently. Such were the origins of the Plymouth Baptist Church.[7]

Elisha Green weathered the storms, though, and even thrived. In the fall of 1884, he was again politically active, speaking for a Republican candidate as he had in 1868. He was chosen on September 5 to be a district convention delegate pledged to William H. Wadsworth for Congress. At that convention, a speaker from Flemingsburg recalled the remarkable address Wadsworth had given there back in 1868 in favor of giving the recently freed slaves the right to vote. His speech, proclaimed the Flemingsburgian, had "sounded the death knell of prohibition of free thought and a free ballot to the African race in this land, and as I look around me I see many a colored face in this audience here assembled which brings a hearty greeting to the man who first in Kentucky strove to bring to them a new and more glorious dawn." Delegate Green's was one of those faces. Registered black Republican voters in Mason County outnumbered whites 999 to 872, so Wadsworth had every reason to court them. But he especially courted Green, an able public speaker and a leader in the black community. In Aberdeen, the Ohio village across the river from Maysville, the Republicans held "an oratorical display" on September 27 in which "some of our Maysville speakers will take part." Elisha Green was one of the two speakers besides Wadsworth.[8]

Wadsworth won his election, thanks to the efforts of black leaders such as Green. But he was the only Republican to do so, the other ten congressional districts remaining or turning Democratic. The *Maysville Evening Bulletin,* a Democratic paper, complained that Wadsworth's opponent "could not overcome the negro vote imported into the district for Wadsworth." Whether imported or not, the number of voters in Mason County had increased by five hundred over past years, and although Wadsworth lost the county by thirty-four votes, historically the Democrats had been winning by five hundred. Thus, those new voters appear to have gone Republican. Aaron Astor writes that "black voters only marginally affected political races in Kentucky," but Wadsworth's victory evidently proved an exception to that rule. Astor also records that from 1870 on, after the passage of the Fifteenth Amendment, granting blacks the vote, "Kentucky Republicans had assembled a viable local party apparatus in eastern Kentucky and in the northern cities along the Ohio River." The results in 1884 bear out this claim, as Wadsworth won Maysville, though falling short in the rest of the county, and of the fourteen counties in the Ninth District, all of the seven that voted Republican were in the east (Lewis, Rowan, Greenup, Carter, Boyd, Johnson, and Martin).[9]

In Bourbon County as well, the Republicans depended on black voters to remain competitive. A Democratic candidate for county judge who had received 81.9 percent of the vote in 1866 saw that portion reduced to 53.5 percent in 1870 because of "first-time black voters supporting the Republican ticket," as Charles L. Davis notes. In 1882, the Republican Party nominated an African American Methodist pastor from Cynthiana to be its standard-bearer in the US congressional race for the Seventh District. Reverend John Wesley Asbury won Paris and Hutchison Station but lost the county 46.6 percent to 53.4 percent and the district as a whole by a greater margin. The *Maysville Evening Bulletin* observed in October 1882: "It is an undeniable fact that the negroes have been gradually drifting into the Democratic ranks, and it is thought that this *coup d'état* will bring them all back to their first love"—before adding, "Where there is any chance of the Republican candidate being elected the nominee is very certain not to be a negro."[10]

Unhappy with Republicans' refusal in most cases to run black candidates, some African Americans had indeed thought of deserting the party, abetted by Democrats who wanted to split their opponents. In 1871, several blacks in Lexington organized a Democratic group. J. Allen Ross, a black man from Frankfort, campaigned throughout the state for Democratic candidates. Victor B. Howard writes that when the Democratic legislature voted to consolidate the school fund so that tax receipts would apply equally to both races, this "removed the last grievance of the Negroes in Kentucky." Several speakers at a Negro Citizens Convention in February 1882 accordingly proclaimed that if a candidate for office "was a friend of Negro education," he should be supported regardless of party.[11]

By contrast to Elisha Green, who once proclaimed on behalf of William Wadsworth that he was "a Republican, from head to foot," the two preachers who led the churches that split off from Green's were of a different persuasion. Of the Reverend R. W. Christian, who once pastored the new Zion Baptist Church in Paris, the *Louisville Courier-Journal* observed that he "has been making Democratic speeches here, and has succeeded in turning many colored people who have hitherto allowed the white Republican leaders to do their thinking for them from the error of their ways." For his pains, Christian was attacked in the streets of Louisville by two Republican workers, who laid him low with a heavy rock, though he survived to continue his Democratic crusade. Reverend B. Andrew Franklin, once of Maysville's Plymouth Baptist, devised a "Fishing Scheme" that encouraged black voters to show their unhappiness with the Republican Party by casting a rod on election day instead of a vote. He and his followers held an enthusiastic mass meeting in Springfield, Missouri, that they began by singing a rousing version of "Shall We Gather at the River?"[12]

A widower since 1880, the sixty-six-year-old Elisha Green remarried on November 27, 1884. The bride was nineteen-year-old Margie J. Mason; born in Virginia in July 1865, she had never known slavery. Editor Craddock of the *Paris Kentuckian* took note of the happy couple, spotted at the Paris train station: "Rev. Elisha Green, the dark colored minister and his very white bride, attracted attention at the depot Tuesday. Being thirty-five years his junior"—the age gap was actually twelve years greater than that—"and looking in her bright red attire so different from his somber dress and color, it was remarked they could outshine Fred Douglass and bride." The celebrated orator, abolitionist, and former slave Frederick Douglass had married his second wife, Helen Pitts, on January 24, 1884. "Though the latter [Mrs. Douglass] is white entirely," wrote Craddock, "it is doubtful if she looks more so than Mrs. Green, whose mother was colored. Mrs. Green is perhaps something like Mrs. Douglass in accomplishments, as she is a teacher. Rev. Green is the one who recovered damages against Prof. Gould for beating him, because he wouldn't give up his seat to ladies. As Prof. Gould has also been accused of desiring a young wife, Green can feel that he is so far ahead of him."[13]

Despite Wadsworth's victory in the congressional contest, the Democrats prevailed in the presidential contest. Nevertheless, on February 28, 1885, Elisha Green and his new bride boarded the train at Maysville to witness the inauguration of Grover Cleveland. An important figure in the local Republican Party, Green was likely the guest of a grateful Congressman Wadsworth.[14]

15

The Buzzards Gather

Perhaps the most insightful and colorful perspective on the Southern Methodist church trial of George T. Gould held in Millersburg in October 1884 was that offered by Harmon Stitt in the columns of the *Bourbon News*. The son of A. G. Stitt, a local doctor, banker, and intimate acquaintance of the Goulds, Harmon at age twenty-two had already been a reporter for at least one newspaper, the *St. Joseph (Missouri) Gazette*. He had no illusions about either Gould's uprightness or his accusers' motives. On September 16, he wrote: "Quite a number of good people in Millersburg deem Dr. Gould a little crooked; but they are charitable enough to be content with thinking so. But that picayunish gang of alleged preachers demand blood. . . . All of their processes of attack and voracity are like the spider's." They will weave a web and patiently wait for Gould to fall into their trap, and then they will devour him. A week later the columnist switched metaphors:

> 'Tis a very roundabout way the Conference has of getting at a moral corpse. It seems that a young, hot-blooded, gay plumaged buzzard has to notify the assembled buzzards that there is moral carrion in a certain locality; then a dignified old buzzard is sent out to sail around and discover if the report is substantiated by facts. If so, several other buzzards are sent for and the carrion tested or tried. If it is, on the whole, considered pretty rotten, it is carried before the next general assembly of

> buzzards and devoured with becoming gusto. Rev. Mr. Walker, of Louisville, sailed slowly and majestically about these diggings last week, scenting for stray odors from the alleged morally defunct Dr. Gould.[1]

The editor of the *Central Methodist,* published in Catlettsburg, Kentucky, was scandalized by this characterization, calling it "the most indecent, scurrilous, and outrageous paragraph which we have ever seen in print . . . not only a flagrant insult to the Methodist Church but to every Christian as well." Stitt delighted in quoting the critique, then pointed out that the offending paragraph "was read before the Gould committee and enjoyed immoderately." The local Methodist pastor even came to the newspaper office "to borrow a paper, stating that he wished to read 'that remarkably funny piece.'" Whatever their faults, the clergy at least had a sense of humor.[2]

In his next installment, Stitt wrote that the central matter of the church trial was "simply a lamentable family affair over which the Conference has no jurisdiction, but is meddling with it under the guise of an 'investigation.'" Mrs. Gould's charge that her husband had abandoned her was false, claimed Stitt, for her letters to him show she still considered him the head of the family, and she could not deny that he never stopped sending her money.[3]

The trial was delayed because Gould's wife did not appear, Stitt informed his readers. Gould had already been absent from his school and pulpit in Las Vegas for three weeks. He could ill afford the drain on his finances caused by having to answer "the charges preferred by people prompted by malice and envy"—his fellow Methodist pastors, the very same individuals who in the trial for drunkenness in March 1880 "lauded Dr. Gould to the sky and vowed before high heaven that he was as pure as the snow and the kindest of husbands and fathers."[4]

If the Methodists thought trying Gould would effect a kind of purification, argued Stitt, they badly miscalculated, for the lurid details of Ella's accusations polluted the public's morals. "The Sunday School children breathe it in. . . . Within the family circle the testimony is talked of . . . so freely that the young who hear it come to regard it a fit subject for conversation." Stitt found fault with Ella for accusing her husband in a public forum and with both of them for not settling their marital problems privately, though it is hard to see how George could have prevented her from taking her case to the conference.

Ella regaled the examining committee with details of her husband's sexual adventures: the nurse girl in Bloomfield, the laundress in Danville, the servant in Maysville, the mulatto in Millersburg. Then there was Texie.

A letter to Texie dated August 18, 1884, eventually demonstrated to be from George, was intercepted, whether by design or bad luck is unclear. He had not signed it, perhaps as a precaution. It was delivered to and opened by Lottie Head, the wife of a cousin of Texie's father. Lottie read it, showed it to her mother, then sent it to Texie. On September 17, George wrote to Texie about this earlier letter and asked her to write to H. P. Walker, the chair of the investigating committee, and tell him whatever she knew about it. She wrote to Walker on September 20, telling him what had happened, saying the letter was so "offensive" that she had destroyed it. The letter, she said, could not have come from Gould because it was not in his handwriting and "contained language I never knew him to address to me." In recent months, she and her uncle and aunt, she claimed, had received other mysterious but similar letters. The letter in question contained "a very extravagant and offensive expression of attachment for the party to whom it was written, and a release of her from a promise to teach." Now she dreaded to open the mail and pleaded that her name not be dragged in the mud.[5]

The August 18 letter from George to Texie was first mentioned in the trial by James W. Wight, the husband of Ella's sister, Aurelia. Because the letter could not be produced, much effort was exerted to find out its contents. Wight testified in October that he had a meeting with Texie on September 25 and asked her why she had destroyed the letter. She replied that there were things in it she did not like. What were they? She replied "that she did not like to tell." He insisted. She finally said, "There were some affectionate things." He asked if it was from Dr. Gould. She said she did not know but admitted that the "part of the letter asking me to come to Las Vegas to teach would lead me to believe that it was." If Wight was being truthful, this admission represents a significant departure from Texie's telling Walker that the letter could not have come from Gould. Wight asked if she was familiar with Gould's handwriting. She was but said that "his writing was not always the same." Wight testified he had approached her more than once about who wrote the letter, and her reply on one occasion was "I do not know" and on another "I do not have to tell."[6]

Lottie Head's mother, having read the letter, told Wight what it said (but at a time when she no longer had it to refer to). He told the court that to the best of his recollection, "the writer asked her to come to Las Vegas to engage in teaching, and that he desired her to live in the house with him but if she could not do that that there was a nice boarding house nearby." That would be the Hotel Buckingham. "That he would certainly marry her after he got his divorce, which would be in about three months. . . . That he was of a jealous disposition. And that he had seen but one person he cared to look upon the second time and that was a fair-haired blonde." Texie was a fair-haired blonde. "The letter wound up by saying I am yours now and forever throughout eternity or words to that effect."[7]

Wight recounted as well a conversation he witnessed between Texie and Mrs. Wight, Ella's sister. "My wife says to her, . . . do you think that it is right for you to come between my sister and her husband?" Texie "burst out crying and says 'I know I have done you wrong, but he loves me and I love him.' My wife then says to her is it not a lustful love? And she says it is." The phrase "lustful love" was crucial, and Gould tried to deny it: "I never told her that I loved her with a lustful love. . . . I put no manner of confidence in the statement that she said her love for me, and my love for her, was a lustful love."[8]

Of course she loved him, Gould said, but not lustfully, for all his students loved him, or most did anyhow. "I published in my catalogue from year to year that my school was governed by love, that I sought to gain the affections of my pupils, and I believe that I succeeded." Of the hundreds of students under his wing in the past twelve years, he claimed, no more than half a dozen did not love him devotedly. "I felt toward them as a father, and they felt towards me as my children. There was more intimacy between me and my school girls than is usual with the President of a school. They even told me of their little love affairs." As for Texie, she was just one among many, though "she is one of the most modest and interesting girls who ever attended my school."[9]

Texie's claim that she had received "so many anonymous letters recently" may have been a ruse to muddy the waters, creating the impression that the August 18 letter was not from Gould but, like the others, from some anonymous crank. That the letter was indeed from Gould is strongly indicated, however—in fact proven beyond doubt—by a detail Ella brought up in a letter she wrote to H. P. Walker on October 14, while the trial was still going on: "There was one point in the letter read by Mrs. Susan Head that did not strike her and that was that the writer said that he had written to the Mrs. and enclosed a letter to Mamie [the Goulds' eldest daughter] but supposed she (Mamie) had not gotten it—as she had not answered it. I received a letter from Dr. G. about that time in which a letter was enclosed for Mamie and she had gone to Shelby [County]; hence, she did not get or answer the letter. How artful it was in him not to use any names, thereby escaping an arrest." Clearly, George wrote the August 18 letter to Texie, for no forger could have known that he had written a letter to his daughter.[10]

Although Gould was able to escape the charge of inebriation in the church trial held in March 1880, he was not so lucky this time. For one thing, in the earlier trial he had somehow managed to restrict the court's attention to whether he was drunk on just one particular day. But now there was no such limitation. Reverend D. A. Beardsley testified in the new church trial that he could smell liquor on Gould's breath when the college students gave a musical and calisthenic performance in Paris in May 1883. Professor A. G. Murphy testified that he was convinced Gould was intoxicated the day on which the previous trial had focused as well as on other occasions. Dr. I. R. Best testified that he had read a statement dated May 10, 1880, and signed by Reverend James E. Letton stating, "I solemnly declare that in the past twelve months I saw G. T. Gould . . . in a state of deep intoxication on spirituous liquors." Letton was too ill at the time of the trial in 1880 to testify or even give a deposition but was unhappy with the trial's result because he was convinced Gould was guilty, and therefore he signed the statement; he died not long after that. Death had also claimed Professor O. P. Moore, who had told Murphy that Gould kept his whisky jug in Moore's office.[11]

Much had changed since Gould's victory in the earlier trial. By now, he had resigned from the college, and the institution's welfare no longer depended on his not being convicted. Mrs. Gould had been actively arousing opinion against him, and so had Professor J. C. C. Newton, as Frank L. Bristow's father, Benjamin F. Bristow, testified. At the Kentucky Conference held a month earlier, in September 1884, the latter said that Newton "was busy in circulating injurious reports against Dr. Gould." His "animus" toward Gould "was very bitter. . . . He seemed to make himself very busy with the members of the Conference in prejudicing their minds" against him. Reverend Bristow asked Newton if he had any personal knowledge to support his argument that Gould was immoral. Newton said he did not but that he put credence in reports he had heard. Many of them came from Ella Gould. He protested that until recently he had been Gould's most faithful supporter. As we know, that changed the moment in late spring 1884 when Gould informed Newton he had tried to fire him in the summer of 1883 and would have done so had Corrington forwarded Gould's letter to him at that time.[12]

Then living in Baltimore, Newton gave a deposition. Concerning the charge of drunkenness, he said, "I know that he [Gould] sometimes indulged in intoxications; this his breath often times made evident, and this I believe was because he was fond of it, as well as because of medicinal necessity; it was doubtless both the one and the other." With regard to Texie Head, he recalled telling Gould of something that he seems to have witnessed: some of the students had written something on the blackboard in a classroom "just over the music room making allusion to the fact that he, Dr. Gould, and the 'young lady' were together in the music room below. To this Dr. Gould made no satisfactory reply, nor did he deny that he ever met the 'young lady' in the music room at night." Newton gave his deposition on September 29; he wrote to H. P. Walker on October 6 with an additional recollection, something he saw with his own eyes: on opening a classroom door, "I found Dr. Gould and Miss Texie Head" in there, "*in the dark* and alone."[13]

Gould could hardly deny that his marriage was a disaster. Indeed, in the lengthy statement he wrote for the church trial he seemed to take pleasure in counting the ways it was. Nor could he deny that he had left his wife. After all, he had gone to New Mexico without her. In the end, he threw himself on the mercy of the court, acknowledging that in his letter to Ella on September 7 he had declared his intention to divorce: "I wrote her I would not live with her, would not be legally bound to her, would take my children from her. If any man among you would have acted differently, said differently, then he has more grace than God has granted to me."[14]

After more than a week of testimony, the committee met past midnight and found Gould guilty of having separated from his wife and of drinking whiskey, both incompatible with being a Methodist preacher. Therefore, he was suspended from his ministerial functions to await the decision of the next annual meeting of the Kentucky Conference in September 1885. On that occasion, a committee would reiterate his expulsion from the ministry and add to it his expulsion from the church.[15]

By then, however, Gould's life would have changed in so many ways that he hardly cared, having long left Kentucky, his wife, and the Southern Methodist Church behind.

16

The Rise and Fall of the Independent Temple

Meanwhile, in New Mexico Frank Bristow was worried. On the steps leading to the door of the Las Vegas Seminary, one of the students overheard him say to George Needham, "Dr. Gould is back in Kentucky and I am here, and I am liable to be arrested at any moment." His fear was unfounded, for the long arm of the law would not be called upon to bring him back as a witness in a church trial. Having probably learned of Gould's defeat, tired of trying to keep the school together in his absence, and not receiving the money he expected from selling tickets to music and calisthenic events, Bristow left Las Vegas for Kentucky on October 28, 1884.[1]

It was around this time that news of the verdict reached Las Vegas. A traveler to the hot springs five miles north of Las Vegas brought a copy of the October 18 issue of the *Paris Kentuckian* and showed it around. It hit the town like a bombshell: "*Dr. Gould Found Guilty.* The trial of Rev. Dr. Gould, at Millersburg, resulted in his being found guilty by a vote of four to one. This subject to confirmation by the Conference next fall, but in the meantime he is debarred from the ministry. He will not return to his school in New Mexico, it being under church influence. The principal charge was desertion of his family." Gould had indeed considered not coming back, but Needham, unaware at first that Gould had been defrocked and therefore was unable to resume management of the school, talked him into returning.[2]

A reporter from the *Las Vegas Daily Optic* went to the Hotel Buckingham and asked to interview Gould's mother. She appeared, full of vinegar and prepared to do battle. Asked if she had any response to the news out of Kentucky, she said she did not, except to complain that the Las Vegas newspapers (the *Las Vegas Daily Gazette* and the *Optic*) were meddling in what did not concern them, that they very well knew that Dr. Gould was coming back, and that "had I known that that *Gazette* reporter was in the house last night I would have kicked him downstairs."[3]

One reason why Gould still remained in Kentucky was his involvement in the publication of Harmon Stitt's pamphlet on the trial. It would consist of the evidence against him by his wife, J. W. Wight, and Professor Murphy, his own written statement, and a speech he gave at the end of the trial. A thousand copies were to be printed, and by November 4 some 772 subscribers had signed up and paid their twenty-five cents. It would come out in mid-December. Dr. I. R. Best was alarmed by the prospect, and on October 22 he wrote to H. P. Walker to ask, "Ought not the committee to take means to suppress it? You are the only parties who have a right to know its contents. The statement, you know, is the vilest piece of composition that was ever presented to any committee, and will be the most obscene that ever greeted any people." The alleged obscenity must have been Gould's frankness about his wife's refusal to comply with his sexual demands and the accusations she made of his sleeping with the servants.[4]

The church was not able to suppress the pamphlet's publication, but the Millersburg post office tried to block its distribution, only to be overruled by the US postmaster general. As of this writing, no copies are extant, though all that is missing from the collected records of the church trial is Gould's final address to the committee. Everything else is preserved in the archives of Kentucky Wesleyan College. The *Optic*, however, did provide an extract from the missing speech:

> God . . . will hold you to as strict an account for the violation of justice in my case as though I were a Vanderbilt in wealth, or a bishop in dignity. Lay not the flattering unction to your souls that this is only an investigation. To me it is a finality. When next the conference meets, I will either be in heaven, or be engaged in that which will make the action of the conference

> of little interest. To me it matters not. I have given to the Methodist church more than I have ever received; but there are those who owe to me their being, who may rise up and call you cursed, who may invoke the vengeance of a justice-loving God upon your heads, if on their names you place a weight undeserved. Then I bid you pause and consult your consciences and your God before you give your verdict.[5]

Elisha Green had a copy, as he states in his autobiography: "Sometime after this Mr. Gould was found guilty of immoral conduct and excluded from the church and conference of which he was a member." And he adds in a footnote: "I have the trial of the above statement," meaning he had a copy of the pamphlet, with its record of the trial. In perusing it, he could savor the collapse of his adversary's reputation. It was not wrong to so rejoice; Moses and the Israelites sang a song of triumph in Exodus 15, and Green doubtless knew the words of spiritual "O Mary, Don't You Weep": "Pharaoh's army got drownded."[6]

When neither persuasion nor the threat of divine vengeance nor a reference to his children's future wrath availed to prevent the investigating committee from finding him guilty, Gould, scheming to keep his Las Vegas income, resorted to misrepresenting that finding. On October 29, he wrote to H. P. Walker to request that Walker say in writing what Gould claimed he had told him in person: that his moral character and his church standing were unaffected by the verdict. Walker wrote back on November 11 to say Gould was wrong; Gould could still pray in church and take communion, but his moral character was indeed impugned by a vote of four to one.[7]

Gould had apparently lied to George Needham, his chief defender in Las Vegas, for the latter issued a statement that was demonstrably false, saying Gould had been acquitted of all charges except deserting his wife, and that although he was suspended from the ministry, it was not on grounds that called his moral character into question. Needham in addition excused Gould's delay in returning to Las Vegas, saying that he had to work out his deep sense of grief and that he had some financial arrangements to make before leaving. One of the latter was to mortgage his entire personal library of 1,500 books for a loan of $275 to be repaid in six months at 8 percent interest. The books were packed in twelve boxes and stored in an upper room of Millersburg Female College. Gould completed that task on November 1.[8]

On November 2, the *Las Vegas Daily Gazette* reported that Needham had received a telegram from Millersburg announcing that Gould would board the train for New Mexico the next day. It also reported that the Las Vegas Seminary's board had appointed Needham as principal in Gould's place, Gould having been denied a transfer to the Colorado Conference because of the Millersburg verdict. The board expressed its regret that Gould could not remain as principal but hoped he would continue as instructor; it emerged later that he would not be allowed to do even that.[9]

Gould arrived at Las Vegas on November 6 and immediately headed for the Hotel Buckingham to see his mother, his son George, and Judge Brigham. A reporter went to the hotel to ask him for a statement. Gould had gone out but was tracked down on the sidewalk. He said he had not yet read the Las Vegas papers and was not eager to do so because it might just make him angry. He added that having only just returned, he had not yet determined what course to pursue.[10]

The next day he published a statement in the *Optic.* He began by saying he had little to add to what Needham had already said on his behalf. He went on to explain that he and his wife had concluded in January to separate rather than continue their unbearable incompatibility and that it was on that express agreement that he had come to New Mexico that summer to begin his duties at the seminary. On September 12, he had received a telegram saying his character had been questioned at the Kentucky Conference meeting then in progress. He took the next train back, expecting to arrive before the meeting ended. But it closed one day earlier than scheduled. He had to await the formation of a special committee of investigation, before which he did not deny the marital separation and could not promise to repair it. The committee, Gould claimed, concluded that the separation was sufficient reason to debar him from the pulpit, but his moral character and church membership were unaffected. This assertion was either a misunderstanding or a lie, for though his church membership at that time was unaffected, his moral character had been challenged. He stated that he had returned to Las Vegas to complete the fall term at the seminary, closing December 5. He had not yet decided whether to stay past that date.[11]

A response from a Las Vegas citizen appeared in the *Optic* a few days later. It focused on the issue of marriage, declaring that many good people would sympathize with Gould's decision to leave his wife. It was "righteous and manly" to do so, for marriages plagued by incompatibility "are not true marriages in the sight of God." The writer expressed the hope that Gould would not keep his light under a bushel just because that committee of Methodist clerics said he should. Maybe he could no longer preach in a Methodist church, but he could still have a public voice, and Las Vegans would love to hear him.[12]

That response seems to have started something. On November 13, Gould discussed it over dinner with three women, who offered him $50 a month to preach. On November 14, they published an open letter in the *Optic* inviting him to do so. He could fulfill a need that no existing churches satisfied. They rented Workingmen's Hall and now invited him to speak there on Sunday.[13]

In the columns of the *Optic* on Saturday, November 15, Gould publicly accepted the invitation. He asserted that Methodist doctrine holds that it is God who calls preachers, not the church, and therefore the Southern Methodist Church cannot take back what she never gave. Freed from denominational shackles, he would preach "as a dying man to dying men"—quoting the Puritan divine Richard Baxter (1615–1691), who wrote those words after he was disbarred from preaching by the Church of England. It took some hutzpah for Gould to liken himself to that seventeenth-century heroic dissenter. Baxter was imprisoned for preaching without permission, having differed from the hierarchy on points of theology; Gould was proposing to preach without the permission he lost because he had abandoned his wife and abused the bottle. He was also suspected, as the *Gazette* had reported in October, "of being too intimate with one of his lady teachers in Kentucky." But he did not address that accusation.[14]

His morning and evening addresses on Sunday, November 16, were an immense success: every seat taken, standing room maxed out, people turned away. The *Optic* compared him to David Swing (1830–1894) and Hiram Thomas (1832–1909), popular Chicago preachers who had broken with their denomination and formed their own churches. Both had found backers to guarantee them a salary based on the rental or sale of seats in the theaters where they held services. Gould undoubtedly saw in them models for his own aspirations, alluding to Thomas's "People's Church" when he declared "I am the people's preacher."[15]

Gould's theology was broad-minded, but just as distinctive was his avowedly "scientific" approach, using history, anthropology, sociology, philosophy, and psychology to demonstrate the supposed truths of the Bible. It gave him ample opportunity to display his learning, and listeners loved it. "He did not depend upon the sayings of the scripture to verify his statements, but argued his points upon a scientific basis," the *Gazette* reported. Using the Bible to prove the Bible, as his church-bound fellow preachers tended to do, was a less-appealing enterprise. Yet Gould would not attack religion; he defended it, taking on the celebrated skeptic Roger Ingersoll (1833–1899), with whose career his listeners were doubtless familiar. He gave a fair hearing to the latter's arguments, then did his best to destroy them. The reporter for the *Gazette* was pleased to write, "Truly, we, a newspaper man, actually left the temple with the happy thought that possibly we might have a soul, and that there was a chance of its being saved." The same reporter noted that "the injustice done him [Gould] by the Kentucky Conference of the Methodist Episcopal Church, South" seemed to have worked in his favor among those who had petitioned him to form his church. The hall was filled to overflowing with an intelligent audience, "the best elements, the most highly educated class of which Las Vegas can boast." Gould found, however, that it was difficult to make himself heard in the low-ceilinged Workingmen's Hall, and it was too small for the anticipated multitudes, and so starting the following Sunday the Independent Temple would hold its services in Ward and Tamme's Opera House.[16]

Services continued at the Independent Temple, which promised "good music, no collections and no sectarian bigotry." Two lectures in early 1885 attracted particular interest, one on the devil and the other on hell. Gould told a delighted audience that both were outdated myths from an earlier epoch of oppression and superstition. The material progress we enjoy in the glorious nineteenth century have made them all nonsense now.[17]

A letter to the editor in the *Optic* in February 1885 pointed out that Gould seemed to have forgotten that in Mark 9:42 Jesus spoke of hell as real, and it expressed the hope that the devil would pay Gould a convincing visit. In the meantime, the letter stated, Gould was leading his listeners to perdition. Though in Gould's view there was no hell, there was a heaven, and, according to a reporter's notes in a subsequent article, "everybody on the right side stands a pretty good show to get on the inside of the pearly gates."[18]

Gould had to deal with the question of what he meant by the right side and took that topic up on March 29 under the title "What Must I Do to Be Saved?" This theme drew his biggest crowd to date. He spent most of the lecture tracing the history of Christian worship through the ages before briefly referring to the question proposed in the title. His answer, breathlessly awaited by the crowd, was that "he agreed with St. Paul when he said, 'Believe in the Lord Jesus Christ and thou shalt be saved, with thy house'"—perhaps too facile an answer to a difficult question. In response to the Gospel of Mark reporting what Jesus said about the unquenchable fires of hell, he said he disagreed with Mark, not addressing the question of whether he disagreed with Jesus.[19]

Tell the people what they want to hear, and they will come. In April, there was talk of building a real temple to house Gould's church. Already on February 15, he was awarded a new six-month contract, and wealthy backers began to pledge monthly contributions. Around the same time, his uncle Thomas Oliver arrived from Kentucky, perhaps beaming with pride at his nephew's success but also worried about the declining health of his sister, Gould's mother.[20]

Another of Gould's Sunday evening lectures, "The Flesh," given on February 28, was likewise a message of comfort, though interestingly with regard not to the world to come but to this one. All religions, he pointed out, hold that to cultivate the spirit one must mortify the flesh through poverty, celibacy, fasting, and penance. There are two reasons for this: the belief that matter is inherently evil and the notion that the gods are best pleased when man sacrifices what is dearest to his heart. Part of what audiences liked in Gould's lectures was the way he took them on guided tours of the bizarre practices of primitive peoples and ancient and exotic cultures, often with attempts at humor. Fakirs and temperance fanatics were in his view alike in their weirdness. His former home church came in for similar ridicule: "Methodists, though they have sadly fallen from grace, started out regarding it as a sin to wear jewelry and costly raiment, and to attend upon anything in the way of worldly amusement. Mr. Wesley was an ascetic of the first class."[21]

But Christianity, as Jesus taught it, ought to be distinguished from all other religions in precisely *not* embracing asceticism, according to Gould. For while John the Baptist subsisted on locusts and wild honey, "the Son of Man came eating and drinking," so much so that some called him a wine bibber and a glutton. Fasting was not for Jesus, who was not a teetotaler but often dined out, gracing by his presence "scenes of festivity and mirth, and even after the guests were well drunk he miraculously increased the supply of wine that the festivities might not be brought to a close." Pursue the middle way, Gould urged, avoiding both self-indulgence and self-denial. To those who can do that, the world is their oyster, for there is no sin in "the reasonable gratification of the natural desires of sight and sound and taste and smell and touch."[22]

His listeners were probably not aware that he was one of those who should abstain. His wife could remember him being too drunk to walk. Though maybe now, with her no longer in his life, he was having to take recourse to the bottle less often. To make sure she would stay away, he had instituted divorce proceedings soon after his arrival in Las Vegas, and now that the six months' residence requirement had passed, they were about to bear fruit. When in Kentucky awaiting the church trial before October 7, he had written to his friend Judge Brigham in Las Vegas to ask about New Mexico divorce law, and Brigham had wired back the good news: "Law all right." The law was remarkably lenient for husbands. After meeting the residency requirement, Gould could as early as February 1885 apply to a New Mexico judge—actually a "master in chancery"—for divorce on the grounds that his wife had abandoned *him*, even though, of course, it had been the other way around. The way the system worked was that although the wife would be summoned to come and prove she had not left her husband, the husband could often pretend he had no knowledge of her whereabouts, and the summons would be published in some obscure New Mexico newspaper of whose existence she was unaware. It was undoubtedly for this reason that instead of going to a chancery court in his native Las Vegas, Gould traveled forty miles north to the town of Mora, located in another county. The closest newspaper, the *Journal Pioneer* of Watrous, never made it out of Mora County. Had he gone to a court in Las Vegas, Ella Gould would have found out about it in time to stop the divorce proceedings, for Gould's adventures were so newsworthy in Paris and elsewhere in

Kentucky (including Maysville, Louisville, and Stanford) that newspapers there received copies of the *Las Vegas Daily Optic* and occasionally published news about him. When it was too late for her to do anything about it, the *Bourbon News* on April 17 conveyed the following item from the *Optic:* "Dr. Gould is now a free man, matrimonially speaking. The master in chancery in his case at the Mora court thought this was the better way out of the difficulty." A week earlier the *Optic* had informed its readers that Gould had gone to Mora but would be back in time for his Sunday sermon; no reason was given for why he had gone.[23]

On the morning of Monday, May 18, he took another trip, this time to Kansas City, Missouri. As he had the previous month, he promised to be back in Las Vegas in time for services on Sunday. The *Optic* took note of his departure and on Thursday, May 21, of his return: "He stepped from the train with a lady whom he introduced as Mrs. Gould upon his arm." They had been married on Tuesday evening at the Central Presbyterian Church of Kansas City. "The young lady who captured the affections of Doctor Gould long months before he came to Las Vegas to make his home was Miss Texie Head, of Howard county, Missouri, but who first became acquainted with the doctor at school in Kentucky, she being one of the instructors therein. She is a blonde, aged nineteen years, a lady of culture and winsome ways. . . . The *Optic* is glad to chronicle this union of hearts, for they have long pined for each other."[24]

The following day, the *Optic* continued to sing the new Mrs. Gould's praises: "Dr. Gould stole a march on the boys by slipping away to Kansas City and marrying the handsomest young lady in seven states. But the Doctor has always been regarded as a man of excellent taste and he has a habit of doing the proper thing at the right time." The *Stanford Interior Journal* reported: "Rev. G. T. Gould, the renegade Methodist preacher who was recently divorced from his wife, was married a few days ago to Miss Texie Head . . . whom he loved and courted during his first marriage. They are now in New Mexico where Gould is trying to start a new denomination, with a very broad creed." Broad enough, the intimation was, to tolerate such behavior.[25]

But it was broad enough as well to draw listeners in large numbers, at least for a while. There were five hundred in attendance at the evening lecture on May 24. Some may have been curious to see Gould's pretty new bride, but two hundred of them were there because he had convinced the local post of the Grand Army of the Republic to let him host their Memorial Day service. Forty Union veterans, marching to the rhythm of their own drum corps, wended their way from the Grand Army Hall, stopping to pick up a contingent of the Catholic Knights of America, then a company of firemen from Hose House Number 2, thence to the Ancient Order of United Workingmen Hall to receive members of the Brotherhood of Railroad Workmen, followed by the Independent Order of Odd Fellows, then more firemen from Hose House Number 1, and finally to the Independent Temple.[26]

Gould addressed the assembly on the subject of "our nation's dead." It may have been a bit awkward for the former would-be Confederate volunteer to lead his former foes in honoring their dead, but he seems to have pulled it off by sounding Lincolnesque. The Civil War president had said in his Second Inaugural Address: "If God wills that [the war] continue until all the wealth piled by the bondsman's two hundred and fifty years of unrequited toil shall be sunk, and until every drop of blood drawn with the lash shall be paid by another drawn with the sword, as was said three thousand years ago, so still it must be said 'the judgments of the Lord are true and righteous altogether.'" Gould said in parallel tones: "Only by the bloody sweat of that four years' Gethsemane of agony could our national sins be atoned; only from that fearful funeral pyre on which was piled our wealth and our richer treasure of the best, the bravest and the noblest of our land—only from the ashes of this pyre could our country, phoenix like, arise and spread her wings for the higher and nobler flight which providence assigned her."[27]

But he had another agenda than Lincoln's. He was repeating in essence what he had preached in a sermon on May 10, to which he gave the title "The Ministry of Evil." War has a purpose, and it is that ministry. "War has been one of the greatest civilizers the world has ever known. I undertake to say that without war, slavery and superstition, man would not today be standing upon the proud eminence of this nineteenth century civilization." God meant for slavery to exist; classical Greece could not have flourished without it. However, its time has come and gone; it should no longer be practiced. But the "white race" is still the superior one. Indeed, he went so far as to argue that the "negro race" is older than Adam; literally so: it predates the Garden of Eden. Nevertheless, Christ died for them, too: "I do not see why Christ could not be the Savior of races that did not descend from Adam just as well as he could of those who did," Gould stated.[28]

Gould was influenced in this particular racist view by Alexander Winchell (1824–1891) and his book *Adamites and Preadamites* (1878) and in this view of war's benefits by William F. Warren, who wrote, "Who can deny the beneficent ministry of war in national development, nay its indispensable necessity?" So broad were Gould's views on good and evil that it is by no means apparent that he was against the latter. In human progress up from "the naked, stone-using, insect-eating savage" to the present glory of nineteenth-century European man, "the highest exponent of the development of the race," there has been an ongoing struggle between good and evil. And evil things sometimes "produce a more beneficial result than do those things which are usually called good." He approvingly quoted ethnologist Hubert Howe Bancroft (1832–1918): "Selfishness does infinitely more for the progress of mankind than philanthropy." A comfortable gospel indeed: be as selfish as you want to be, for God will make it right.[29]

How Christian was the Independent Temple? Its declaration of principles aligns it in large measure with the Ethical Culture Movement founded by Felix Adler (1851–1933) in New York in 1877. "Our creed: The Bible, which each one is entitled to interpret for himself. Our object: To make better men and women of ourselves. Our pledge: To do all the good we can and as little evil, both to ourselves and to our fellow men; endeavoring to keep before us the Golden Rule as the standard of our conduct." The Independent Temple extended an invitation to those wishing to drop "sectarian shibboleths." Gould here shows the influence of one of his early teachers, Robert Milligan of Kentucky University, who said of his school that he wished to avoid "sectarian bias" and to make the Bible "its own interpreter." Milligan was a member of the Disciples of Christ, who believed in "no creed but Christ." Gould's adoption of the Bible as his only creed came close to the Disciples' belief with the Gospel of John that Jesus is the eternally existing Word of God. In creating the Independent Temple, Gould may have been returning to his origins after decades in the wilderness of the Southern Methodist Church.[30]

The services at the Temple were more entertaining than religious. Yet they did include such musical expressions of piety as "I Love to Tell the Story," "Come, Thou Fount of Every Blessing," and "Blest Be the Tie

That Binds," and each service began with the Doxology. Great care was taken with the musical performances by soloists and the choir. I. N. Donaldson, "the silver-tongued minstrel of the Wizard Oil Troubadours," came from Los Angeles to begin a year's contract with the Temple, a longer term than even the mere six months Gould was awarded. Donaldson would prepare and conduct the choir and sing weekly solos such as "Where Is My Wandering Boy Tonight?," "Jesus, Lover of My Soul," "Almost Persuaded," and "I Would Not Live Alway," the latter specially arranged to the tune of "The Last Rose of Summer," to which it was not normally sung. The lilt of the tune may have countered somewhat the morbidity of the text: "I would not live alway; no, welcome the tomb. / Since Jesus hath lain there, I dread not its gloom." Donaldson sang the song about the wandering boy "in such a pathetic strain that several ladies in the audience wept copiously." The Wizard Oil Troubadours were a traveling medicine show act, fancily dressed in pinstriped trousers, frock coats, spats, patent leather shoes, and top hats. Wizard Oil was a cure-all containing mostly alcohol but also more alarming ingredients such as chloroform, ammonia, and turpentine. The poet James Whitcomb Riley ("Little Orphant Annie") and songwriter Paul Dresser ("On the Banks of the Wabash, Far Away") were once Wizard Oil performers.[31]

The revivalist flavor of a hymn such as "Almost Persuaded" may seem at odds with the liberal theology of the Independent Temple, but listeners there could thrill to the drama of the battle for the soul's conversion, just as they could weep for the wandering boy. They didn't have to take the hymn literally to find it entertaining.

Soon after arriving in Las Vegas, Texie Head attended a "sociable social" at the palatial residence of a Temple supporter. After an attempt at a fund-raising concert in January fell through, this was the first successful public event of an increasingly active group of Independent Temple women. They went on to organize five money-making events from July to November. Texie doubtless found much to occupy her in their midst, whether it was what she had envisaged in coming to New Mexico or not. On July 20, they put on a fête at the Opera House. At fifty cents a ticket, the audience was entertained by quartets, trios, duets, solos, tableaux, and a comic recitation. Then refreshments were served, the chairs were cleared away, and dancing went on until the wee hours of the morning. The orchestra played waltzes, quadrilles, schottisches, and a polka, concluding with "Home, Sweet Home," perhaps an indication that it was time for those still dancing to return there.[32]

Gould got an opportunity to put himself before the entire community at a well-attended memorial service for Ulysses S. Grant on July 26. This time all the churches and all the patriotic societies attended. According to *Optic* editor Russ Kistler, Gould had "a pleasant voice and a slow distinct delivery." He was not fiery but worked his charm by eloquent repetition, reasonable arguments, and abundant and at times amusing illustrations drawn from his wide reading.[33]

But how did this son of the South and an erstwhile Confederate sympathizer approach the task of eulogizing the general who had crushed the rebellion? The answer is that Gould did the least eulogizing he could get away with, and then he simply changed the subject. His speech was not about Grant at all; it was about death. He took as his text Job 14:14, "If a man die, shall he live again?" After spending much of his sermon reminding his listeners that they too will perish, he affirmed his belief in a general resurrection. It was not a particularly Christian resurrection; it was no different from the Old Testament version: "Thy dead men shall live, together with my dead body shall they arise. Awake and sing, ye that dwell in dust: for thy dust is as the dew of herbs, and the earth shall cast out the dead" (Isaiah 26:19), Grant with the rest of them. In fact, he was probably right now chatting with Robert E. Lee, dead since 1870. Gould minimized the death toll of the war, saying that more had perished since it ended than had fallen on the field of battle.[34]

What little praise he gave Grant was to note his genius and tenacity, that he had saved the nation, and that he had won the reverence of his foes. But, Gould said, we have heard enough encomiums of the man in the long death watch of his final illness, and if anyone needed to hear them now, they just weren't paying attention. Thus did he escape the demands of the occasion, though he seemed to have impressed at least some in his audience all the same.[35]

The Independent Temple concert on August 28 netted $80. It was decided to add a new enticement for the next one. They would award $700 in prizes, selling that many tickets at a dollar each. Somehow they managed to make $400, quite an improvement over their previous effort. Prizes included a house and lot, a diamond ring, a violin, a clarinet, a piccolo, a cornet, two music stands, nine chromolithographs suitable for framing, and a magic lantern complete with slides. Gould himself won a lady's watch to give Texie. In fact, of the nineteen prizes listed in the *Gazette* on September 22, seven went to church members, including the house and lot. The *Optic* took note of this outcome, and it caused some grumbling. As a consequence, it was announced that for the October 10 raffle Temple members would not be allowed to buy any chances.[36]

In his first Sunday-evening lecture after the September 21 raffle and the revelation in the *Gazette* the following day that many of the prizes had gone to the Temple itself and its members, Gould addressed the issue. He argued that casting lots was biblical. Proverbs 16:33 tells us that in any game of chance the result is in God's hands. Therefore, to cast lots or throw dice is a good way to find out what God wants. Thus did Aaron to find the right scapegoat, the Israelites to apportion Canaan real estate, King Saul to find a guilty culprit, and Jesus's disciples to pick Judas's replacement. In purely ethical terms, there was no difference between gambling and investing money in a risky commercial enterprise. It might be considered getting something for nothing, but so was lending money at interest. Buying life insurance is a form of playing the odds. Gould then specifically brought up the topic of church raffles and concluded they were just fine.[37]

It was all very well to speak from the Temple pulpit in favor of gambling, but the odds of success were about to turn against the church and its pastor. For they now had a rival: "Las Vegas has another new preacher," the *Optic* announced on September 25, 1885. To the degree that Gould's popularity was based on his novelty, this was a strike against him. Reverend Thomas L. Gulick had arrived in town to found a new Congregational church. Like the Temple worshippers but unlike both the Northern and Southern Methodists, the Congregationalists were a church with a liberal theology. Unlike the Methodists, the Episcopalians, and the Catholics, they had no hierarchy; they lived up to their name as congregation based. When Gulick had graduated from Andover Seminary in 1868, the denomination was experiencing a struggle between old orthodoxy and new progressivism, and the latter was winning. Gulick was evidently a product of that new generation, having, as the *Las Vegas Daily Gazette* put it, a "broad Christian faith." The same adjective had been applied, and appropriately so, to the Temple, and it was true even when said back in Kentucky with a sneer: "Gould, the renegade Methodist preacher . . . is trying to start a new denomination, with a very broad creed," an allusion, on the occasion of his marrying his former student, to his broad views on divorce.[38]

The rest of the *Gazette*'s description of the new church in town likewise echoed what Gould had said of the Independent Temple's preaching to the unchurched, and it is clear that the Temple and the Congregationalists were aiming at the same demographic, an educated elite of the city unhappy with traditional evangelical religion: "There is a large number of Christian people here who have no abiding church home. Many of these have, by education and preference, a leaning towards the Congregational order; others would most naturally affiliate with this broad Christian faith." On October 11, the new Congregational church would hold its first service in the same building where the Temple got its start.[39]

The following Sunday, October 18, both morning and evening services at the Temple were mysteriously canceled, for different reasons. According to the *Optic*, "Bad weather interfered in the morning and in the evening the Opera House was not opened in time." There was no mention of inclement weather in either paper or that any other church had failed to meet. The reason given for the evening lecture's cancellation was equally suspect.[40]

The real reason was probably the excitement generated by yet another new preacher, the one at the First Methodist church, who gave his inaugural sermons that morning and evening. This was not the Southern Methodist church attached to the Female Seminary but the regular Methodist church, part of the northern-based denomination from which the southern branch had seceded in 1844. The First Methodist church had been "densely thronged" the night before, when a reception was held for the new pastor, Winchester D. Kistler, the brother of the *Optic*'s editor. On October 24, he would join his brother on the masthead as coproprietor of the paper.[41]

Enticed by not just one but two new preachers in town, Gould's flock seemed to at least temporarily desert him. On the heels of the failure to meet on Sunday, October 18, on Tuesday October 20 a headline stated that the "Grand Gift Promenade Concert and Oyster Supper" the Independent Temple was supposed to have held that evening was postponed until the following Tuesday. The Temple had probably not sold enough tickets to part with the $500 in prizes. Organizers may have been counting on selling the remaining tickets on October 18, but there was no one at the Temple that Sunday to sell them to. On October 27, the raffle and concert were indeed held and reportedly "largely attended." But the Temple would never organize another giveaway. On November 16, the ladies gave "an anniversary promenade" at the Opera House—celebrating the Temple's beginning on that date in 1884. But there was no raffle. In light of such discouragement, it comes as no surprise to read in the *Stanford Interior Journal* of October 27 that "George Gould, son of Rev. G. T. Gould, who is clerking in a drug store out at Las Vegas, New Mexico, has written to his mother at Shelbyville, in which he says: 'Father has about run his course here. Where he will turn next, God only knows.'"[42]

As the Independent Temple venture began to collapse in late 1885, George T. Gould took to selling typewriters, but that venture would not be sufficient to support his family. He landed the job of city editor at the *Las Vegas Daily Gazette* and began work in January 1886, interviewing tradesmen, farmers, immigrants, and jail inmates awaiting trial. He reviewed a production of *Uncle Tom's Cabin* at the Opera House featuring plantation singers, trick donkeys and massive bloodhounds, and an excellent Topsy. The donkeys were inferior to any burro you could find on a Las Vegas street, he wrote, and the play lacked unity, yet the plantation singers were a pleasant reminder of his North Carolina childhood. "But the frequent passage of some of the negroes, with their hats on, between the audience and the stage, even while the play was going, was an insult to the ladies and gentlemen of the audience which should not have been tolerated." Like Elisha Green on the Kentucky Central train, these actors apparently did not know their place.[43]

But the *Gazette* was having financial difficulties, and it folded not long after George and Texie's son Robin was born in April. By August, however, Gould was hired by Russ Kistler, editor of the other paper in town, the *Optic*. Gould's official title was business manager, but Kistler knew him to be an excellent wordsmith and employed him in that capacity, too, although secretly. Gould was a Democrat, and Kistler a Republican, and Gould was obliged to write Republican-leaning editorials. He performed those duties for two years, having a family to support and a job that paid well. The family was growing: a second son, Ralf, was born in January 1888.[44]

In July of that year with the financial backing of local Democrats, Gould left the *Optic* to create a new paper more in line with his politics. The *Las Vegas Courier* supported Grover Cleveland for president, and Gould was a candidate for county school superintendent but lost. So, too, did Cleveland, and the *Courier* went out of business in December. In March 1889, Gould became editor of the *Trinidad Advertiser* in Trinidad, Colorado, a six-hour journey by train from Las Vegas. Then in May he found a better situation with the *Democrat* in Albuquerque, and his family moved there to join him.[45]

In June, a statement appeared in the *Democrat* that so offended Russ Kistler, his former boss at the *Las Vegas Daily Optic,* that Kistler dropped the mask of professional courtesy and said what he really thought of his former protégé. "Little Doctor Gould," he wrote, alluding to the shortness of Gould's stature at five foot five, "has failed at everything he ever attempted." The list of failures would include the Millersburg Female College, the Las Vegas Female Seminary, the Independent Temple, and, according to Kistler, his current profession: "His consuming self esteem leads him into the ludicrous delusion that he is a newspaper man. He has never learned even the rudiments of journalism." On top of that, he was "an apostate from the religion he professed and preached."[46]

This judgment came from a man who had known him for nearly four years, who "has frequently, under the influence of misguided judgment, spoken in complimentary terms of him, and has always honestly wished that despite his faults and failings he might do well. But Gould can't appreciate favors of this kind. He would, under the influence of his vicious temper, bite the hand that fed him every day of the year. He has no more sense of gratitude than a snake." As for his writing ability, stated Kistler, it might do for the public rostrum, but in a newspaper it was deathly boring. A reader, he complained, described Gould's articles for the *Optic* as "long, dreary," and "scholastic," written on topics of no earthly interest.[47]

Kistler soon realized that Gould had not in fact written the offending sentence and that he had been attacking the wrong man, and so he tried to take back what he had written about Gould, but his sketch of Gould's character was nevertheless right on the money. Gould was indeed a failure, prone to anger, envious, ungrateful, selfish, and ignorant of the newspaper business. He never learned much on the job, convinced he already knew everything he needed to know and seeing no need to improve.

Nevertheless, he continued to ply the journalistic trade, returning to the *Optic* in October 1890 but abandoning it to become postmaster of East Las Vegas, a separate though neighboring town, from 1894 to 1898. He was hired back to the *Optic* under new management but was fired after attacking Max Frost, a powerful behind-the-scenes figure in territorial politics in Santa Fe, who sued the *Optic* for defamation. Gould relocated to a newspaper in El Paso, Texas, where his sons went to high school and his daughter, Alice, was born in 1900.[48]

He returned to Las Vegas to edit a newspaper there in 1903; in 1905, he became editor of the *Albuquerque Citizen,* and his family joined him in Albuquerque. But by 1907 he and Texie were living apart, she in the city and he at a nearby ranch. The reason for the separation, according to Gould's grandson Warren Gould, was "his drinking." They appear to have reunited, however, by the summer of 1911, when Texie and Alice were living with him at the ranch (by this point, the sons, Robin and Ralf, were grown up and living on their own).[49]

But Gould's health was failing. The sixty-nine-year-old Gould was walking down an Albuquerque street the morning of Monday, November 20, 1911, when he was seen to stagger and fall. He was carried into a store and within a few minutes died. He "had been under the care of his friends and physicians for the past year on account of his heart," but that day he "eluded his watchers and, being a man of much more than ordinary energy, over-exerted himself, which brought on the fatal attack." The nature of his exertion remains a mystery.[50]

In the decade after her husband's death, Texie Gould lived in Albuquerque with Ralf and Alice. Ralf was working as a railway mail clerk and would do so his entire career. Robin earned a bachelor of science degree in journalism from the University of Missouri, returned to El Paso to work as business manager for the *El Paso Herald,* married Katherine Warren in El Paso in 1912, and subsequently entered the Christian ministry. The *Herald* had paid his college expenses, and he worked for the paper until he paid it back. He was pastoring a church in St. Joseph, Missouri, in 1918 when he decided to become a chaplain in the army.[51]

On June 7, 1922, Alice Gould married Howell Stevens Faw of Albuquerque. Robin performed the ceremony, and Ralf gave the bride away. In

1928, the Faws moved to Big Spring, Texas, and Ellen, as Texie now called herself, went with them: the US Census of 1930 finds them all there and indicates that Mr. Faw owned a lumber company. In 1937, Faw partnered with E. L. Gibson to open an appliance store, but the Gibson–Faw concern stopped advertising in the spring of 1938, so it is not clear what if any source of income the Faws had at that point. In July 1941, a round of farewell parties in Big Spring marked the Faws' departure for Oklahoma City, where daughter Jacqueline was already attending college and where Howell Faw's parents were then living. But by 1942 the Faws were in Little Rock, Arkansas, and Texie had moved back to Albuquerque.[52]

In 1945 Texie was again living with the Faws, now in Houston, Texas, where Howell Faw was working for the US General Accounting Office. In 1947, he switched to the Hughes Tool Company, located in Houston and owned by tycoon, pilot, and film director Howard Hughes. In 1967, Hughes brought Faw to Las Vegas, Nevada, to become treasurer of the Desert Inn, the first of several hotels he bought there. The *Las Vegas Sun* of March 3, 1968, printed a photo of the Faws at a gala at the Sands Hotel, Alice wearing a mink coat.[53]

Asked what he could remember of his grandmother, Warren Gould replied: "I knew Texie Ellen briefly during a visit she made to Baltimore when we were living there. We got along very well. This was not the case with Grandmother and my Mother [Mrs. Robin Gould]. Texie Ellen was known to be feisty and proud of her children."[54]

Ralf, Texie's firstborn, spent fifty years with the US Postal Transportation Service, sorting mail in railroad cars traveling between New Mexico, Arizona, and Texas; he died in Albuquerque in 1974. Reverend Robin Gould served Methodist churches in Missouri, Oklahoma, Virginia, Maryland, and Delaware. He inherited both his father's eloquence and his predisposition to heart failure, dying of it at age sixty-three in 1950. Their sister, Alice, enjoyed the glamour of the other Las Vegas until Howard Hughes's death put an end to that adventure. The Faws retired to Oklahoma City, where Alice died in 1995.[55]

Texie passed away at age eighty-six on March 8, 1952, at her daughter's home in Houston.[56]

Frank Leslie Bristow, as noted, seeing that with Gould's defrocking he too would be out of a job at the seminary, left Las Vegas in late October 1884 and returned to Kentucky, probably to his parents in Covington. That would have freed him from the need to make a living for a few months, but he eventually found short-term employment providing music for a Methodist camp meeting at High Bridge in July 1885. A site of remarkable natural beauty, High Bridge derived its name from the railroad trestle connecting Jessamine and Mercer Counties, which was nearly three hundred feet above the Kentucky River, for a time the highest such bridge in the world. Thousands of sightseers had been coming there since the span's construction in 1877 to picnic on the grounds on the cliff, and between 1879 and 1883 Southern Methodists held camp meetings there in midsummer. Bristow had been organist and music director for the meeting in 1882, the summer after his initial arrival in Millersburg.[57]

Bristow continued to live in Covington, though little is known of his activities in 1886, apart from providing music for various gospel meetings and revivals. His fortunes got a major boost in July 1887, when the Music Teachers' State Association elected him president. This indicates he must have been engaged for some time in either public or private music teaching. In 1888, he was again hired for High Bridge, his name prominently featured right next to the preacher's, Sam Jones, in the advertising for the camp meeting.[58]

In 1889, he finally landed a good position as professor of music in the Covington public schools. His previous election to the presidency of the Music Teachers State Association as well as his growing reputation as a composer had doubtless burnished his credentials. His compositional output, however, was limited to sacred songs for the church and comic ones for the stage; no string quartets or symphonies emerged from his pen. His "Old Grapevine Swing" would be adopted by the vaudeville male–female duo known as Hines and Remington, and Hines would say it proved the greatest hit of his career.[59]

To his public-school teaching Bristow brought his expertise in gymnastics as a public spectacle, producing a calisthenic entertainment at the Covington Odd Fellows Hall on May 2, 1890, in which one hundred schoolchildren took part. In 1891, his 106-page collection of calisthenic exercises was published. He returned to High Bridge in 1890, and his association with the campground would in one way or another continue for the next fifteen years. It was now a private concern, the Southern Methodist Church having washed its hands of the affair because of the drinking and prostitution that it attracted in the nearby bushes and woods and that no draconian measures seemed able to eradicate.[60]

So enamored was Bristow of the site that he wed a wealthy widow to buy it. His marriage to Emily Buford took place on June 24, 1891, and in August he signed the contract to purchase High Bridge. Her former husband, Vincent Shinkle, was not as wealthy as Bristow may have thought, though, having gone bankrupt shortly before his death, but Emily was nevertheless a society belle and her father, Ambrose Buford, a man of means. A daughter, Ninita, was born to the Bristows on April 15, 1892.

Frank kept running the camp meetings at High Bridge, hiring musicians and star evangelists. In the summer of 1898, however, he put his wife in charge and stayed away from the campground so that the two could divorce on grounds of abandonment. But in September she surprised him by suing for divorce on grounds of mental cruelty, asserting that he had accused her of infidelity. After running High Bridge for a summer, she discovered that she liked the work and was now trying take the property away from him. The bitter dispute was finally resolved on the original grounds, the divorce granted on November 30 leaving him in sole possession of the site. He was granted rights to visit their child, but Ninita repeatedly refused to go for a walk with her father when he came for that purpose.

Ambrose Buford, offended by Frank's having said in court that his father-in-law was in league with Emily to rob him of High Bridge, attacked him at a chance meeting on January 12, 1899, pounding him with his fists and cane. Bristow escaped and had Buford arrested. Two months later, Bristow had another run-in with a member of his former wife's family, who accused his former brother-in-law, Frank, of owing him money and provoked him to fisticuffs, in which Frank drew a knife and cut him on the neck, face, and hand.[61]

Bristow had always been prone to violence, as we saw in what transpired on June 8, 1883. In 1900, the Covington School Board admonished him for assaulting a student who had disrespected him. His racism had never disappeared, either, for the school board was obliged to hire a teacher for the black pupils he refused to teach, even though teaching them was in his job description.[62]

In 1900, he sold High Bridge to his sister, who five years later sold it at a profit to the Queen and Crescent Railroad, which over the years had transported tens of thousands to the site. The company turned it into pleasure park with dining facilities and a handsome dance hall.[63]

Frank L. Bristow died at age sixty-nine on November 11, 1914, a week after losing an election for a seat on the Covington School Board.

Ninita Bristow, inheriting her mother's looks and her father's musical talent, became an actress in plays and musical comedies, occasionally performing on Broadway but more often touring in vaudeville and stock companies across the East and Midwest. In 1913, she had a minor role in a silent film, *The Inside of the White Slave Traffic.* She gave up her acting career to marry a wealthy industrialist from Duluth in 1923; after his death in 1935, she tried to make a comeback but does not appear to have succeeded. In 1939, she took up residence with her mother at the fashionable Grosvenor Hotel in Manhattan and continued to live there after Columbia University turned it into a student dormitory. She told a reporter for the *New York Times* in 1971 that she preferred the company of young people to those who were stuck in the past. She died at age eighty-one on June 1, 1973.[64]

17

The Venerable Pastor

Fleeing a sex scandal in Louisville, Reverend B. Andrew Franklin found a new pulpit in Maysville, as we have seen, creating or at least profiting from a split in Elisha Green's church in August 1884 to form Plymouth Baptist. The church rented space from the Amazon Fire Company on East Second Street and grew from ten to seventy-three members in its first year. In May 1885, Franklin conducted a revival at Green's other breakaway church in Paris and formed a partnership with its pastor, Reverend R. W. Christian—who had succeeded and perhaps displaced Green's hand-picked successor, W. R. Davis—to publish the *Gold Eagle*, a "politico-religious journal." In June, the *Maysville Evening Bulletin* was impressed by the journal's quality and quoted from an article entitled "The Colored People of Maysville," undoubtedly written by Franklin, that said they were "thrifty, active and enterprising . . . generous, impulsive and good natured," that they "love education and set a high premium on intelligence. Many of them have comfortable homes and are well to do in life."[1]

Franklin was, in other words, characterizing them as upwardly mobile and middle class, along the lines of both their Louisville namesake (the Plymouth Congregational Church that broke away from the Center Street Colored Methodist Episcopal Church)—and the members of Green's Paris church who had left it to form what became Zion Baptist. Franklin's role in creating Plymouth was publicly acknowledged by both him and the congregation: "It was my pleasure to be in the organization of the Plymouth Church," he wrote. "Dr. Franklin," they declared, "found us only ten in number and not even organized into a regular church; he assisted in our organization and became our first pastor."[2]

Under his leadership, Plymouth increased its visibility. For each of two nights in June 1885, the church sold four hundred tickets to a "grand metropolitan concert" of out-of-town actors and musicians. In August, Franklin organized a ten-day camp meeting in Dietrich Park along the Ohio River in east Maysville; one of the speakers was his Paris friend R. W. Christian. The Plymouth camp meetings would continue for years, long after Franklin's departure, and consistently attract thousands.

Despite his efforts on their behalf, the Plymouth congregation was unable to pay Franklin a regular salary, and in September 1885 he left Maysville for Murfreesboro, Tennessee, where he had been offered a pulpit that paid $1,000 a year. Before his departure, Plymouth took up a collection to buy him a suit of clothes. They amassed $50, most of which was contributed by the town's white citizens. He had not told them whether he would accept the Tennessee offer, and they granted him a leave of absence in the hope he would return. But he apparently took the new job right away, for he represented the Mufreesboro church at a Missionary Baptist convention in Chattanooga in October, where he took the opportunity to attend a Republican rally and make "a splendid speech" that "created the only enthusiasm of the evening."[3]

Franklin made a visit to Maysville to run the Plymouth camp meeting in late August 1886 and in December returned to assume once more the pulpit of the church. By now, he was claiming to have invented a new patent medicine, Franklin's Boss Lightning Cure, good for rheumatism, neuralgia, "and all manner of aches and pains." He announced he would build a factory to manufacture it in Maysville, employ a thousand traveling salesmen, and send a medicine show with musicians around the country to promote it. But his Maysville pastorate was soon over, for by March 1887 he had relocated to Terre Haute, Indiana, where he was at the Third Baptist Church and still selling his patent medicine.

Reverend W. M. Jamison became pastor of Plymouth in his place, and on September 7, 1887, he and two of his deacons went to ask Elisha Green if their church could temporarily hold services at Bethel. The Plymouth congregation had purchased the building where they had been renting space, but it would take a few weeks to get it ready for services. It had originally been a Presbyterian church, then became a fire hall, and would again be a house of worship once repairs were made and pews installed.[4]

Their request and Green's eventual refusal caused "a great deal of gossiping," as Green acknowledged in an article he published in the *Maysville Evening Bulletin* to explain himself before the public. The gossip stemmed not just from the refusal but from three years of rivalry, Plymouth's birth having come at Bethel's expense. To make matters worse, the new church had "gone against Baptist usages," Green charged, by taking in members that Bethel had expelled—for defective morality or belief—and for that reason he would not give his consent without bringing the question before his members. When he did, they voted no.[5]

The Plymouth deacons replied with a newspaper notice of their own, saying that they had found another church to meet in, one whose people had a more Christian spirit than Bethel: Scott Methodist, the African American church on Fourth Street a few blocks east of Green's. The deacons alluded to ill feeling between them and Bethel's pastor: "The Plymouth Church has done all that she could do to make reconciliation with Elder Green before she was and since she has been a church." To his accusation that they had taken in excluded members, they demanded to know who those members were, claimed that issue was not the true reason for Bethel's refusal, and hinted that "we may be caused to tell in the future" what that reason was, darkly hinting at trouble to come. But nothing further surfaced in the press.[6]

Back in September 1885, Green had taken part in the dedication of a black Baptist church at Marshall Station, near Lewisburg; had held a revival at Bethel in February 1886; and had given a temperance speech in Washington in July. In April 1887, he added fourteen members to his Paris church and in June baptized four for Bethel. In September 1887, he engaged in the aforementioned public dispute with Plymouth Baptist, and that fall was busy dictating his memoirs to his former Paris associate Rice B. Butler.[7]

Life of the Rev. Elisha W. Green was published in January 1888 by the printing office of the *Maysville Republican,* which said of the book that it "is of interest to the general reader as showing the possibility of development of the race to which the author belongs. It is of especial interest as showing that in Kentucky, slave State though she was, the colored people had only the kindest of treatment from very many leading white citizens."[8] Yes, some had treated him kindly, but that "very many" did was an exaggeration. Green did have some "leading white citizens" to thank in the book, and he thanked them: A. M. January, Lewis Collins, and the rest of the thirteen Maysville citizens who had advanced him the money to buy his wife and two of his children. But his autobiography bears ample witness to the mistreatment he received from whites day in and day out, leading citizens or not.

Life concludes with a detailed account of what happened on the train and the subsequent trial, indicating that, apart from his second marriage, nothing occurring in the three years since then was nearly as important. Gould and Bristow thus gave his book its final chapter, and in his court victory over them he was able to end his life story on a triumphal note.

The rivalry with Plymouth continued. On the afternoon of Sunday, April 1, 1888, both churches baptized new members in the river, Bethel at the foot of Wall Street and, two blocks away, Plymouth at the foot of Market Street. These dueling rites were conducted within sight of each other, Green's church edging out Plymouth by a score of nine to eight.[9]

Green continued to baptize new members, helped lay the cornerstone for a church in Flemingsburg, attended meetings in Frankfort and Louisville, and raised money for the debts and expenses of Bethel Baptist, whose handsome brick edifice had been dedicated in 1875. And he kept taking the train between Maysville and Paris. Their earlier troubles forgotten, the Paris congregation noted with satisfaction his thirty-five-year anniversary with them in 1890 and said they expected him to remain their pastor as long as he lived. Later that year the two churches in Paris and Maysville announced an upcoming celebration to commemorate his joint pastorate.[10]

In November 1889, however, Green suffered the loss of his sister Harriet, who perished when her clothing caught fire in her house, which was near Green's Maysville church. This is the sister he had rescued from slavery by buying her for $600 on December 13, 1853, when he himself was still a slave.[11]

In April 1892, he performed a wedding at Bethel Baptist that drew more white guests than black. In its write-up, the *Maysville Public Ledger* expressed nostalgia for the antebellum era: "It was the gathering of a goodly number of white persons to witness the union of two colored people. . . . It was typical of the by-gone days when good masters and kind mistresses were wont to show their appreciation for faithful servants; for the bride of the occasion had nursed most of the mothers and children who were present with their gifts and their good wishes for her future happiness." The bride was born in 1850; a soldier for the Union, the groom had fought to end slavery. It is likely that neither was as enamored of the by-gone days as the white spectators were.[12]

Green, "the venerable Pastor of the church, pronounced the ceremony in a very simple yet impressive manner. Miss Lida Berry presided at the organ." Berry, a local piano teacher and frequent accompanist at the Washington Opera Theater and at social events in white homes and churches, was white. She may have been engaged to play for this event by one or more of the seventeen white women the reporter went on to name. "There were comparatively few colored persons present, and those of the better class. Among the whites were some of those most prominent in society, and as leaders in good works."[13]

Blacks and whites worshipping together was not unheard of in Maysville. But while black churches occasionally invited whites to attend on special occasions such as the Bethel wedding and revivals, blacks had for some time been unwelcome in white houses of worship. Plymouth Baptist for years held camp meetings in a city park that drew as many as 5,000 participants and typically invited both races to attend. The same church held a "rally day" in January 1888, with guest preachers at both morning and afternoon services, the more prominent one appearing at the latter. They invited "both white and colored," adding: "Seats will be reserved at 2:30 p.m. for the whites," suggesting that they thought the latter would be more likely to come if they had their own space.[14]

Gone were the days when the young Elisha Green could attend services at the white Baptist churches in May's Lick and Maysville or at the Presbyterian church. The *Indianapolis Freeman,* an African American newspaper, reported what happened when in the spring of 1891 two black women tried to visit the white Baptist church on Market Street that fifty years earlier had welcomed Green and given him a license to preach:

> Two of our most highly respectable ladies visited the Baptist church (white) last Sunday, and occupied one of the back seats. They had been seated only a few minutes when the sexton, who by the way was colored, was ordered to tell them they would have to vacate, which they did. Now the dirtiest "poor white trash" in Maysville, smelling as they do of the grease and dirt of the cotton factory, can occupy pews right up under the noses of the "white folks" and they grin and bear it, but when educated, refined and cleanly dressed colored people dare to occupy a back pew, they are very soon hoisted out; but this is the first offense of the kind to which our people have been subjected, and causes not a little comment.[15]

As the first such offense the *Freeman* could recall, it was indicative of a change in the times. The Jim Crow age had arrived.

In this era of increasing segregation, blacks and whites occupying the same train cars was soon to be illegal. The separate-coach bill passed the Kentucky Senate on March 31 and then the House of Representatives on May 20, 1892, and the governor signed it into law on May 24; it would take effect on October 1, 1893.[16]

Agitation to introduce the bill was sparked by a single unfortunate but misreported event. Christine McEwan, a socially prominent twenty-four-year-old from Frankfort, was returning home on a special excursion train from the Satellites of Mercury parade and ball in Louisville in the morning hours of October 2, 1891, when she was wounded by a stray bullet from the pistol of Wes Watson, an African American. Early reports gave various accounts of how and why this happened. All versions, however, agreed that the train was occupied by both white and black passengers and was so crowded that many were standing in the aisles. According to the *Frankfort Roundabout* of October 3, a black man was occupying a seat while white women were still standing; a white man asked him to give it up; he refused; they argued; the black man finally left and went to the platform connecting this car with another. According to this story, a few minutes later he opened the door, aimed a pistol where the white man had been standing, fired, and missed, and the bullet hit Miss McEwan under her left eye and lodging in her neck. The shooter jumped from the train and escaped.[17]

Although incorrect in some particulars, this version at least had the virtue of not trying to incite race hatred. Unlike in other accounts, the reporter did not blame the black race, did not mischaracterize blacks as drunken hoodlums, and did not advocate for a law separating whites and blacks on Kentucky trains. He did make a couple of pertinent points, however. One was that murder and mayhem on excursion trains were becoming all too common and that such trains should be provided with officers empowered to make arrests and eject drunken passengers. The other was that any "man, white or black," who draws a pistol in a railroad car where women and children are present should be thrown out the window with the train chugging at full speed.[18]

According to the *Louisville Courier-Journal,* however, the trouble allegedly began when a white man named William Wiley momentarily left his female companion to get a drink of water. When he returned, he found that a black man, Wes Watson, had taken his place. When Watson refused to leave, Wiley jerked him out of the seat. Watson's friends became angry; one of them pulled a knife and came in Wiley's direction. "There was a great deal of excitement, and suddenly Watson drew a pistol and fired." From another part of the car came a woman's scream.[19]

The *Cincinnati Enquirer* adopted this completely false version, adding its own sauce of fearmongering in alleging that a "train panic [was] caused by colored rioters." The *Owensboro Messenger* urged a lynching: "The Men Charged with the Crime . . . SHOULD BE PROMPTLY HUNG," screamed its headline. The *Louisville Courier-Journal* called for a separate-coach law and observed that what happened to Miss McEwan had given "a great impetus" to the demand for such a law. Petitions were circulating and newspapers editorializing over the "outrage."[20]

Others joined the chorus. The *Breckenridge News* reported that McEwan's injury had prompted the state railroad commissioners to consider a rule requiring separate coaches, and it argued that if they did not issue one, the next legislature should impose it. The *Mt. Sterling Advocate* said newspapers from every part of the state were reporting that Kentuckians thought the time had come for the legislature to act. The railroad commissioners did indeed make that recommendation and cited the McEwan incident as its justification: "On excursion trains particularly, breaches of the peace have frequently occurred, and sometimes passengers have been injured or killed. A notable instance of outrageous conduct is to be found in the recent shooting of a young lady of Frankfort by a colored man."[21]

That breaches of decorum were more likely to occur on a special excursion train than on a regularly scheduled one stands to reason. Passengers traveled more often in ones and twos on the latter but in larger groups on the former. A holiday spirit prevailed on an excursion train made up of friends going to the same destination; alcohol flowed, and consequently bad things could happen. But in the year 1891, with the exception of the McEwan case, not one of these bad things happened to whites at the hands of blacks. The crimes were black on black and white on white. On September 18, on an excursion train composed entirely of African Americans traveling from Louisville to a Lexington "colored fair," shots were fired, resulting in one man killed and another wounded. No white people were endangered.[22]

On April 28, the Busy Bee Club of the First Baptist Church of Owensboro, Kentucky, organized an all-day excursion to Louisville. There were five hundred white passengers in seven coaches, with many standing in the aisles. "There was never a better collection of people on an excursion," according to the *Owensboro Messenger*, "until at Lodiburg a menagerie of the hillbillies with which that country is afflicted got on board. They were drunk at the time, but kept comparatively quiet on the trip to Louisville." On the return journey, however, a ruckus started when a young man from Owensboro passing through the aisle happened to bump the elbow of a hillbilly playing his fiddle. The men from Lodiburg rose as one and declared war on the Bees, vowing to clean out the train. Instead, they were escorted off at the next station, but they riposted by shooting out a train window, narrowly missing an Owensboro passenger. And they managed to get back on the train by catching the last car as it drew out of the station.[23]

The miscreants behaved for a while but then resumed their reign of terror, marching through the ladies' cars threatening vengeance. As the train neared Lodiburg, they announced they would shoot up a car. Men and boys hid under their seats, and confusion reigned. At their home town, they disembarked of their own accord, but not without firing three or more times at the train, again shattering a window. As the train left the station, a young man made to pull the bell rope, saying those ruffians should be dealt with, but a woman grabbed him and begged him to let the train proceed now that they had escaped the enemy.[24]

The separate-coach law would not have prevented this near tragedy unless it required separate coaches for drunken rustics. The *Stanford Interior Journal* made just such an observation. Rather than segregating passengers by skin color, "the better plan would be . . . to have a separate coach for drunken and disorderly passengers of either race. The negroes are much less dangerous in this regard than the whites, who, in the mountains especially, are so wont to draw their guns, take possession of the trains and put the ladies and other passengers in fear of their lives." The *Maysville Evening Bulletin* made a similar argument: "Railroad companies ought to adopt rules excluding drunken people from their trains. The lives of passengers are too often endangered by roughs crazed with liquor."[25]

A separate-coach law would not have prevented Christina McEwan's injury, for the conductor had originally placed Wes Watson and the other blacks in a separate coach before Watson fired the shot. This fact emerged in the opinion written by James R. Grace (1834–1896), the appellate judge who heard the railroad company's appeal of the judgment rendered November 28, 1891, ordering it to pay McEwan $18,000 in damages. Grace found that judgment excessive and on May 31, 1895, ordered a new trial. His detailed account of what happened is the only clear and complete one we have. According to him, the earlier news stories about Watson, like Elisha Green, not giving up his seat for white ladies standing in the aisle or about a white male passenger returning from the water cooler to find Wes Watson sitting next to his date were bogus. So, too, were claims that Watson had initiated the violence.

According to Judge Grace, because of tension between white and black passengers in the third car from the engine, the one where McEwan was seated, the conductor made the black passengers go into the fourth car. This was thirty to forty-five minutes before the confrontation that led to Watson's shooting his pistol. There was at least one white passenger already in the fourth car when the black passengers were brought in. His name was McHotton. He was seated in the middle of the car and "became offended at some negro leaning on his seat." Judge Grace noted that it is uncertain whether the offending leaner was Watson. McHotton began to attack that passenger and then attacked two or three others, "knocking them forward out of that car, across the platform between that and the third car, knocking down two or three" of those he had pushed into the third car, including Watson. The conductor returned, put the black passengers back into the fourth car, left McHotton in the third, locked the door, and went into the fourth car to learn something from the black passengers there of how the fight started. Then he heard a shot. "The evidence shows that this shot was fired by Watson," standing on the platform between the cars (profiting from the conductor having unlocked the door of the fourth car in order to enter it), "through the glass door or transom of the third car, and at McHotton, striking and wounding plaintiff."[26]

In making the black passengers move to the fourth car, the conductor had essentially made the third car a white car and the fourth car a black one, as if the separate-coach law were already in effect. This unfortunately did not prevent Watson from leaving the fourth car to stand on the platform connecting it to the third car and firing through the glass window in the locked door at McHotton, who was seated in the third car. That glass obstruction may have changed the path of the bullet enough to prevent it hitting McHotton and make it strike McEwan.

When Wes Watson's trial was held on March 25, 1892, he "entered a partial plea of guilty to the charge of willful shooting, and through his attorney acknowledged that the testimony would warrant his being sentenced to the penitentiary for one year, and this punishment was assessed against him." Had he been tried in the heat of the excitement the previous year, he would likely have received harsher punishment.[27]

Although friends and family feared Christine McEwan might die from the gunshot wound to her head, she lived safely through another six decades, passing away at age eighty-four on October 27, 1951. She never married.[28]

The *Maysville Evening Bulletin,* despite its Democratic leanings, did not support the bill. "This separate coach idea is all a piece of nonsense, and the Legislature ought to sit down on it. Texas has tried it, is tired of it. What is needed more is a law making all train employees officers of the law and compelling them to eject from passenger coaches all roughs, toughs and drunken desperadoes, black and white, unless they behave themselves properly."[29]

In the Kentucky Senate debate, several spoke in opposition to the legislation, one senator calling it "a farce bill." Another "eulogized the negro, and the faithful servant he has been. He thought the bill did not represent the sober judgment of the people of the State." But another, "an old-fashioned Democrat, said he favored the bill. In after years he wanted his record so that his descendants might know that he was opposed to placing negroes upon an equality with whites," a statement that revealed what was really behind the bill: not public safety but white supremacy. Another argued "that provisions have already been made for separate schools, separate churches, and that it was going but little farther, and in the right direction, for separate railroad coaches." But at least as far as churches were concerned, such provisions did not have the force of law.[30]

Protests against the bill continued throughout 1892 and 1893 and beyond. Before its passage, African Americans in Lexington boycotted merchants who favored the bill, with the result that "the 'white folks' are firing their colored servants and employees." In Danville, a boycott was applied against merchants who had signed a petition in favor of the bill. Two of them claimed they had not signed it and procured a letter from their local state senator attesting to that fact. Preparations for similar protests were under way in Ashland. In Maysville, a mass meeting was held at Scott Methodist Church to send delegates to a state convention to take steps to test the constitutionality of the law.[31]

The railroads were not in favor of the law because it would cost them money and not provide a return. The Louisville and Nashville Railway reluctantly purchased new passenger cars, but the Chesapeake and Ohio announced they would not "until they are compelled to do so, as their trains are now as heavy as they can pull."[32]

Meanwhile, Green's health was declining. The *Maysville Evening Bulletin* of February 3, 1893, reported that he had been "ill several days, and was not able to fill his pulpit at Paris last Sunday." He was perhaps incapacitated until April, when he returned "sincere thanks to his many friends in his congregation and others who were so kind to him during his sickness." He celebrated his recovery by traveling with his wife to Petersburg, Pennsylvania. He journeyed to Louisville to preach at the funeral of his colleague W. M. Jamison on Sunday, April 23. Jamison, it will be recalled, was B. A. Franklin's successor at the competing Plymouth Baptist church in Maysville and had called on Green in 1887 to convey his church's request to use Bethel for services until Plymouth's new building was ready. But Jamison was not one of the Plymouth members who had signed the angry note in the Maysville press attacking Green for his refusal. In the notice he put in the *Evening Bulletin,* Green took pains to note that "as far as the pastor, Elder Jamison, is concerned, we are good friends. I try to do right by everybody, and, if I miss it, it is not of the heart." At the time of his death, Jamison was pastor of Zion Baptist in Louisville.[33]

On June 7, 1893, Green, "weak in body but of sound mind and disposing memory," wrote his last will and testament. To Margie, his wife, he bequeathed the Bugle Alley house and lot. At her death, the property would be sold for the benefit of his three living daughters, Amanda, Caroline, and Catherine, and of the children of his deceased daughters Eveline, Charlotte, and Mariah. He owned three other lots, all on West Fourth Street. Catherine lived on one, and he willed it to her; he gave the other two to Amanda and Caroline, respectively. There is no mention of sons. We know that Thomas died in the Cincinnati riots in 1884; John had been sold south before emancipation, and Green was unable to find him; Elisha Jr., who had been returned to his father after he escaped to Ohio during the Civil War, must have died before 1893; Marshall, of whom there is but one mention in *Life,* must likewise have been dead. Green's book collection was significant enough to merit separate mention: "I will that my library remain in the house where it now is for the use of my wife during her life, and at her death to be equally divided between my living daughters."[34]

As the notorious separate-coach law went in effect October 1, 1893, opposition intensified, particularly in Maysville. A Citizen Rights Association was formed and resolved "that in vindication of our manhood and womanhood we urge upon our people in general the necessity of their refraining from traveling by rail, and adopt instead the boats and common vehicles, even though it be inconvenient." The association contributed money for contesting the law's constitutionality, and it further resolved to "thank the members of the Plymouth Baptist Church and Scott Methodist Church and Order of Oddfellows for the use of their hall." Bethel Baptist was not among those mentioned, for Green, weakened by illness and his approaching end, had yielded leadership in the struggle to a new generation. He had fought his battle already and had paid the price in bodily injury. In addition, opposition to the separate-coach law came primarily from the black middle class, as Anne

Marshall observes, which is how Plymouth's pastor B. A. Franklin described his congregation.[35]

The *Maysville Public Ledger* endorsed the effort to overturn the law through the courts and predicted that it would be "'knocked out,' as most of the acts of the last disgraceful Legislature have been." Alas, that prophecy was not fulfilled as the US Supreme Court in 1900 upheld the law, citing *Plessy v. Ferguson* (163 US 537 [1896]), which had established the "separate but equal" doctrine that lasted for six decades.[36]

The struggle to undo the separate-coach law, despite boycotts and some initial victories—Judge John Watson Barr's ruling in 1894 that the law interfered with interstate commerce and a similar ruling by Judge James Breathitt of Hopkinsville, both of which were later overturned—came to fruition only when the federal government began to attack segregation in public transportation. In *Morgan v. Virginia* (328 US 373) in 1946, the Supreme Court ruled that segregation on buses interfered with interstate commerce, precisely what Barr and Breathitt had argued five decades earlier. The majority opinion was written by Stanley F. Reed (1884–1980), who by coincidence had been growing up in Maysville when Elisha Green was still living there and was a boy of nine years at the time of Green's death. In 1955, the Interstate Commerce Commission outlawed segregation on trains, ruling that separate but equal was not equal. The Separate Coach Act was finally repealed by the Kentucky legislature in 1966.[37]

Rosa Parks's refusal to give up her seat on a Montgomery, Alabama, bus in 1955 gave rise to a bus boycott that nearly bankrupted the bus company and led to a ruling by the Supreme Court in 1956 that the city ordinance requiring segregation on its buses was unconstitutional. The boycott was a milestone in the civil rights movement. As Merlene Davis pointed out in an article in 2005, Elisha Green deserves recognition as a forerunner of Parks. She was arrested, and he was physically attacked for the same reason: not giving up their seats for newly arriving white passengers.[38]

In retrospect, the twenty years from the opening of the Kentucky Central line in 1873 to his death in 1893 during which Elisha Green could freely take the train between Maysville and Paris, recognized, respected, and in 1883 defended by the personnel of the Kentucky Central Railroad, seem a lost golden age. In January 1898, Governor William O. Bradley of Kentucky regretted its passing. The first Republican to occupy that office, he argued for repeal of the Separate Coach Act, but his bill did not get even a second reading in the Democrat-dominated legislature. "From 1865 to 1892," he wrote, "notwithstanding the prejudices and heart burnings that grew out of the civil war, it never occurred to the General Assembly that such a measure should be passed. The inspiration grew out of the fact that a drunken negro fired from a passing train in Frankfort, wounding an estimable young woman." He got one of his facts wrong, as we know—the bullet that struck Christine McEwan came from the train she was in (that is, from the platform separating her car from the next), not from a passing train—but he correctly placed the blame for the law on that one incident, misrepresented as it was. "While this was most reprehensible, it furnished no excuse, much less justification, for the passage of a law aimed at a whole race of people, generally most kindly disposed." The intent of that law, he wrote, was to "taunt" black citizens "and burn more deeply, if possible, upon their foreheads the humiliating brand of slavery."[39]

Elisha Green's presence on the Kentucky Central train on June 8, 1883, was not a test case meant to overturn an unjust law, for the law did not yet exist. His refusal to yield to Gould and Bristow's demands was simply the assertion of his manhood, far from the only one in his long and notable life.

Green succumbed to asthma at his Maysville home at two o'clock on the morning of November 1, 1893. His funeral on November 3 was one of the largest ever held in Maysville. Bethel church was filled to overflowing, and many stood outside. A large number had come from Paris.[40]

He lies in the Maysville Cemetery beside Susan, his first wife. Just a few feet away, trains rumble by daily. Death spared him the indignity of having to travel in a separate coach.[41]

Afterword

Margie Green, Elisha's widow, was living in the Bugle Alley house at the time of the US Census of 1900 but had passed away by the time the house was sold on April 24, 1909, for $375 to Albert Marshall and his wife. Green's will had stipulated that "upon her death said property should be sold by his executor," and the deed transfer declares that "the said wife of said Green has since died."[1]

The will indicated that none of his sons and only three of his daughters were alive in 1893: Amanda, Catherine, and Caroline. Amanda married John T. Coleman in 1884, but we know nothing about her after 1893. A Maysville newspaper reported in 1901 that "Mrs. Cady Fox, a daughter of the late Rev. Elisha Green, died in Chicago Tuesday night," October 15—evidently referring to Catherine.

Caroline married Madison Baber on December 6, 1871. The Babers were living in Maysville when their first child, Madison W. Baber, was born on June 10, 1873. By 1880, they had moved to Adams Township, Clinton County, Ohio, near Wilmington. On October 8, 1896, young Madison married Bertha Morris of Yellow Springs, Ohio, where she had been born on September 23, 1873. Her father, Isadore Morris, had been a slave in Virginia and had reached Ohio on the underground railroad. Her mother, Evaline, had also been a Virginia slave, the property of the family of Moncure Conway (1832–1907), who disowned him when he became an outspoken abolitionist, radicalized by the capture of fugitive slave Anthony Burns in Boston in 1854 while Conway was a student at Harvard. When some thirty slaves from the Conway plantation escaped to Washington, DC, in July 1862, he conceived the idea of transporting them to Yellow Springs, a community he had visited when he was a Unitarian minister in Cincinnati and where he correctly surmised they would be welcome. He bought their tickets and accompanied them on a harrowing train journey through slave territory to southwest Ohio—an overground underground railroad. The result was a progressive and enduring black community in Yellow Springs.[2]

Caroline Green Baber's daughter-in-law, Bertha Morris, was interviewed in 1968 at age ninety-five. Like Caroline's father, she remained faithful to the Republican Party. "I never voted Democrat until the last presidential election when Goldwater ran. He told us what he was going to do to Negroes and I voted against him."[3]

Caroline died in nearby Xenia on July 2, 1920.

Elisha Green is still etched in local memory in both Maysville and Paris. Bethel Baptist now occupies the former Forest Avenue School in Maysville's East End. Its original brick building on West Fourth, dedicated May 17, 1875, was destroyed by fire on January 19, 1977. The congregation of First Baptist in Paris still meets in the brick church erected in 1858 on Eighth Street. The church that broke away, Zion Baptist, is located on the same street just a block away. In their annual commemorations, both proudly trace their origins to Elisha Green, Zion still insisting that only a desire to meet every Sunday caused them to reject his leadership and strike out on their own. The other break-away church, Plymouth Baptist in Maysville, closed its doors in 1910.[4]

But Maysville's public recollection of Green risks being clouded by some erroneous information. His headstone in the Maysville Cemetery misspells his name ("Greene" for "Green") and gives the date of his death as 1892 instead of 1893. The historical marker placed at the site of the old Bethel Baptist Church building at 127 West Fourth Street says he died in 1889. After correctly noting that he was born into slavery in Bourbon County, the marker errs in stating, "Elisha Green grew up in Mason County at 'Glen Alice' farm outside Maysville." Green was ten years old when he arrived in Mason County, having already done his growing up in Bourbon. His childhood was over when he assumed his hated domestic duties at John L. Kirk's house. He was thirty years old when John Porter Dobyns built Glen Alice in 1848, so he could not have grown up there. It was (and is) a beautiful octagon-shaped house but had no farm.

Paris should have a historical marker for Green, especially one that honors his role in creating an entire neighborhood for the town. But Claysville was razed in the 1970s, replaced by modern public housing,

Bethel Baptist Church, Maysville, KY, date unknown (Kentucky Gateway Museum Center, Maysville)

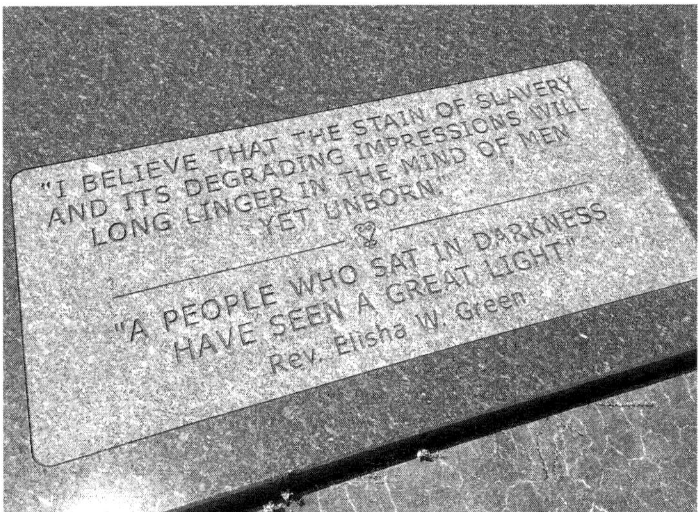

Two statements by Elisha W. Green engraved at the memorial for Bethel Baptist Church, Maysville, KY, 2020. (Photograph by Elizabeth Runyon)

and officially renamed Garrett Morgan Place in 2000. Descendants of the original residents still live there. Centerville, six miles west, has a marker that names him as a founder of the First Baptist Church but does not mention that he was born nearby.[5]

By contrast to George T. Gould and Frank L. Bristow, Elisha Green was a man of genuine and deep piety. Their religiosity, when they had it, was just a way to make a living. They prospered from white privilege; he overcame the disadvantages of being born a slave. Over the course of their lives, they descended into irrelevance, but through hard work, perseverance, and personal courage he rose from obscurity and passed his final moments in the loving embrace of his community.

Acknowledgments

I am deeply indebted to Warren Gould for family reminiscences and to Neil Allen Bristow for information about Frank L. Bristow and other members of the Bristow family. Charles L. Davis's articles on the Gould–Green encounter and George T. Gould's presidency of Millersburg Female College form the kernel of this book, and he has given me good advice on pursuing his leads. Jeannie McKinley of the Citizens' Committee for Historic Preservation of Las Vegas, New Mexico, has furnished information on Gould's life in that city.

Sharon Fields of the Paris-Bourbon County Public Library provided insight on the local black community, especially on the two congregations that trace their origin to Elisha Green, and facilitated my access to the library's collection of local history and microfilmed newspapers. I am grateful as well for the library's invitation to speak on my work in progress.

Richard Weiss, archivist of Kentucky Wesleyan College in Owensboro, opened up his treasure trove of documents from Gould's church trial. The New Mexico State University Library in Las Cruces gave me access to its collection of Gould's sermons and speeches. Miami University Library, Oxford, Ohio, was very helpful in providing access to its collections and interlibrary loan microfilmed documents and newspapers; I especially wish to thank librarian Mary Hubbard for her constantly cheerful assistance. Staff at the Circuit Clerk offices of Jessamine, Bourbon, and Mason Counties in Kentucky were efficient and helpful. I also gratefully acknowledge the assistance of Susan Brown, director of libraries at Transylvania University.

Thanks to Cheryl L. Caskey, director of the Hopewell Museum in Paris, Kentucky, for providing old photographs of the Paris Courthouse, the train depot, and Millersburg Female College. Thanks likewise to C. J. Hunter, director of the Kentucky Gateway Museum Center in Maysville, for permission to use a photograph of Bethel Baptist Church and to his top-notch staff, especially Kay Chamness, Sue Ellen Grannis, and Myra Hardy, for the many occasions when they assisted my research there.

I am exceedingly grateful to Natalie O'Neal, acquisitions editor of the University Press of Kentucky, for her encouragement and for shepherding the manuscript through the reading process; to the anonymous readers who invested so much time, effort, and expertise in helping me get it into shape; and to my most helpful copy editor, Annie Barva.

Finally, enormous thanks to my wife, Elizabeth Smart Runyon, for essential technical assistance and for helping me weed out the bad and improve the good. I have learned it's always best to follow her advice.

Notes

Introduction

1. Elisha Green, *Life of the Rev. Elisha W. Green, One of the Founders of the Kentucky Normal and Theological Institute—Now the State University at Louisville; Eleven Years Moderator of the Mt. Zion Baptist Association; Five Years Moderator of the Consolidated Baptist Educational Association; and over Thirty Years Pastor of the Colored Baptist Churches of Maysville and Paris. Written by Himself.* (Maysville, KY, 1888), 59. Despite the claim in the title, Green did not actually write the book but dictated it to an amanuensis, whose full identity had been unknown until now. Green calls him "Brother Butler"; he was Rice B. Butler, a former clerk of Green's Paris church who later earned a ministerial degree and served as pastor of a church in Versailles, Kentucky, from 1908 to 1934. Green gives him credit for "many utterances of elegant diction" in *Life,* thus leaving us in doubt as to which words are whose. Details of Butler's career can be found in C. H. Parrish, *Golden Jubilee of the General Association of Colored Baptists in Kentucky: The Story of 50 Years' Work from 1865–1915* (Louisville, KY: Mayes Printing, 1915), 207–8.

2. Charles L. Davis, "Green v. Gould (1884) and the Construction of Postbellum Race Relations in a Central Kentucky Community," *Register of the Kentucky Historical Society* 105, no. 3 (Summer 2007): 383–416, and "Confronting a Petty Tyrant: Patriarchy and Protest at Millersburg Female College, 1880–1884," *Register of the Kentucky Historical Society* 115, no. 3 (Summer 2017): 349–76.

1. On the Auction Block

1. Green, *Life,* 1. Six miles west of Paris lies the village of Centerville, which got its name from being halfway between Paris and Georgetown and between Cynthiana and Lexington.

2. Green, *Life,* 2; J. Winston Coleman, *Slavery Times in Kentucky* (Chapel Hill: University of North Carolina Press, 1940), 85. Three patrollers were killed, and several horses had to be destroyed when this tactic was used in Lincoln

County ("Indiana, Arnold-Woodson," 1936, manuscript/mixed material, vol. 5 of Federal Writers' Project, US Work Projects Administration, "Slave Narratives: A Folk History of Slavery in the United States from Interviews with Former Slaves," manuscripts, Library of Congress, Manuscripts Division, Washington, DC, at https://www.loc.gov/item/mesn050/, informant: Frank Cooper, image 61).

3. Green, *Life,* 2. On whether the Vesey conspiracy was real or merely alleged, see Michael P. Johnson, "Denmark Vesey and His Co-Conspirators," *William and Mary Quarterly* 58, no. 4 (Oct. 2001): 915–76; Coleman, *Slavery Times in Kentucky,* 85–86.

4. Lowell H. Harrison and James C. Klotter, *A New History of Kentucky* (Lexington: University Press of Kentucky, 1997), 168; Kenneth H. Williams and James Russell Harris, "Kentucky in 1860: A Statistical Overview," *Register of the Kentucky Historical Society* 103, no. 4 (Autumn 2005): 751, 748, 749.

5. Harold D. Tallant, "Slavery," in *The Kentucky Encyclopedia,* edited by John E. Kleber (Lexington: University Press of Kentucky, 1992), 827, and *Evil Necessity: Slavery and Political Culture in Antebellum Kentucky* (Lexington: University Press of Kentucky, 2003), 63.

6. Tallant, *Evil Necessity,* 63, 64.

7. Marion B. Lucas, *A History of Blacks in Kentucky,* vol. 1: *From Slavery to Segregation, 1760–1891* (Frankfort: Kentucky Historical Society, 1992), 43, emphasis in original; J. Blaine Hudson, *Fugitive Slaves and the Underground Railroad in the Kentucky Borderland* (Jefferson, NC: McFarland, 2002), 19.

8. Coleman, *Slavery Times in Kentucky,* 145, 173–75.

9. Green, *Life,* 2–3.

10. Green, *Life,* 2; Coleman, *Slavery Times in Kentucky,* 155–56.

11. Green, *Life,* 1; Caroline R. Miller, *Slavery in Mason County, Kentucky: A Century of Records 1788–1888,* 2 vols. (Maysville, KY: National Underground Railroad Museum, 2001), 1:274, 294.

12. Will Book G, pp. 242, 344, Mason County Circuit Clerk's Office, Maysville, KY. My great-grandfather's great-grandfather, Daniel Runyon (1750–1815), was the father of Asa Randolph Runyon (1789–1858), who bought a slave when Elisha Green was sold. Because Asa was born from a different mother, he is not my ancestor.

13. Green, *Life,* 1, 2.

14. William M. Towery, "My Dobyns/Berry/Porter/Hitt/Vaughan and Allied Families," typescript, 2004, Kentucky Historical Society Library, Frankfort, 23 (on Frances Amanda Kirk's birth); Green, *Life,* 1; Francis Frederick, *Autobiography of Rev. Francis Frederick* (Baltimore, 1869), 9.

15. John H. Spencer, *A History of Kentucky Baptists,* 2 vols. (Cincinnati, 1885), 1:203; Green, *Life,* 16; Z. T. Cody, *History of May's Lick Baptist Church* (Maysville, 1890), 22, 27; Alexander Campbell, *Memoirs of Alexander Campbell,* 2 vols., ed. Robert Richardson (Cincinnati, 1898), 2:330.

16. Green, *Life,* 12, quoting Vaughan; Cody, *History of May's Lick Baptist Church,* 39.

17. Green, *Life,* 31, 59.

18. *Baptist Memorial and Monthly Record* 4 (1845): 238; Parrish, *Golden Jubilee,* 262.

19. On the May's Lick church's unhappiness with Warder's absences, see *Baptist Memorial and Monthly Record* 4 (1845): 237–38.

2. I Desired to Read the Word of God

1. Green, *Life,* 3. Elizabeth Sisson, born in Virginia in 1791, is described in both the 1840 and 1850 US Census as having two sons but no husband. See Elizabeth Sisson, Mason County, KY, US Census, 1840, microfilm, National Archives and Records Administration (NARA), Washington, DC, records made available through FamilySearch, website of the Church of Jesus Christ of Latter-day Saints, database with images, at https://www.familysearch.org/ark:/61903/1:1:XHYP-YT5; Elizabeth Sisson, Mason County, KY, US Census, 1850, microfilm, NARA, FamilySearch, at https://www.familysearch.org/ark:/61903/1:1:M656-BLD. On John Porter Dobyns's motive for moving from Flemingsburg to Maysville, see John Livingston, *Biographical Sketches of Distinguished Americans, Now Living* (New York, 1853), 208. Dobyns and Livingston's other contributors probably wrote their own biographical sketches for the volume, and then Livingston edited and put their words in the third person. Livingston cites classical precedents for this practice: "Many, from the remotest period, have even been their own historians, persuaded that in speaking of themselves they should display an honest confidence in their integrity" (John Livingston, *Portraits of Eminent Americans Now Living,* vol. 4 [New York, 1854], 6).

2. G. Glenn Clift, *History of Maysville and Mason County* (Lexington, KY: Transylvania Printing, 1936), 174, 143–44 (reference to Michaux), 148 (quote from Cuming); Jean Calvert and John Klee, *Maysville, Kentucky: From Past to Present in Pictures* (Maysville, KY: Mason County Museum, 1983), 5, 6.

3. Clift, *History of Maysville and Mason County,* 153, 155, 156–57.

4. Clift, *History of Maysville and Mason County,* 181, quoting Cummings; Karl Raitz and Nancy O'Malley, *Kentucky's Frontier Highway: Historical Landscapes along the Maysville Road* (Lexington: University Press of Kentucky, 2012), 66, 64.

5. Livingston, *Biographical Sketches,* 208.

6. Ann Hagedorn, *Beyond the River: The Untold Story of the Heroes of the Underground Railroad* (New York: Simon and Schuster, 2002), 135–39.

7. Hagedorn, *Beyond the River,* 178–79, 230.

8. Green, *Life,* 9, 59–60.

9. Livingston, *Biographical Sketches,* 209; Green, *Life,* 9, 15–16.

10. Green, *Life,* 3.

11. Green, *Life,* 4, 16.

12. *Lexington Intelligencer,* Sept. 4, 1841, reprinted in *North American and Daily Advertiser* (Philadelphia), Sept. 21, 1841.

13. *Cincinnati Enquirer,* Sept. 4, 1841; *North American and Daily Advertiser* (Philadelphia), Sept. 21, 1841.

14. *Cincinnati Daily Gazette,* reprinted in the *Massachusetts Spy* (Worcester), June 2, 1841.

15. Green, *Life,* 5.

16. Martin H. Smith, *History of the Maysville Baptist Church* (Maysville, KY, 1875), 5, 7.

17. Green, *Life,* 18, 19.

18. Green, *Life,* 19.

19. *Louisville Daily Courier,* Oct. 7, 1852; George M. Apperson, "Lincoln, the Churches, and Memphis Presbyterians," *American Presbyterians* 72, no. 2 (Summer 1994): 102.

20. Mark Auslander, *The Accidental Slaveowner: Revisiting a Myth of Race and Finding an American Family* (Athens: University of Georgia Press, 2011), 201, 90, 323.

21. John Nelson Norwood, *The Schism in the Methodist Episcopal Church 1844: A Study of Slavery and Ecclesiastical Politics* (Alfred, NY: Alfred University Press, 1923), 133–34; April E. Holm, *A Kingdom Divided: Evangelicals, Loyalty, and Sectionalism in the Civil War Era* (Baton Rouge: Louisiana State University Press, 2017), 67–68.

22. Holm, *A Kingdom Divided,* 76; Norwood, *The Schism,* 142 n.

23. Norwood, *The Schism,* 143–44; Calvert and Klee, *Maysville, Kentucky,* 18.

3. More Than One Path to Freedom

1. Green, *Life,* 23.

2. Lucas, *A History of Blacks in Kentucky,* 1:104–5.

3. Green, *Life,* 15; *Louisville Daily Courier,* Jan. 25, 1850; Miller, *Slavery in Mason County,* 2:160.

4. *Kimball & James Business Directory for the Mississippi Valley* (Cincinnati, 1844), 332; *Maysville Eagle* quoted in *Louisville Daily Courier,* July 8, 1845, and Oct. 21, 1844; *Louisville Daily Courier,* June 29, 1849.

5. Margaret Walsh, *The Rise of the Midwestern Meat Packing Industry* (Lexington: University Press of Kentucky, 2015), 29, 15; *Louisville Daily Courier,* Nov. 17, 1848; Livingston, *Biographical Sketches,* 210; Clift, *History of Maysville and Mason County,* 185, quoting *Lexington Observer and Reporter.*

6. Clift, *History of Maysville and Mason County,* 199, 201.

7. Carl Schmidt and Ellen Puerzer, "More about Octagons," *Lexington Herald-Leader,* Dec. 26, 1998; Jean Calvert and John Klee, *The Towns of Mason*

County: Their Past in Pictures (Maysville, KY: Maysville and Mason County Library Historical and Scientific Association, 1986), 87.

8. Green, *Life,* 11; Livingston, *Biographical Sketches,* 209. Alice Dobyns was born on March 3, 1843, and died on March 16, 1923 (Alice Dobyns Orr, 1923, Alabama Deaths, 1908–1974, database, based on data from the Alabama Department of Health, Montgomery, FamilySearch, at http://FamilySearch.org/ark:/61903/1:1:JD2Y-XHF). Having started with Green, Alice Dobyns Orr taught school in Kentucky and Alabama for the rest of her life. President Warren Harding was in Birmingham in 1921 when he chanced to see a newspaper article about her career and sent her a congratulatory letter on White House stationery that she proudly read to her pupils (*Maysville Public Ledger,* Nov. 12, 1921). On forging passes, see Diane Perrine Coon, "Freedmen's Bureau Schools," in *The Encyclopedia of Northern Kentucky,* ed. Paul A. Tenkotte and James C. Claypool (Lexington: University Press of Kentucky, 2009), 370.

9. "Florida Narratives," vol. 3 of Federal Writers' Project, US Work Projects Administration, "Slave Narratives: A Folk History of Slavery in the United States from Interviews with Former Slaves," Manuscript Division, Library of Congress, Washington, DC.

10. Green, *Life,* 5–6.

11. Miller, *Slavery in Mason County,* 1:269, 274, 294, 244, 255, 262, 265, ii.

12. *Anti-Slavery Bugle* (Salem, OH), Apr. 3 (quoting letter to the *Maysville Eagle*) and Dec. 18, 1852; Miller, *Slavery in Mason County,* 2:158–63.

13. *Anti-Slavery Bugle,* Apr. 3, 1852, quoting *Ripley Bee* and *Maysville Eagle.*

14. *Louisville Courier,* Sept. 22, 1853, quoting *Maysville Eagle; Anti-Slavery Bugle,* June 12, 1852.

4. I Belong to Mr. Green

1. Green, *Life,* 9–10; Deed Book 62, p. 414, Mason County Circuit Clerk's Office, Maysville, KY.

2. Miller, *Slavery in Mason County,* 1:317–18; *Maysville Eagle,* Aug. 14, 1854.

3. Green, *Life,* 9, 28, 6; Coleman, *Slavery Times in Kentucky,* 100.

4. Green, *Life,* 29, 6.

5. Green, *Life,* 7.

6. Green, *Life,* 12.

7. "Virtually all of today's American Saddlebreds somehow trace to Grey Eagle," Anne Peters writes. "Foaled in 1835, Grey Eagle helped establish Kentucky's reputation as a premier source of great horses, but his influence on the American Thoroughbred went far beyond racing" ("From War Horse to Saddle Horse," *American Saddlebred Magazine,* Nov.–Dec. 1998; see also Anne Peters, "Pedigree Analysis: Grey Eagle," *Bloodhorse,* Jan. 9, 2015, at https://www.

bloodhorse.com/horse-racing/articles/109985/pedigree-analysis-grey-eagle). On Dobyns's retirement, see *Louisville Daily Courier,* July 6, 1855.

8. Miller, *Slavery in Mason County,* 1:322; Green, *Life,* 13, 33; Lucas, *A History of Blacks in Kentucky,* 1:114; Marshall T. Green, Mason County, KY, US Census, 1850, microfilm, NARA, FamilySearch, at https://www.familysearch.org/ark:/61903/1:1:M656-BG3.

9. *Louisville Journal,* June 15, 1856, and Oct. 30, 1852; *Louisville Daily Courier,* July 8, 1858, and Apr. 9, 1857; Lucas, *A History of Blacks in Kentucky,* 1:104–5, 1:9.

10. Lucas, *A History of Blacks in Kentucky,* 1:113; Green, *Life,* 13–14.

11. Green, *Life,* 14.

12. Green, *Life,* 14–15, 26; Darrell E. Bigham, *On Jordan's Banks: Emancipation and Its Aftermath in the Ohio River Valley* (Lexington: University Press of Kentucky, 2006), 33.

13. Green, *Life,* 29.

14. J. Foster Barbour, quoted in the *Maysville Public Ledger,* June 20, 1917.

15. Green, *Life,* 4.

16. Green, *Life,* 10.

17. Green, *Life,* 10.

18. Green, *Life,* 10.

19. *Louisville Daily Courier,* Mar. 5, 1860. In the meantime, on November 29, 1859, Dobyns's sixteen-year-old daughter, Alice, Elisha's writing teacher, married her father's bookkeeper, who later divorced her, obliging her to earn her own living as a teacher.

20. Elisha Green, Susan Green, Thomas Green, and Catherine Green, Maysville, Mason County, KY, US Census, 1860, microfilm, NARA, FamilySearch, at https://familysearch.org/ark:/61903/1:1:MZ13–7LR; Green, *Life,* 4.

5. The Interests of My People

1. Green, *Life,* 13; *Maysville Weekly Bulletin,* Sept. 18, 1862.

2. Harrison and Klotter, *A New History of Kentucky,* 180.

3. Lucas, *A History of Blacks in Kentucky,* 1:298; Green, *Life,* 33; *Proceedings of the State Convention of Colored Men Held at Lexington, Kentucky, in the A. M. E. Church, November 26th, 27th, and 28th, 1867* (Frankfort, KY, 1867), 5, 13; J. Michael Rhyne, "'We Are Mobed & Beat': Regulator Violence against Free Black Households in Kentucky's Bluegrass Region, 1865–1867," *Ohio Valley History* 2, no. 1 (Spring 2002): 30–41, C. J. True quoted on 35.

4. Deed Book 70, p. 524, Mason County Circuit Clerk's Office, Maysville, KY; Margie Green, Maysville, Mason County, Kentucky, US Census, 1900, microfilm, NARA, FamilySearch, at https://familysearch.org/ark:/61903/1:1:M9HW-MP1.

5. Green, *Life,* 26.

6. Green, *Life,* 30–31.

7. Lucas, *A History of Blacks in Kentucky,* 1:178; Green, *Life,* 19–20. Palmer resigned on April 1, 1866, so this settlement between Green and Reid must have occurred before then.

8. Green, *Life,* 21.

9. Green, *Life,* 21.

10. Green, *Life,* 24; Elisha Green, Maysville, Mason County, Kentucky, US Census, 1870, microfilm, NARA, FamilySearch, at https://familysearch.org/ark:/61903/1:1:MXWG-H1R.

11. Green, *Life,* 37. In the US Census of 1870 (see note 10), Elisha Jr. gave his age as twenty-one.

12. Green, *Life,* 25.

13. Deed Book 5, Bourbon County Circuit Court, Paris, KY; Green, *Life,* 25; H. E. Everman, *Bourbon County since 1865* (Richmond, KY: H. E. Everman, 1999), 37, 39, 279.

14. Lucas, *A History of Blacks in Kentucky,* 1:207; Miller, *Slavery in Mason County,* 1:339.

15. Green, *Life,* 33–37. Green says the meeting took place in 1866, and it is true that a similar meeting was held in Lexington in March of that year, but the lengthy description he provides is clearly of the event in 1876. He may well have also attended the one in 1866, but he does not mention both.

16. "Freedmen's Bureau Records of Persons and Articles Hired, 1865–1872," database with images, FamilySearch, at https://familysearch.org/ark:/61903/1:1:Q2QP-WRF8; Lucas, *A History of Blacks in Kentucky,* 1:233; Rhyne, "'We Are Mobed & Beat,'" 37; Coon, "Freedmen's Bureau Schools," 370.

17. *Louisville Daily Courier,* June 22, 1868; William H. Wadsworth, *Speech of Hon. W. H. Wadsworth, at Flemingsburg, Kentucky, June 13, 1868* (Washington, DC, 1868), 6, 7.

18. Green, *Life,* 32.

19. Green, *Life,* 32.

20. Green, *Life,* 39.

21. Green, *Life,* 39–40.

22. Green, *Life,* 39–40.

23. Green, *Life,* 40.

24. Green, *Life,* 40–41.

25. Henry Davenport Northrop et al., *The College of Life or Practical Self-Educator: A Manual of Self-Improvement for the Colored Race . . . Giving Examples and Achievements of Successful Men and Women of the Race* (N.p., 1896), 55; Lewis S. Hammond, Baltimore, MD, US Census, 1860, microfilm, NARA, FamilySearch, at https://familysearch.org/ark:/61903/1:1:M696–63K; *United States Naval Enlistment Rendezvous,* 1855–1891; *Baltimore Sun,* Mar. 7, 1872; *Cincinnati Enquirer,* Apr. 26, 1872.

26. Green, *Life,* 41.

27. Deed Book 75, pp. 517, 90, 302, Mason County Circuit Clerk's Office, Maysville, KY.

28. *New York Times,* June 16, 1876; Ross A. Webb, *Benjamin Helm Bristow: Border State Politician* (Lexington: University Press of Kentucky, 1969), 235–36.

29. Green, *Life,* 43–44.

30. Green, *Life,* 44; *Cincinnati Enquirer,* May 20, 1876.

31. Green, *Life,* 44–45.

32. Green, *Life,* 45.

33. Green, *Life,* 50–51.

34. Green, *Life,* 51, 20.

35. *Maysville Evening Bulletin,* Feb. 6, 1882.

36. *Maysville Evening Bulletin,* July 15, 1882.

6. The Confederacy or the Church?

1. *Methodist Episcopal Church South v. Rev. George T. Gould,* church trial, Millersburg, October 1884 (hereafter *MECS v. GTG*), a collection including a transcript of the trial and other records (letters, depositions, and statements written by Gould and others), Kentucky Wesleyan College, Owensboro, trial transcript, 179–80; Thomas M. Oliver, Raleigh, Wake County, NC, US Census, 1850, microfilm, NARA, FamilySearch, at https://www.familysearch.org/ark:/61903/1:1:M4B2-ZDR; George Golds [Gould], Raleigh, Wake County, NC, US Census, 1850, microfilm, NARA, FamilySearch, at https://www.familysearch.org/ark:/61903/1:1:M4B2-BVC.

2. Richard M. Pope, *Lexington Theological Seminary: A Brief Narrative* (Lexington, KY: Lexington Theological Seminary, 1973), 7.

3. *Second Annual Announcement of Kentucky University* (Harrodsburg, KY, 1860), 17.

4. Matthew Simpson, ed., *Cyclopedia of Methodism, Embracing Sketches of Its Rise, Progress, and Present Condition* (Philadelphia, 1883), 416.

5. George T. Gould, "The Blue and the Gray, Delivered at the Ninth Annual Session of the Encampment of the G. A. R., Department of New Mexico, April 7th, 1892," George T. Gould Papers, New Mexico State University Library, Las Cruces.

6. John W. Cunningham, "A Preacher's Experiences during the Civil War" (1903), reprinted in *Kentucky Explorer Magazine,* Mar. 2001, 66–67.

7. Cunningham, "A Preacher's Experiences," 66–67; *Minutes of the Annual Conferences of the Methodist Episcopal Church, South for the Year 1862* (Nashville, TN, 1862), 368.

8. William Henry Perrin, *History of Bourbon, Scott, Harrison, and Nicholas Counties, Kentucky* (Chicago, 1882), 510; *Minutes of the Annual Conferences of the Methodist Episcopal Church, South for the Year 1862; Minutes of the Forty-*

Seventh Session of the Kentucky Annual Conference of the Methodist Episcopal Church, South (Shelbyville, KY, 1867), *Minutes of the Forty-Ninth Session of the Kentucky Annual Conference of the Methodist Episcopal Church, South* (Shelbyville, KY, 1869); *Minutes of the Fifty-First Session of the Kentucky Annual Conference of the Methodist Episcopal Church, South* (Cincinnati, 1871), *Minutes of the Fifty-Second Session of the Kentucky Annual Conference of the Methodist Episcopal Church, South* (Louisville, KY, 1872).

9. Walter B. Stevens, *Centennial History of Missouri,* 6 vols. (St. Louis, MO: S. J. Clarke, 1921), 3:733; Mary Ann McCaffrey quoted in *New York Daily Herald,* Mar. 28, 1879.

10. George T. Gould, "Statement of George T. Gould," Oct. 15, 1884, 9–10, *MECS v. GTG.* Gould wrote out the statement and handed it to the committee sitting in judgment of him at the trial.

11. Gould, "Statement," 9–10, 30, *MECS v. GTG;* Ella Gould, testimony, trial transcript, 26, *MECS v. GTG.*

12. Ella Gould, testimony, trial transcript, 5, *MECS v. GTG;* Gould, "Statement," 58, *MECS v. GTG.*

13. Ella Gould, testimony, trial transcript, 6–8, *MECS v. GTG;* Gould, "Statement," 60–61, *MECS v. GTG.*

14. Ella Gould, testimony, trial transcript, 11–12, *MECS v. GTG.*

15. *Las Vegas (New Mexico) Daily Optic,* July 17, 1885; *Paris Kentuckian,* Mar. 17, 1880; D. A. Beardsley, testimony, trial transcript, 136, *MECS v. GTG; Maysville Republican,* Dec. 30, 1871.

7. Millersburg Beckons

1. Deed Book 60, pp. 356, 431, 432; Deed Book 61, pp. 49, 138; Mortgage Book 5, pp. 195, 279–80, 281, 533, all in Bourbon County Circuit Court, Paris, KY.

2. Thomas Oliver, testimony, trial transcript, 166–68, 181–82, *MECS v. GTG.*

3. Alma Bridwell White, *The Story of My Life,* vol. 1 (Zarephath, NJ: Pillar of Fire, 1919), 270–71; Craig Friend, *Along the Maysville Road: The Early American Republic in the Trans-Appalachian West* (Knoxville: University of Tennessee Press, 2005), 249.

4. Friend, *Along the Maysville Road,* 265; Raitz and O'Malley, *Kentucky's Frontier Highway,* 207.

5. Alvin Fayette Lewis, *History of Higher Education in Kentucky* (Washington, DC, 1899), 236–39; Davis, "Confronting a Petty Tyrant," 354.

6. Gould "Statement," 76, *MECS v. GTG;* Ella Gould, testimony, trial transcript, 12–13, *MECS v. GTG.*

7. Ella Gould, testimony, trial transcript, 52–53, *MECS v. GTG.*

8. *Minutes of the Forty-Ninth Session of the Kentucky Conference of the Methodist Episcopal Church, South,* 32–33.

9. *Minutes of the Kentucky Conference of the Methodist Episcopal Church, South* (Shelbyville, Ky., 1878), 18.

10. *Paris Kentuckian,* Jan. 17, 1877.

11. *Stanford (Kentucky) Interior Journal,* Jan. 3 and Sept. 19, 1879.

12. *Washington (DC) Evening Star,* Mar. 18, 1879.

13. *New York Daily Herald,* Mar. 19, 1879.

14. *Washington Evening Star,* Mar. 21, 1879.

15. *Washington (DC) Post,* Mar. 22, 1879; *St. Louis Post-Dispatch,* Mar. 24, 1879; Alice A. Olliver [Oliver], 1857, Kentucky Births and Christenings, 1839–1960, database, based on data collected by the Genealogical Society of Utah, Salt Lake City, FamilySearch, https://familysearch.org/ark:/61903/1:1:FWKP-3XJ; *Philadelphia Times,* Mar. 22, 1879; *New York Daily Herald,* Mar. 28, 1879; Alice Harget in household of Willie Harget, White Oak, Onslow, NC, US Census, 1880, microfilm, NARA, FamilySearch, at https://familysearch.org/ark:/61903/1:1:MCX6–526.

16. *Philadelphia Times,* Mar. 19, 1879; *Washington Evening Star,* Mar. 21, 1879; *Baltimore Sun,* Mar. 29, 1879; *New York Daily Herald,* Mar. 29, 1879.

17. *New York Daily Herald,* Mar. 25, 1879; *Chicago Tribune,* Mar. 25, 1879; *Southern Argus* (Selma, AL), Apr. 4, 1879.

18. *New York Daily Herald,* Mar. 25, 1879.

19. Ottilie Assing to Frederick Douglass, Apr. 1, 1879, General Correspondence, Frederick Douglass Papers, Manuscript Division, Library of Congress, Washington, DC.

20. Paul Kahan, *Amiable Scoundrel: Simon Cameron, Lincoln's Scandalous Secretary of War* (Lincoln: University of Nebraska Press, 2016), 280. For a more sympathetic appraisal of the "Widow Oliver's" claims, see Patricia Miller, *Bringing Down the Colonel: A Sex Scandal of the Gilded Age, and the "Powerless" Woman Who Took on Washington* (New York: Farrar, Straus and Giroux, 2018), 50–51.

21. *Memphis Daily Appeal,* Apr. 1, 1879; *Baltimore Sun,* Mar. 22, 1879.

22. J. C. Meininger, "School Girls Dream" (piano piece) (Cincinnati, 1880); Thomas Oliver, testimony, trial transcript, 188–89, *MECS v. GTG; Paris Kentuckian,* Nov. 10, 1880; *Washington Evening Star,* Apr. 15, 1879. The police caught the culprits, and Oliver recovered everything but a few cents.

8. An Accusation Dodged

1. *Paris Kentuckian,* Mar. 3, 1880; George T. Gould, "The Soul and Its Immortality," Feb. 29, 1880, George T. Gould Papers, New Mexico State University Library, Las Cruces.

2. *Paris Kentuckian,* Mar. 17, 1880; *Cincinnati Commercial,* Apr. 15, 1880.

3. *Cincinnati Commercial,* Mar. 19, 1880, which provides quotations from the trial but not the entire transcript.

4. *Cincinnati Commercial,* Mar. 19, 1880.

5. *Cincinnati Commercial,* Mar. 19, 1880.
6. *Cincinnati Commercial,* Mar. 19, 1880.
7. *Cincinnati Commercial,* Mar. 19, 1880.
8. *Cincinnati Commercial,* Mar. 19, 1880.
9. *Paris Kentuckian,* Mar. 31, 1880; Davis, "Confronting a Petty Tyrant," 362, quoting the statement signed by the ten Millersburg Female College faculty members.
10. *Cincinnati Commercial,* Apr. 15, 1880.
11. Gould, "Statement," 23, *MECS v. GTG; Paris Kentuckian,* Mar. 17, 1880.
12. Gould, "Statement," 23–24, *MECS v. GTG;* on Ella's miscarriage: Ella Gould, testimony, trial transcript, 28, *MECS v. GTG.*
13. "Murphy is my enemy": Gould, "Statement," 73, *MECS v. GTG* (Gould later thought better of this confession and marked it out in his written statement); A. G. Murphy, testimony, trial transcript, 64, *MECS v. GTG;* Moore's Millersburg appointment: *Minutes of the Kentucky Conference of the Methodist Episcopal Church, South* (1878), 21. The *Stanford Interior Journal* of October 17, 1879, announced that "Mr. O. P. Moore, of Crab Orchard Springs, formerly instructor of modern languages at the Kentucky Wesleyan and Female Colleges, Millersburg, has consented to teach a class in German in Stanford if satisfactory arrangements can be perfected." Moore later began a school in Crab Orchard.
14. *Paris Kentuckian,* Oct. 17, 1880, and Sept. 7, 1881.
15. *Cincinnati Commercial,* Apr. 15, 1880; *Paris Kentuckian,* Apr. 21, 1880.

9. Let the Past Be Buried

1. *Paris Kentuckian,* June 16, 1880.
2. Meininger, "School Girls Dream."
3. *Paris Kentuckian,* Nov. 17, 1880.
4. *Paris Kentuckian,* Nov 17, 1880.
5. *Paris Kentuckian,* Sept. 29 and Nov. 17, 1880.
6. *Paris Kentuckian,* Oct. 6, Nov. 15 and 17, 1880; Jan. 6, 1881.
7. Thomas Oliver, testimony, trial transcript, 167, *MECS v. GTG.*
8. Gould, "Statement," 13–14, *MECS v. GTG;* Ladies' Missionary Society of Corsicana, Texas: *Paris Kentuckian,* Dec. 15, 1880.
9. *Paris Kentuckian,* Oct. 20, 1880.
10. Julia Pratt to Merrill Pratt, Nov. 23, 1872, quoted in Curtis J. Evans, *The Conquest of Labor: Daniel Pratt and Southern Industrialization* (Baton Rouge: Louisiana State University Press, 2014), 232.
11. *Stanford (Kentucky) Interior Journal,* Oct. 23, 1874; Feb. 16, 1875; and Aug. 13, 1880.
12. *Stanford Interior Journal,* Oct. 15, 1880.
13. *Paris Kentuckian,* June 22, 1881. Hiram Bassett was listed among the Millersburg Female College faculty on the cover of Meininger's piano piece

"School Girls Dream," published in 1880, a list probably reflecting the personnel as of September that year. He was grand master of the Millersburg Masonic Lodge, of which Gould had been a member since 1873 (Perrin, *History of Bourbon, Scott, Harrison, and Nicholas Counties,* 395).

14. *Paris Kentuckian,* Dec. 7, 1881.

15. *Paris Kentuckian,* Nov. 9, 1881.

16. "A Card from Mrs. Tarrant," *Paris Kentuckian,* Dec. 7, 1881.

17. "A Card from Mr. Gould," *Paris Kentuckian,* Dec. 7, 1881; "A Card from Mrs. Tarrant" (second card), *Paris Kentuckian,* Dec. 7, 1881.

18. "A Card from Mr. Gould," Dec. 7, 1881.

19. "A Card from Mr. Gould," Dec. 7, 1881.

20. "A Card from Mrs. Tarrant," Dec. 7, 1881.

21. "A Card from Mrs. Tarrant" (second card), Dec. 7, 1881.

22. "A Card from Mrs. Tarrant" (second card), Dec. 7, 1881.

23. "A Card from Mrs. Tarrant" (second card), Dec. 7, 1881.

24. *Stanford Interior Journal,* Feb. 7, 1882; *Bourbon News* (Paris, KY), May 9, 1882; *Paris Kentuckian,* May 31, 1882.

25. *Paris Kentuckian,* Jan. 25, 1882; Gould, "The Soul and Its Immortality."

10. Copperheads and Pearly Gates

1. Franklin Bristow, in household of B. F. Bristow, Morgan [possibly an error in the record because no such town existed], Morgan County, IL, US Census, 1850, microfilm, NARA, FamilySearch, at https://www.familysearch.org/ark:/61903/1:1:M858-165; Frank Bristow, in entry for B. F. Bristow, Morgan, Morgan County, IL, US Census, 1860, microfilm, NARA, FamilySearch, at https://familysearch.org/ark:/61903/1:1:MXHZ-CKY; *Minutes of the Sixty-Eighth Session of the Kentucky Conference of the Methodist Episcopal Church, South* (Frankfort, KY, 1888), 51.

2. Charles H. Rammelkamp, "The Reverberations of the Slavery Conflict in a Pioneer College," *Mississippi Valley Historical Review* 14, no. 4 (Mar. 1928): 447–61.

3. *Fort Smith (Arkansas) Times,* Dec. 31, 1906; Illinois Veterans, databases, Illinois State Archive, Springfield, at http://cyberdriveillinois.com/departments/archives/databases/home.html.

4. Ross A. Webb, "Bristow, Francis Marion," in *Kentucky Encyclopedia,* ed. Kleber, 124–25; Webb, *Benjamin Helm Bristow,* 22.

5. Don Harrison Doyle, *The Social Order of a Frontier Community: Jacksonville, Illinois, 1825–70* (Carbondale: University of Illinois Press, 1978), 234.

6. *Fort Smith Times,* Dec. 31, 1906.

7. *Fort Smith Times,* Dec. 31, 1906.

8. Robert Hartje, "Van Dorn Conducts a Raid on Holly Springs and Enters Tennessee," *Tennessee Historical Quarterly* 18, no. 2 (June 1959): 126; *Fort Smith Times,* Dec. 31, 1906.

9. *Fort Smith Times,* Dec. 31, 1906.

10. *Fort Smith Times,* Dec. 31, 1906.

11. *Fort Smith Times,* Dec. 31, 1906.

12. W. R. Stevenson, "Capture of Holly Springs, Miss.," *Confederate Veteran Magazine* 9 (1901): 134; *Fort Smith Times,* Dec. 31, 1906.

13. In an autobiographical sketch submitted to his college literary society, Bristow wrote that he "was on the march to the sea with Sherman" (*Catalogue of Phi Alpha Society: 1845–1890,* vol. 23 [Jacksonville, IL, 1890], 65–66). This information is confirmed in "Histories of Illinois Civil War Regiments and Units," in *Report of the Adjutant General of the State of Illinois* (1900–1902), at http://www.old-new-orleans.com/ILLINOIS_CW_reghist.pdf.

14. James J. Barnes and Patience P. Barnes, "Was Illinois Governor Richard Yates Intimidated by the Copperheads during the Civil War?," *Journal of the Illinois State Historical Society* 107, no. 3 (Fall–Winter 2014): 321–45; Doyle, *Social Order of a Frontier Community,* 237–38; *Chicago Tribune,* Sept. 16, 1863; *Jacksonville (Illinois) Journal,* Sept. 17, 1865, cited in Doyle, *Social Order of a Frontier Community,* 237–38.

15. *Chicago Tribune,* Sept. 2 and 3, 1863; Barnes and Barnes, "Was Illinois Governor Richard Yates Intimidated by the Copperheads during the Civil War?," 326.

16. *Chicago Tribune,* Sept. 24, 1863.

17. *Chicago Tribune,* Nov. 10, 1863.

18. *History of Morgan County, Illinois* (Chicago, 1878), 265; *Minutes of the Sixty-Eighth Session of the Kentucky Conference of the Methodist Episcopal Church, South* (1888), 51; Roy Hunter Short, *Methodism in Kentucky* (Rutland, VT: Academy Books, 1979), 26.

19. *Catalogue of Phi Alpha Society,* 65–66; Moses E. Lard, "Patterson Institute, at North Middletown, Ky.," *Lard's Quarterly: Devoted to the Propagation and Defense of the Gospel* 4 (July 1867): 285.

20. Bristow, autobiographical sketch, in *Catalogue of Phi Alpha Society; Tuscaloosa (Alabama) Gazette,* Dec. 11, 1873; Frank Leslie Bristow, "Daisey Dell" (song) (Cincinnati, 1874); *Tuscaloosa (Alabama) Weekly Times,* May 12 and June 23, 1875.

21. *Tuscaloosa Weekly Times,* May 31, 1876.

22. *Shelby Sentinel* (Columbiana, AL), May 10, 1877; *Marion (Alabama) Commonwealth,* Aug. 30, 1877; *Selma (Alabama) Times-Argus,* Sept. 7, 1877; *Tuscaloosa Gazette,* Mar. 7 and Aug. 8, 1878.

23. *Tuscaloosa (Alabama) News,* Sept. 25, 1879.

24. *Tuscaloosa News,* Dec. 18, 1879.

25. Frank Leslie Bristow, "The Little Cadet" (song) (Cincinnati, 1880); *Weekly Democratic Statesman* (Austin, TX), Jan. 22; *Galveston (Texas) Daily News,* June 26, 1880.

26. *Memphis Daily Appeal,* Sept. 8, 22, and Apr. 20, 1881. "The neighbors of the State female college buildings are much mixed up just now, the topic being where it will be best to convert the college into a public asylum for the insane, a colored female institute, or a more desirable purpose" (*Memphis Public Ledger,* Apr. 29, 1881).

27. *Paris Kentuckian,* Feb. 1 and 8, 1882.

28. *Bourbon News* (Paris, KY), Mar. 14, 17, and 21, 1882.

29. *Bourbon News,* Apr. 11, 21, 1882. There were two Millersburg correspondents for the *Bourbon News,* Harlan Vimont (1861–1897) and Harmon Stitt (1862–1938). Vimont had at one time been the town constable; Stitt was the son of Dr. A. G. Stitt (*Bourbon News,* June 22, 1883, and July 6, 1888).

30. *Boone County (Kentucky) Recorder,* May 24, 1951, kindly communicated to the author by Neil Allen Bristow.

31. *Paris Kentuckian,* Mar. 8, 1882.

32. Frank Leslie Bristow, *Calisthenic Exercises and Marches with Pleasing Drill Songs and Music Suitable for Schools, Colleges, Private Entertainments, and Public Exhibitions* (Cincinnati, 1891).

33. J. Madison Watson, *Watson's Manual of Calisthenics: A Systematic Drill-Book without Apparatus, for Schools, Families, and Gymnasiums, with Music to Accompany the Exercises* (New York, 1864); Jan Todd, *Physical Culture and the Body Beautiful: Purposive Exercise in the Lives of American Women 1800–1870* (Macon, GA: Mercer University Press, 1998), 253; Dio Lewis, *The New Gymnastics for Men, Women, and Children* (Boston, 1862); Bristow, *Calisthenic Exercises,* 75.

34. Frank Leslie Bristow, "Marche Calisthenique" (piano piece) (Cincinnati, 1882); *Paris Kentuckian,* June 21, 1882.

35. Frank Leslie Bristow, "Ain't I Glad" (song) (Cincinnati, 1880); *Paris Kentuckian,* July 19, 1882.

36. *Louisville Courier-Journal,* July 19, 1882.

37. *Paris Kentuckian,* Sept. 6, 1882; *Bourbon News,* Sept. 12, 1882.

38. *Maysville Evening Bulletin,* Sept. 7, 1882; Frank L. Bristow, "Sweet Rest at Home" (song) (Cincinnati, 1883).

11. Delicacy, Refinement, Propriety

1. *Bourbon News* (Paris, KY), June 9, 1882; [George T. Gould], [auto]biographical sketch in Perrin, *History of Bourbon, Scott, Harrison, and Nicholas Counties,* 510.

2. *Report of the Commissioner of Education Made to the Secretary of the Interior for the Year 1882* (Washington, DC, 1883), 476; *Paris Kentuckian,* July 26, 1882.

3. Advertisement quoted in *New York Sun,* July 19, 1882.

4. As printed in the *Paris Kentuckian,* Aug. 9, 1882.

5. Idress Head Alvord, *Head, Descent of Henry Head (1697–1770) in America* (Columbia, MO: I. H. Alvord, n.d. [c. 1949]), 203.

6. *Bourbon News,* Sept. 29; *Paris Kentuckian,* Oct. 4, 1882; *Paris Kentuckian,* Jan. 10, 1883.

7. *Paris Kentuckian,* Sept. 20 and Oct. 25, 1882; *Bourbon News,* Nov. 28, 1882; *Paris Kentuckian,* Dec. 27, 1882.

8. *Paris Kentuckian,* Jan. 31, 1883; Gould, "Statement," 65, *MECS v. GTG.*

9. *Bourbon News,* Feb. 2 and 13, 1883.

10. *Bourbon News,* Feb. 27, 1883.

11. *Bourbon News,* Feb. 23 and Mar. 2, 1883.

12. *Bourbon News,* May 1, 1883; *Paris Kentuckian,* May 2, 1883; Frank Leslie Bristow, *The Little Shaking Quakers* (musical comedy sketch) (Cincinnati, 1883).

13. *Bourbon News,* May 22, 1883; *Paris Kentuckian,* May 30, 1883.

14. *Paris Kentuckian,* June 9, 1883.

15. Gould, "Statement," 35–36, *MECS v. GTG.*

16. Gould, "Statement," 33–34, *MECS v. GTG.*

17. Kentucky Central Railroad time table published in the *Maysville Evening Bulletin* on June 2, 1883.

12. June 8, 1883, and Its Aftermath

1. John Barbour, deposition submitted to Court of Common Pleas, Bourbon County, KY, from Paxton, IL, Feb. 28, 1884, Kentucky Department for Libraries and Archives, Public Records Division, Frankfort. I am grateful to Professor Charles L. Davis for providing a copy of this deposition and several related documents.

2. *Paris Kentuckian,* June 9, 1883; *Bourbon News* (Paris, KY), June 12, 1883; Green, *Life,* 55.

3. Green's statement was published in the *Maysville Evening Bulletin,* June 15, 1883.

4. *Bourbon News,* June 12, 1883.

5. Barbour, deposition.

6. Green, *Life,* 51–52.

7. Davis, "Green v. Gould," 403–4, 406; see also Charles L. Davis, "The Railroad Expansion Controversy in Postbellum Bourbon County: Conflicting Economic Interests and Ideological Perspectives among Urban and Rural Elites," *Register of the Kentucky Historical Society* 112, no. 1 (Winter 2014): 51–82.

8. "A Card from Dr. Gould," *Maysville Evening Bulletin,* June 22, 1883.

9. "A Card from Dr. Gould," June 22, 1883.

10. "A Card from Dr. Gould," June 22, 1883.

11. Green, *Life,* 54.

12. *Paris Kentuckian,* June 20, 1883; Gould, "Statement," 52, *MECS v. GTG;* Frank Leslie Bristow, "Eyebright" (song) (Cincinnati, 1883); *Cartersville (Georgia) American,* Nov. 11, 1884.

13. *Paris Kentuckian,* June 20, 1883; *Maysville Evening Bulletin,* June 15, 1883.

14. *Lexington Transcript,* June 19, 1883, quoted in Green, *Life,* 56; *Bourbon News,* June 29, 1883.

15. *Maysville Eagle,* reprinted in the *Bourbon News,* June 15, 1883.

16. *Maysville New Republican,* quoted in Green, *Life,* 57–58.

17. *Vanceburg (Kentucky) Courier,* reprinted in *Bourbon News,* July 3, 1883.

18. "Not at or near Vanceburg": quoted in *Bourbon News,* July 6, 1883; "among its trustees": O. G. Ragan, *History of Lewis County* (Cincinnati, OH: Jennings and Graham, 1912), 225; further on Taylor's dispute with Gould: Davis, "Confronting a Petty Tyrant."

19. *Carlisle (Kentucky) Mercury,* reprinted in *Maysville Evening Bulletin,* June 15, 1883.

20. *Cynthiana (Kentucky) News,* reprinted in *Bourbon News,* July 3, 1883; *Maysville Evening Bulletin,* June 22, 1883; *Cincinnati Enquirer,* July 17, 1883; *Maysville Evening Bulletin,* September 6, 1883.

21. *Paris Kentuckian,* July 4, 1883.

22. *Paris Kentuckian,* Mar. 12, 1884.

23. *Bourbon News,* June 12 and 15, 1883.

24. *Bourbon News,* June 15 and 8, 1883.

25. Ella Gould, testimony, trial transcript, 97–98, *MECS v. GTG.*

26. Gould, "Statement," 36–37, *MECS v. GTG.*

27. Gould, "Statement," 37, *MECS v. GTG.*

28. Gould, "Statement," 37, *MECS v. GTG.*

29. *Paris Kentuckian,* July 7, 1883; *Bourbon News,* June 19, 1883. However, the trial would have been delayed anyway because Gould and Bristow argued that they wanted to call some of the students as witnesses, but the students would not be back in town until the fall.

30. *Vanceburg Courier,* quoted in the *Bourbon News,* July 27, 1883; *Bourbon News,* July 10, 1883; Davis, "Confronting a Petty Tyrant," 352.

31. *Bourbon News,* July 19, 1883.

32. Davis, "Green v. Gould," 386.

33. Gould, "Statement," 37, *MECS v. GTG.*

34. Gould, "Statement," 30–31, *MECS v. GTG.*

35. Gould, "Statement," 52, *MECS v. GTG.*

36. Gould, "Statement," 53, *MECS v. GTG.*

37. Gould, "Statement," 53, *MECS v. GTG.*

38. *Bourbon News,* Oct. 2, 1883.

39. *Bourbon News,* Nov. 17, 1883; *Semi-weekly Bourbon News* (Paris, KY), Jan. 25, 1884.

40. Gould, "Statement," 15–18, *MECS v. GTG.*

41. Gould, "Statement," 18, *MECS v. GTG.*

42. *Paris Kentuckian,* Jan. 30, 1884; J. C. C. Newton, deposition, Sept. 29, 1884, *MECS v. GTG;* Gould, "Statement," 45, *MECS v. GTG;* Ella Gould, testimony, trial transcript, 25–26, *MECS v. GTG.*

43. Davis, "Green v. Gould," passim; *Paris Kentuckian,* Mar. 12, 1884.

44. Davis, "Green v. Gould," 402.

45. *Paris Kentuckian,* Mar. 12, 1884.

46. Green, *Life,* 58.

47. Victor B. Howard, "The Black Testimony Controversy in Kentucky, 1866–1872," *Journal of Negro History* 5812 (Apr. 1973): 140–65; Melissa Milewski, "From Slave to Litigant: African Americans in Court in the Postwar South, 1865–1920," *Law and History Review* 30, no. 3 (Aug. 2012): 724; Green, *Life,* 58–59.

48. *Paris Kentuckian,* March 12, 1884.

49. Order Books, Mar. 18, 1884, Bourbon County Court of Common Pleas, Paris, KY. Gould was charged costs of $15.94; Bristow, $15.43. Gould's friend Dr. A. G. Stitt confirmed that Gould had to pay court costs (testimony, trial transcript, 161, *MECS v. GTG*).

50. *Bourbon News,* Mar. 11, 1884.

51. *Cincinnati Enquirer,* Apr. 1, 1884.

52. *Cincinnati Enquirer,* Mar. 30, 1884; *New York Tribune,* Apr. 1, 1884.

53. *San Antonio Light,* Apr. 2 and 5, 1884; Gould, "Statement," 19–20, *MECS v. GTG; Paris Kentuckian,* Apr. 28, 1884.

54. *Bourbon News,* Apr. 29; *Maysville Evening Bulletin,* May 5, 1884.

55. *Bourbon News,* May 27, 1884.

56. Gould, "Statement," 54–57, *MECS v. GTG.*

57. *Bourbon News,* June 3, 1884; *Paris Kentuckian,* Feb. 9, 1881.

58. *Bourbon News,* June 3, 1884.

59. *Paris Kentuckian,* June 11, 1884; George T. Gould, "She Hath Done What She Could," June 4, 1884, George T. Gould Papers, New Mexico State University Library, Las Cruces.

60. *Paris Kentuckian,* June 11, 1884; Ella Gould, testimony, trial transcript, 52–53, *MECS v. GTG.*

61. Newton, deposition, Sept. 29, 1884, *MECS v. GTG.*

62. D. A. Beardsley, testimony, trial transcript, 128, 133, *MECS v. GTG.*

63. *Paris Kentuckian,* June 11, 1884.

13. Go West

1. *Paris Kentuckian,* June 11, 1884; Ella Gould to Texie Head, June 9 and 24, 1884 (a single letter written on two different days), *MECS v. GTG.*

2. Gould, "Statement," 21–22, *MECS v. GTG.*

3. Gould, "Statement," 46, *MECS v. GTG;* J. C. C. Newton, deposition, Sept. 29, 1884, *MECS s. GTG.*

4. Ella Gould to Texie Head, June 9 and 24, 1884, *MECS v. GTG.*

5. Ella Gould to Texie Head, June 9 and 24, 1884, emphasis in original.

6. Mortgage Book 5, p. 533, and Inventory Book C, pp. 6–7, Bourbon County Circuit Court, Paris, KY; *Paris Kentuckian,* June 21, 1884.

7. George T. Gould to Reverend M. Evans, July 8, 1884, and Ella Gould to George T. Gould, August 5, 1884, *MEGS v. GTG.*

8. *Las Vegas (New Mexico) Daily Gazette,* July 30, 1884; *Las Vegas (New Mexico) Daily Optic,* Jan. 22, 1885.

9. *Las Vegas Daily Gazette,* July 31, 1884; Gould, "Statement," 3–4, *MECS v. GTG.*

10. Lynn Irvin Perrigo, *Gateway to Glorieta: A History of Las Vegas, New Mexico* (Santa Fe, NM: Sunstone Press, 2010), 74–75.

11. *Las Vegas Daily Gazette,* Sept. 2, 1885; May 18, 1884; Jan. 15, 1885.

12. Ella Gould to George T. Gould, Aug. 5, 1884, *MECS v. GTG.*

13. *Las Vegas Daily Optic,* Aug. 7, 1884; *Las Vegas Daily Gazette,* Aug. 16 1884; letter to the editor, *Las Vegas Daily Optic,* Aug. 19, 1884; Needham: *Las Vegas Daily Optic,* Sept. 4, 1884.

14. *Stanford (Kentucky) Interior Journal,* Aug. 15, 1884.

15. George T. Gould, "Brochure for the Las Vegas Female Seminary 1884–85," *MECS v. GTG.*

16. George T. Gould to Texie Head, Aug. 15, 1884, and Texie Head to George T. Gould, Aug. 18, 1884, *MECS v. GTG.*

17. *Las Vegas Daily Gazette,* Aug. 28, Sept. 6 and 7, 1884.

18. George T. Gould to Ella Gould, Sept. 7, 1884, *MECS v. GTG.*

19. George H. Gould to Ella Gould, Sept. 16, 1884, *MECS v. GTG.*

20. *Las Vegas Daily Optic,* Sept. 19, 1884; *Las Vegas Daily Gazette,* Sept. 21 and 27, 1884.

21. *Las Vegas Daily Gazette,* Sept. 23, 1884; *Las Vegas Daily Optic,* Oct. 11 and 27, 1884.

22. *Las Vegas Daily Optic,* Oct. 27, 1884.

14. Rebellious Flocks

1. Parrish, *Golden Jubilee,* 282; *Maysville Evening Bulletin,* May 21, 1885.

2. Sharon Fields to the author, personal communication, Nov. 25, 2019.

3. Green, *Life,* 46; *Hickman (Kentucky) Courier,* Aug. 7, 1885; Parrish, *Golden Jubilee,* 283; Elijah P. Marrs, *Life and History of the Rev. Elijah P. Marrs* (Louisville, 1885), 120; *Maysville Evening Bulletin,* July 21, 1885; *Louisville Courier-Journal,* Feb. 9, 1885.

4. *Maysville Evening Bulletin,* Sept. 28, 1887; Benjamin D. Berry Jr., "The Plymouth Congregational Church of Louisville, Kentucky," *Phylon* 42, no. 3 (1981): 224–32, quote from 225.

5. Marrs, *Life and History of the Rev. Elijah P. Marrs,* 133; *Louisville Courier-Journal,* July 15, 1884.

6. *Springfield (Missouri) Leader and Press,* Dec. 22, 1891; *New York Times,* Sept. 30, 1873; *New York Daily Herald,* May 2, 1874.

7. *Louisville Courier-Journal,* Feb. 6, 1885.

8. *Maysville Evening Bulletin,* Sept. 15, Oct. 1, Sept. 19 and 27, 1884.

9. *Maysville Evening Bulletin,* Nov. 17, 1884; *Louisville Courier-Journal,* Nov. 12, 1884; Aaron Astor, *Rebels on the Border: Civil War, Emancipation, and the Reconstruction of Kentucky and Missouri* (Baton Rouge: Louisiana State University Press, 2012), 229, 220–21.

10. Charles L. Davis, "Racial Politics in Central Kentucky during the Post-Reconstruction Era: Bourbon County, 1877–1899," *Register of the Kentucky Historical Society* 109, no. 4 (Autumn 2010): 358, 359 n. 20, 365–66; *Maysville Evening Bulletin,* Oct. 2, 1882.

11. Victor B. Howard, "Negro Politics and the Suffrage Question in Kentucky, 1866–1872," *Register of the Kentucky Historical Society* 72, no. 2 (Apr. 1974): 133, 133 n. 91.

12. *Louisville Courier-Journal,* Nov. 2, 1888; *Springfield Leader and Press,* Jan. 15, 1892.

13. Elisha Green and Margie J. Mason, married November 27, 1884, Kentucky Marriages, 1785–1979, database, based on data collected by the Genealogical Society of Utah, Salt Lake City, FamilySearch, at https://familysearch.org/ark:/61903/1:1:F4S1-SJX; *Paris Kentuckian,* Jan. 3, 1885.

14. *Maysville Evening Bulletin,* Feb. 28, 1885.

15. The Buzzards Gather

1. *Bourbon News* (Paris, KY), Sept. 16 and 23, 1884. Harman Stitt (1862–1938) shared credit for these columns with Harlan Vimont (1861–1897), who had been the town constable but left that position to be a guard at a distillery because that job paid more (*Bourbon News,* July 10, 1883). Stitt was a graduate of Kentucky Wesleyan, and after a journalistic career in Missouri, Texas, Colorado, and California, he became a lawyer and later a distinguished and wealthy judge (*Cincinnati Enquirer,* July 16, 1938). Lacking that education and experience, Vimont probably contributed little more than his name to their joint

journalistic venture. At the conclusion of the trial, they would team up to edit, print, and sell as a pamphlet copies of Gould's statement to the committee and of some of the more salient testimony.

2. *Bourbon News,* Oct. 28, 1884.

3. *Bourbon News,* Sept. 30, 1884.

4. *Bourbon News,* Oct. 7, 1884.

5. Texie Head to H. P. Walker, Sept. 20, 1884, *MECS v. GTG.*

6. James W. Wight, testimony, trial transcript, 44, *MECS v. GTG.*

7. Wight, testimony, trial transcript, 50–51, *MECS v. GTG.*

8. Wight, testimony, trial transcript, 32, *MECS v. GTG;* Gould, "Statement," 49–50, *MECS v. GTG.*

9. Gould, "Statement," 50, 49, *MECS v. GTG.*

10. Ella Gould to H. P. Walker, Oct. 14, 1884, *MECS v. GTG.*

11. A. G. Murphy, testimony, trial transcript, 60, *MECS v. GTG;* James E. Letton, signed statement, May 10, 1880, *MECS v. GTG.* O. P. Moore died in London on February 4, 1883 (*Bourbon News,* March 9, 1883).

12. Benjamin Franklin Bristow, testimony, trial transcript, 112, *MECS v. GTG.*

13. J. C. C. Newton, deposition, *MECS v. GTG;* J. C. C. Newton to H. P. Walker, October 6, 1884, *MECS v. GTG,* emphasis Newton's.

14. Gould, "Statement," 79, *MECS v. GTG.*

15. "Verdict in Gould Case, Sept. 12, 1885," *MECS v. GTG.*

16. The Rise and Fall of the Independent Temple

1. *Las Vegas* (*New Mexico*) *Daily Gazette,* Oct. 28 and 31, 1884.

2. *Las Vegas* (*New Mexico*) *Daily Optic,* Oct. 17, 1884; *Las Vegas Daily Gazette,* Oct. 29, 1884.

3. *Las Vegas Daily Optic,* Oct. 28, 1884.

4. *Bourbon News* (Paris, KY), Nov. 4, 1884; I. R. Best to H. P. Walker, Oct. 22, 1884, *MECS v. GTG;* Gould, "Statement," 29, *MECS v. GTG.*

5. *Maysville Evening Bulletin,* Dec. 18, 1884; Gould's speech: *Las Vegas Daily Optic,* Dec. 23, 1884.

6. Green, *Life,* 59, 59 n.

7. George T. Gould to H. P. Walker, Oct. 29, 1884, and H. P. Walker to George T. Gould, Nov. 11, 1884, *MECS v. GTG.*

8. *Las Vegas Daily Gazette,* Oct. 31, 1884; Mortgage Book 8, p. 163, Bourbon County Circuit Court, Paris, KY.

9. *Las Vegas Daily Gazette,* Nov. 2, 1884.

10. *Las Vegas Daily Optic,* Nov. 8, 1884. It is odd that the *Optic* ran this story on November 8, by which time it was out of date, given the statement from Gould the paper printed on November 7 (see note 11). The Saturday paper normally ran to more pages, so perhaps the story on November 8 may have simply been used as filler.

11. *Las Vegas Daily Optic,* Nov. 7, 1884.
12. *Las Vegas Daily Optic,* Nov. 11, 1884.
13. *Las Vegas Daily Optic,* Nov. 14, 1884, and Jan. 26, 27, 1885.
14. *Las Vegas Daily Optic,* Nov. 15, 1884; *Las Vegas Daily Gazette,* Oct. 28, 1884.
15. *Las Vegas Daily Optic,* Nov. 17 and 15, 1884.
16. *Las Vegas Daily Gazette,* Nov. 18, 1884.
17. *Las Vegas Daily Optic,* Feb. 16, 1885.
18. *Las Vegas Daily Optic,* Feb. 26 and Mar, 23, 1885.
19. *Las Vegas Daily Optic,* Mar. 30, 1885.
20. *Las Vegas Daily Optic,* Apr. 7 and Feb. 16, 17, 1885.
21. *Las Vegas Daily Optic,* Feb. 28, 1885; George T. Gould, "The Flesh," Feb. 28, 1885, George T. Gould Papers, New Mexico State University Library, Las Cruces.
22. Gould, "The Flesh."
23. *Las Vegas Daily Optic,* Jan. 23 and 30, Mar. 9, Apr. 8, 1885; *Bourbon News,* Apr. 17, 1885; length of residence required for divorce in New Mexico: *Las Vegas Daily Optic,* July 29, 1884. In its editorial on March 9, the *Optic* complained about the divorce law, arguing that the residency requirement be increased from six months to two years to discourage eastern husbands from flocking to New Mexico for a quickie divorce.
24. *Las Vegas Daily Optic,* May 21, 1885.
25. *Las Vegas Daily Optic,* May 22, 1885; *Stanford (Kentucky) Interior Journal,* May 29, 1885.
26. *Las Vegas Daily Optic,* May 25, 1885.
27. Abraham Lincoln, Second Inaugural Address, Mar. 4, 1865, National Park Service, at https://www.nps.gov/linc/learn/historyculture/lincoln-second-inaugural.htm; Gould's address to the Las Vegas post of the Grand Army of the Republic: *Las Vegas Daily Optic,* May 25, 1885.
28. George T. Gould, "The Ministry of Evil," May 10, 1885, Gould Papers, New Mexico State University Library.
29. Gould, "The Ministry of Evil"; Alexander Winchell, *Adamites and Preadamites* (Syracuse, NY, 1878); William F. Warren, *Ministry of Evil: An Examination of the Popular Bitter-Sweet Theology* (New York, 1859), 14; Hubert Howe Bancroft, *The Native Races of the Pacific States,* vol. 2 (San Francisco, 1883), 24.
30. *Las Vegas Daily Gazette,* Jan. 4, 1885; Robert Milligan, *Second Annual Announcement of Kentucky University* (Harrodsburg, KY, 1860).
31. *Las Vegas Daily Optic,* Mar. 27 and June 22, 1885.
32. *Las Vegas Daily Optic,* May 27 and July 21, 1885; *Las Vegas Daily Gazette,* July 18 and 21, 1885.
33. *Las Vegas Daily Gazette,* July 26, 1885; *Las Vegas Daily Optic,* July 27, 1885.

34. *Las Vegas Daily Optic,* July 27, 1885.

35. *Las Vegas Daily Optic,* July 27, 1885.

36. *Las Vegas Daily Gazette,* Sept. 22, 1885; *Las Vegas Daily Optic,* Aug. 29, Sept. 18 and 23, Oct. 14, 1885.

37. *Las Vegas Daily Gazette,* Sept. 22, 1885; George T. Gould, "Games and Gaming," Sept. 21, 1885, Gould Papers, New Mexico State University Library.

38. *Las Vegas Daily Optic,* Sept. 25, 1885; David E. Swift, "Conservative versus Progressive Orthodoxy in Latter 19th-Century Congregationalism," *Church History* 16, no. 1 (Mar. 1947): 22–31; "*broad* Christian faith": *Las Vegas Daily Gazette,* Oct. 7, 1885, emphasis added; *Stanford Interior Journal,* May 29, 1885.

39. *Las Vegas Daily Gazette,* Oct. 7, 1885; *Las Vegas Daily Optic,* Oct. 10, 1885.

40. *Las Vegas Daily Optic,* Oct. 19 and 17, 1885.

41. *Las Vegas Daily Optic,* Oct. 17 and 24, 1885.

42. *Las Vegas Daily Optic,* Oct. 20 and 28, 1885; *Las Vegas Daily Gazette,* Nov. 15, 1885; *Stanford Interior Journal,* Oct. 27, 1885.

43. *Las Vegas Daily Optic,* Nov. 3, 1885, and Jan. 20, 1886; *Las Vegas Daily Gazette,* Jan. 24, Feb. 4, 5, 17, and Apr. 18, 1886.

44. *Las Vegas Daily Optic,* Apr. 3, June 12, Aug. 8, 1886; Oct. 24, 1887; and Jan. 30, 1888.

45. *Santa Fe Herald,* July 14 and Oct. 1, 1888; *Rio Grande Republican* (Las Cruces, NM), Dec. 22, 1888; *Las Vegas Daily Optic,* May 20, 1889.

46. *Las Vegas Daily Optic,* June 25, 1889.

47. *Las Vegas Daily Optic,* June 25, 1889.

48. *Las Vegas Daily Optic,* Oct. 13, 1890, and Jan. 30, 1894; *Rio Grande Republican,* Feb. 11, 1898; *Las Vegas Daily Optic,* Oct. 8, 1898; *Albuquerque Citizen,* Dec. 3, 1898, and Mar. 29, 1899; *Alamogordo (New Mexico) News,* Sept. 21, 1899; *El Paso Times,* Oct. 10, 1899; family arrives in El Paso: *Las Vegas Daily Optic,* Oct. 31, 1899; Gould editor of the *El Paso Evening News: Albuquerque Citizen,* Dec. 6, 1899, and *El Paso Times,* Feb. 10, 1900; Alice: *El Paso Times,* July 14, 1905.

49. *Albuquerque Citizen,* Jan. 7, 1903; *El Paso Herald,* Mar. 28, 1905; extract from *Albuquerque City Directory,* 1907, printed in *Albuquerque Citizen,* Apr. 27, 1907; Warren Gould to the author, email, May 31, 2017; *Albuquerque Journal,* July 21, 1911.

50. *El Paso Herald,* Nov. 20, 1911; *Albuquerque Journal,* Nov. 21, 1911.

51. Warren Gould to the author, email, May 31, 2017; *Albuquerque Journal,* Aug. 13, 1918.

52. *Albuquerque Journal,* June 11, 1922; Howell S. Faw, Big Spring, Howard County, TX, US Census, 1930, microfilm, NARA, FamilySearch, at https://familysearch.org/ark:/61903/1:1:CMYR-ZT2; *Big Spring (Texas) Daily Herald,* Mar. 19, 1937, and July 24, 1941; *Daily Oklahoman* (Oklahoma City), Apr. 25, 1942; *Albuquerque Journal,* Sept. 17, 1942.

53. *Albuquerque Journal,* Sept. 19, 1945; *San Francisco Examiner,* Apr. 30, 1968 ("After 20 years with the Hughes Tool Co. in Houston, Howell Faw, now 65, assumed the treasurership of the hotel after Hughes bought it"); *Las Vegas (Nevada) Sun,* Mar. 3, 1968, and July 2, 1968 ("Congrats to Hughes Exec Howell Faw on His 21st Ann'y with HH").

54. Warren Gould to the author, email, May 31, 2017.

55. *Albuquerque Journal,* May 3, 1956, and Mar. 24, 1974; *Wilmington (Delaware) News Journal,* May 16, 1950; *Daily Oklahoman,* Apr. 27, 1995.

56. Ellen Gould, Harris, Texas, Mar. 8, 1952, Texas Death Index, 1903–2000, database, based on data from the Texas Department of Health, State Vital Statistics Unit, Austin, collected by Ancestry.com, FamilySearch, at https://familysearch.org/ark:/61903/1:1:VZ6D-HP3. The first Mrs. George T. Gould, Mary Elenor Fullenwider Gould, died on November 18, 1920, at age seventy-five while on a visit to her daughter, Jane Gould Fitch, in Nicholasville, Kentucky. Jane, born in January 1884, had married J. Norton Fitch in 1905. He would hold various offices in Kentucky state government and have extensive land holdings in Jessamine County. Jane died in 1967 (*Richmond [Kentucky] Daily Register,* Nov. 22, 1920; *Louisville Courier-Journal,* June 8, 1905, and Oct. 26, 1956). George H. Gould, who accompanied his father to New Mexico, was born in 1870 in Bloomfield, Kentucky. He lived with his father in Las Vegas for six years, where he worked at a drugstore. He then returned to Kentucky to live with his mother and graduated from the Louisville College of Pharmacy in 1890. He became a pharmacist, then bought his own drugstore in downtown Louisville around the turn of the century. In 1913, he founded a pharmaceutical manufacturing company and died a wealthy man in 1950. His brother, Kenneth, joined him in that enterprise and died in Louisville in 1961. Their sister, Mary Aurelia "Mamie" Gould, born in 1872, married a photographer from Lafayette, Indiana, and died in 1936 (*Louisville Courier-Journal,* June 12, 1950, and Oct. 21, 1961; *Las Vegas Daily Optic,* Dec. 23, 1897; *Louisville Courier-Journal,* Nov. 6, 1936).

57. William Ellis, "High Bridge," in *The Kentucky Encyclopedia,* ed. Kleber, 428–29; Howard Curry, *High Bridge: A Pictorial History* (Lexington, KY: Feeback Printing, 1984); *Louisville Courier-Journal,* July 18, 1882.

58. *Louisville Courier-Journal,* July 3, 1887; *Maysville Evening Bulletin,* June 26, 1888.

59. *Cincinnati Enquirer,* July 6, 1889, and Oct. 5, 1890; Frank L. Bristow, "The Old Grapevine Swing" (song) (Cincinnati, 1885).

60. *Louisville Courier-Journal,* July 23, 1885; *Cincinnati Enquirer,* May 3, 1890; *Stanford Interior Journal,* July 18, 1890; Bristow, *Calisthenic Exercises.*

61. *Cincinnati Enquirer,* Jan. 13 and Mar. 10, 1899.

62. *Cincinnati Enquirer,* Dec. 21, 1900, and Jan. 9, 1901.

63. Deed Book 19, p. 573, Jessamine County Circuit Court, Nicholasville, KY; *Danville (Kentucky) Advocate,* Apr. 9, 1906.

64. On Ninita Bristow's acting career, see *Brooklyn Daily Eagle,* Mar. 30, 1913; *Reading (Pennsylvania) Times,* Dec. 28, 1915; *Hartford (Connecticut) Courant,* Oct. 6, 1916; *Baltimore Sun,* Oct. 19, 1919; *Berkshire Eagle* (Pittsfield, MA), Oct. 11, 1921; *Minneapolis Star Tribune,* Oct. 8, 1922; *Bridgeport (Connecticut) Telegram,* Feb. 12, 1923. On Broadway, she appeared in *Marry the Poor Girl,* which ran for eighteen performances at the Little Theatre (later named the Helen Hayes Theatre) on 240 W. Forty-Fourth Street in September and October 1920 (*New York Daily News,* Sept. 27, 1920). On Ninita Bristow's marriage and later life, see *Des Moines Register,* Oct. 13, 1923; *Chicago Tribune,* Sept. 9, 1935; *Louisville Courier-Journal,* July 21, 1940; *New York Times,* Nov. 21, 1971; Ninita Reis, June 1973, United States Social Security Death Index, database, based on US Social Security Administration, Death Master File, database, National Technical Information Service, Alexandria, Virginia, FamilySearch, at https://familysearch.org/ark:/61903/1:1:JYM9-F26,.

17. The Venerable Pastor

1. *Maysville Evening Bulletin,* June 12, 1885.

2. *Maysville Evening Bulletin,* Nov. 27, 1886, and Sept. 2, 1885.

3. *Maysville Evening Bulletin,* Sept. 2, 9, and 10, 1885; *Chattanooga (Tennessee) Daily Times,* Oct. 7 and 13, 1885.

4. *Maysville Evening Bulletin,* Oct. 14, 1887.

5. *Maysville Evening Bulletin,* September 19, 1887.

6. *Maysville Evening Bulletin,* Sept. 28, 1887.

7. *Maysville Evening Bulletin,* Sept. 1, 1885; Feb. 6 and July 28, 1886; Apr. 13 and June 20, 1887.

8. *Maysville Republican,* reprinted in the *Louisville Courier-Journal,* Jan. 27, 1888.

9. *Maysville Evening Bulletin,* Apr. 2, 1888.

10. *Maysville Evening Bulletin,* Apr. 2, May 16, July 24, Aug. 17, 1889; Feb. 4, 1888; Mar. 14, Apr. 29, Oct. 21, 1890.

11. *Maysville Evening Bulletin,* Nov. 26, 1889.

12. *Maysville Public Ledger,* Apr. 28, 1892; Spencer Hubbard, United States Census of Union Veterans and Widows of the Civil War, 1890, database with images, microfilm, NARA, FamilySearch, at https://familysearch.org/ark:/61903/1:1:K8S6-WPJ; Sarah Hubbard, in household of Spencer Hubbard, Minerva, Mason County, KY, US Census 1900, microfilm, NARA, FamilySearch, at https://familysearch.org/ark:/61903/1:1:M9HW-5T5.

13. *Maysville Public Ledger,* Apr. 28, 1892. Berry's race is given as white in the US Census of 1910 (Lida Berry, Maysville, Mason County, KY, US Census, 1910, microfilm, NARA, FamilySearch, at https://familysearch.org/ark:/61903/1:1:M266-S7Z), and my mother, who knew her in the 1940s, recollected her as white. She taught out of her home at 215 W. Second Street (e.g., *Maysville*

Evening Bulletin, Sept. 16, 1893) and played the organ at the Southern Methodist Church (*Maysville Evening Bulletin,* Nov. 29, 1899; her connection with that church was also noted in *Maysville Evening Bulletin,* Mar. 30 and May 31, 1887).

14. *Maysville Evening Bulletin,* Sept. 4, 1886. Plymouth issued similar invitations in *Maysville Evening Bulletin,* July 30, 1887, and July 25, 1891; seats reserved for the whites: *Maysville Evening Bulletin,* Jan. 18, 1888.

15. *Indianapolis Freeman,* May 2, 1891.

16. George C. Wright, *A History of Blacks in Kentucky,* vol. 2 (Frankfort: Kentucky Historical Society, 1992), 70.

17. *Frankfort (Kentucky) Roundabout,* Oct. 3, 1891.

18. *Frankfort Roundabout,* Oct. 3, 1891.

19. *Louisville Courier-Journal,* Oct. 3, 1891.

20. *Cincinnati Enquirer,* Oct. 3, 1891; *Owensboro (Kentucky) Messenger,* Oct. 3, 1891; *Louisville Courier-Journal,* Oct. 10, 1891.

21. *Breckenridge News* (Cloverport, KY), Oct. 14, 1891; *Mt. Sterling (Kentucky) Advocate,* Oct. 27, 1891; *Twelfth Report of the Railroad Commissioners of Kentucky, for the Year 1891* (Frankfort, KY, 1891), 51.

22. *Owensboro Messenger* and *Frankfort Roundabout,* Sept. 19, 1891.

23. *Owensboro Messenger,* Apr. 29, 1891.

24. *Owensboro Messenger,* Apr. 29, 1891.

25. *Louisville Courier-Journal,* Nov. 29, 1891; *Stanford (Kentucky) Interior Journal,* Dec. 4, 1891; *Maysville Evening Bulletin,* Nov. 7, 1891.

26. *South Western Reporter,* 1895, 465–67.

27. *Louisville Courier-Journal,* Mar. 26, 1892.

28. Christine W McEwan, died Oct. 27, 1951, burial at Frankfort Cemetery, Frankfort, Franklin County, KY, BillionGraves Index, database, FamilySearch, at https://familysearch.org/ark:/61903/1:1:KXB1–327.

29. *Maysville Evening Bulletin,* Jan. 28, 1892.

30. *Maysville Evening Bulletin,* Mar. 30, 1892.

31. Bill passed and signed: Anne E. Marshall, "Kentucky's Separate Coach Law and African American Response, 1892–1900," *Register of the Kentucky Historical Society* 98, no. 3 (Summer 2000): 249; Lexington boycott: *Maysville Evening Bulletin,* Apr. 7, 1892; Danville: *Maysville Public Ledger,* June 17, 1892; Ashland: *Maysville Public Ledger,* June 20, 1892; Maysville: *Maysville Public Ledger,* June 16, 1892.

32. *Maysville Public Ledger,* May 31 and June 28, 1892.

33. *Maysville Evening Bulletin,* Feb. 3, Apr. and 10, 1893; *Louisville Courier-Journal,* Apr. 22, 1893; *Maysville Evening Bulletin,* Sept. 19 and 28, 1887.

34. Will Book Y, p. 269, Mason County Circuit Clerk's Office, Maysville, KY.

35. *Maysville Evening Bulletin,* Oct. 25, 1893; Marshall, "Kentucky's Separate Coach Law," 247.

36. *Maysville Public Ledger,* Oct. 31, 1893; Marshall, "Kentucky's Separate Coach Law," 257.

37. Catherine A. Barnes, *Journey from Jim Crow: The Desegregation of Southern Transit* (New York: Columbia University Press, 1983), 46, 98–99.

38. Merlene Davis, "The Bluegrass Had Its Own Rosa Parks," *Lexington Herald-Leader,* Oct. 30, 2005. I am indebted to my friend Wes Mallory for pointing out the parallel with regard to newly arriving white passengers.

39. William O. Bradley, "Message to General Assembly Session 1898," in *Public Documents of Governor William O. Bradley* (Louisville, 1899), 108–9.

40. *Maysville Evening Bulletin,* Nov.1 and 3, 1893; *Maysville Public Ledger,* Nov. 4, 1893.

41. Green's headstone reads:

ELISHA W. GREENE [*sic*]
1816–1892 [*sic*]
ORDAINED 1845
ORGANIZED BETHEL
BAPTIST CHURCH 1844

Afterword

1. Margie Green, Maysville, Mason County, KY, US Census, 1900, microfilm, NARA, FamilySearch, at https://familysearch.org/ark:/61903/1:1:M9HW-MP1; Deed Book 111, pp. 442–43, Mason County Circuit Clerk's Office, Maysville, KY.

2. Moncure Conway, *Autobiography: Memories and Experiences,* 2 vols. (Boston: Houghton, Mifflin, 1904), 1:175, 357–63.

3. *Xenia (Ohio) Daily Gazette,* Sept. 24, 1968.

4. Vicki Bolden and John Klee, "Bethel Baptist Church," in *The Encyclopedia of Northern Kentucky,* ed. Tenkotte and Claypool, 85; the author's visits to both Paris churches' anniversary celebrations in August and September 2019; *Maysville Public Ledger,* Sept. 30, 1910.

5. Garrett Morgan (1877–1963), an African American who invented the first three-color traffic signal and developed an early gas mask, was born in Claysville.

Bibliography

Archival Materials

Barbour, John. "Deposition of Rev. John Barbour, Paxton, Illinois, Feb. 26, 1884." Copy in the author's files.

Bourbon County Circuit Court. Paris, KY.

Deed Books 60, 61.

Inventory Book C.

Mortgage Books 5, 8.

Bourbon County Court of Common Pleas. Paris, KY.

Order Books.

FamilySearch. Website of the Church of Jesus Christ of Latter-day Saints. At http://FamilySearch.org.

Alabama Deaths, 1908–1974. Database. Based on data from the Alabama Department of Health, Montgomery.

BillionGraves Index. Database.

Freedmen's Bureau Records of Persons and Articles Hired, 1865–1872. Database.

Kentucky Births and Christenings, 1839–1960. Database. Based on data collected by the Genealogical Society of Utah, Salt Lake City.

Kentucky Marriages, 1785–1979. Database. Based on data collected by the Genealogical Society of Utah, Salt Lake City.

Kentucky Death Records, 1911–1965. Database. Based on data from the Kentucky Office of Vital Statistics, Frankfort.

Texas Death Index, 1903–2000. Database. Based on data from the Texas Department of Health, State Vital Statistics Unit, Austin, collected by Ancestry.com.

United States Census of Union Veterans and Widows of the Civil War, 1890. Database with images. Microfilm. National Archives and Records Administration (NARA), Washington, DC.

United States Social Security Death Index. Database. Based on US Social Security Administration, Death Master File, database, National Technical Information Service, Alexandria, VA.

US Census, 1840, 1850, 1860, 1900, 1910, 1930. Microfilm. National Archives and Records Administration (NARA), Washington, DC.

Illinois State Archive. Springfield.

Illinois Veterans. Databases. At http://cyberdriveillinois.com/departments/archives/databases/home.html.

Jessamine County Circuit Court. Nicholasville, KY.

Deed Book 19.

Kentucky Department for Libraries and Archives. Public Records Division. Frankfort.

Barbour, John. Deposition. Court of Common Pleas, Bourbon County, KY, Feb. 28, 1884.

Kentucky Historical Society Library. Frankfort.

Towery, William M. "My Dobyns/Berry/Porter/Hitt/Vaughan and Allied Families." Typescript, 2004.

Kentucky Wesleyan College, Owensboro.

Methodist Episcopal Church South v. Rev. George T. Gould (*MECS v. GTG*). Transcript of church trial, Millersburg, KY, Oct. 1884, as well as other records that are not part of the trial transcript, such as depositions, statements, testimony, and letters.

Library of Congress, Manuscript Division. Washington, DC.

Douglass, Frederick, Papers. General Correspondence.

Federal Writers' Project. US Work Projects Administration. "Slave Narratives: A Folk History of Slavery in the United States from Interviews with Former Slaves." Manuscripts.

Vol. 3: "Florida Narratives." Manuscript. At https://www.loc.gov/item/mesn030.

Vol. 5: "Indiana, Arnold–Woodson." 1936. Manuscript/mixed material. At https://www.loc.gov/item/mesn050/.

Library of Congress, Geography and Map Division. Washington, DC.

Map of Paris. In *Atlas of Bourbon, Clark, Fayette, Jessamine, and Woodford Counties, Ky.* Philadelphia, 1877.

Mason County Circuit Clerk's Office. Maysville, KY.

Deed Books 62, 70, 75, 90, 111.

Will Books G and Y.

New Mexico State University Library. Las Cruces.

Gould, George T., Papers.

Gould, George T. "The Blue and the Gray, Delivered at the Ninth Annual Session of the Encampment of the G. A. R., Department of New Mexico, April 7th, 1892."

———. "The Flesh." Feb. 28, 1885.

———. "Games and Gaming." Sept. 21, 1885.

———. "The Ministry of Evil." May 10, 1885.

———. "She Hath Done What She Could." June 4, 1884.
———. "The Soul and Its Immortality." Feb. 29, 1880.

Periodicals

Alamogordo (New Mexico) News
Albuquerque Citizen
Albuquerque Journal
Anti-Slavery Bugle (Salem, OH)
Baltimore Sun
Baptist Memorial and Monthly Record
Berkshire Eagle (Pittsfield, MA)
Big Spring (Texas) Daily Herald
Boone County (Kentucky) Recorder
Bourbon News (Paris, KY)
Breckenridge News (Breckenridge County, KY)
Bridgeport (Connecticut) Telegram
Brooklyn Daily Eagle
Carlisle (Kentucky) Mercury
Cartersville (Georgia) American
Chattanooga (Tennessee) Daily Times
Chicago Tribune
Cincinnati Commercial
Cincinnati Daily Gazette
Cincinnati Enquirer
Cynthiana (Kentucky) News
Daily Oklahoman (Oklahoma City)
Danville (Kentucky) Advocate
Des Moines Register
El Paso Herald
El Paso Times
Fort Smith (Arkansas) Times
Frankfort (Kentucky) Roundabout
Galveston Daily News
Hartford (Connecticut) Courant
Hickman (Kentucky) Courier
Indianapolis Freeman
Jacksonville (Illinois) Journal
Kentucky Conference Journal
Kentucky Explorer Magazine
Las Vegas (New Mexico) Daily Gazette
Las Vegas (New Mexico) Daily Optic
Las Vegas (Nevada) Sun

Lexington Intelligencer
Lexington Transcript
Louisville Courier-Journal
Louisville Daily Courier
Marion (Alabama) Commonwealth
Massachusetts Spy (Worcester)
Maysville Eagle
Maysville Evening Bulletin
Maysville New Republican
Maysville Public Ledger
Maysville Weekly Bulletin
Memphis Daily Appeal
Memphis Public Ledger
Minneapolis Star Tribune
Mt. Sterling (Kentucky) Advocate
New York Daily Herald
New York Sun
New York Times
New York Tribune
North American and Daily Advertiser (Philadelphia)
Owensboro (Kentucky) Messenger
Paris Kentuckian
Philadelphia Times
Reading (Pennsylvania) Times
Richmond [Kentucky] Daily Register
Rio Grande Republican (Las Cruces, NM)
San Antonio Light
San Francisco Examiner
Santa Fe Herald
Selma (Alabama) Times-Argus
Shelby Sentinel (Columbiana, AL)
Semi-weekly Bourbon News (Paris, KY)
Southern Argus (Selma, AL)
South Western Reporter
Springfield (Missouri) Leader and Press
Stanford (Kentucky) Interior Journal
St. Louis Post-Dispatch
Tuscaloosa (Alabama) Gazette
Tuscaloosa (Alabama) News
Tuscaloosa (Alabama) Weekly Times
Vanceburg (Kentucky) Courier

Washington (DC) Evening Star
Washington (DC) Post
Weekly Democratic Statesman (Austin, TX)
Wilmington (Delaware) News Journal
Xenia (Ohio) Daily Gazette

Published Primary and Secondary Sources

Alvord, Idress Head. *Head, Descent of Henry Head (1697–1770) in America.* Columbia, MO: I. H. Alvord, n.d. [c. 1949].

Apperson, George M. "Lincoln, the Churches, and Memphis Presbyterians." *American Presbyterians* 72, no. 2 (Summer 1994): 97–107.

Astor, Aaron. *Rebels on the Border: Civil War, Emancipation, and the Reconstruction of Kentucky and Missouri.* Baton Rouge: Louisiana State University Press, 2012.

Atlas of Bourbon, Clark, Fayette, Jessamine, and Woodford Counties, Ky. Philadelphia, 1877.

Auslander, Mark. *The Accidental Slaveowner: Revisiting a Myth of Race and Finding an American Family.* Athens: University of Georgia Press, 2011.

Bancroft, Hubert Howe. *The Native Races of the Pacific States.* Vol. 2. San Francisco, 1883.

Barnes, Catherine A. *Journey from Jim Crow: The Desegregation of Southern Transit.* New York: Columbia University Press, 1983.

Barnes, James J., and Patience P. Barnes. "Was Illinois Governor Richard Yates Intimidated by the Copperheads during the Civil War?" *Journal of the Illinois State Historical Society* 107, no. 3 (Fall–Winter 2014): 321–45.

Berry, Benjamin D., Jr. "The Plymouth Congregational Church of Louisville, Kentucky." *Phylon* 42, no. 3 (1981): 224–32.

Bigham, Darrell. E. *On Jordan's Banks: Emancipation and Its Aftermath in the Ohio River Valley.* Lexington: University Press of Kentucky, 2006.

Bolden, Vicki, and John Klee. "Bethel Baptist Church." In *The Encyclopedia of Northern Kentucky,* edited by Paul A. Tenkotte and James C. Claypool, 85. Lexington: University Press of Kentucky, 2009.

Bradley, William O. *Public Documents of Governor William O. Bradley.* Louisville, 1899.

Bristow, Frank Leslie. "Ain't I Glad" (song). Cincinnati, 1880.

———. *Calisthenic Exercises and Marches with Pleasing Drill Songs and Music Suitable for Schools, Colleges, Private Entertainments, and Public Exhibitions.* Cincinnati, 1891.

———. "Daisey Dell" (song). Cincinnati, 1874.

———. "Eyebright" (song). Cincinnati, 1883.

———. "The Little Cadet" (song). Cincinnati, 1880.

———. *The Little Shaking Quakers* (musical comedy sketch). Cincinnati, 1883.

———. "Marche Calisthenique" (piano piece). Cincinnati, 1882.

———. "The Old Grapevine Swing" (song). Cincinnati, 1885.

———. "Sweet Rest at Home" (song). Cincinnati, 1883.

Calvert, Jean, and John Klee. *Maysville, Kentucky: From Past to Present in Pictures.* Maysville, KY: Mason County Museum, 1983.

———. *The Towns of Mason County: Their Past in Pictures.* Maysville, KY: Maysville and Mason County Library Historical and Scientific Association, 1986.

Campbell, Alexander. *Memoirs of Alexander Campbell.* 2 vols. Edited by Robert Richardson. Cincinnati, 1898.

Catalogue of Phi Alpha Society: 1845–1890. Vol. 23. Jacksonville, IL, 1890.

Clift, G. Glenn. *History of Maysville and Mason County.* Lexington, KY: Transylvania Printing, 1936.

Cody, Z. T. *History of May's Lick Baptist Church.* Maysville, KY, 1890.

Coleman, J. Winston. *Slavery Times in Kentucky.* Chapel Hill: University of North Carolina Press, 1940.

Collins, Lewis. *Historical Sketches of Kentucky.* Maysville, KY, 1847.

Conway, Moncure. *Autobiography: Memories and Experiences.* 2 vols. Boston: Houghton, Mifflin, 1904.

Coon, Diane Perrine. "Freedmen's Bureau Schools." In *The Encyclopedia of Northern Kentucky,* edited by Paul A. Tenkotte and James C. Claypool, 370–71. Lexington: University Press of Kentucky, 2009.

Cunningham, John W. "A Preacher's Experiences during the Civil War" (1903). Reprinted in *Kentucky Explorer Magazine,* Mar. 2001.

Curry, Howard. *High Bridge: A Pictorial History.* Lexington, KY: Feeback Printing, 1984.

Davis, Charles L. "Confronting a Petty Tyrant: Patriarchy and Protest at Millersburg Female College, 1880–1884." *Register of the Kentucky Historical Society* 115, no. 3 (Summer 2017): 349–76.

———. "Green v. Gould (1884) and the Construction of Postbellum Race Relations in a Central Kentucky Community." *Register of the Kentucky Historical Society* 105, no. 3 (Summer 2007): 383–416.

———. "Racial Politics in Central Kentucky during the Post-Reconstruction Era: Bourbon County, 1877–1899." *Register of the Kentucky Historical Society* 109, no. 4 (Autumn 2010): 347–81.

———. "The Railroad Expansion Controversy in Postbellum Bourbon County: Conflicting Economic Interests and Ideological Perspectives among Urban and Rural Elites." *Register of the Kentucky Historical Society* 112, no. 1 (Winter 2014): 51–82.

Davis, Merlene. "The Bluegrass Had Its Own Rosa Parks." *Lexington Herald-Leader,* Oct. 30, 2005.

Doyle, Don Harrison. *The Social Order of a Frontier Community: Jacksonville, Illinois, 1825–70.* Carbondale: University of Illinois Press, 1978.
Ellis, William. "High Bridge." In *The Kentucky Encyclopedia,* edited by John E. Kleber, 428–29. Lexington: University Press of Kentucky, 1992.
Evans, Curtis J. *The Conquest of Labor: Daniel Pratt and Southern Industrialization.* Baton Rouge: Louisiana State University Press, 2014.
Everman, H. E. *Bourbon County since 1865.* Richmond, KY: H. E. Everman, 1999.
Frederick, Francis. *Autobiography of Rev. Francis Frederick.* Baltimore, 1869.
Friend, Craig. *Along the Maysville Road: The Early American Republic in the Trans-Appalachian West.* Knoxville: University of Tennessee Press, 2005.
Green, Elisha. *Life of the Rev. Elisha W. Green, One of the Founders of the Kentucky Normal and Theological Institute—Now the State University at Louisville; Eleven Years Moderator of the Mt. Zion Baptist Association; Five Years Moderator of the Consolidated Baptist Educational Association; and over Thirty Years Pastor of the Colored Baptist Churches of Maysville and Paris. Written by Himself.* Maysville, KY, 1888.
Hagedorn, Ann. *Beyond the River: The Untold Story of the Heroes of the Underground Railroad.* New York: Simon and Schuster, 2002.
Harrison, Lowell H., and James C. Klotter. *A New History of Kentucky.* Lexington: University Press of Kentucky, 1997.
Hartje, Robert. "Van Dorn Conducts a Raid on Holly Springs and Enters Tennessee." *Tennessee Historical Quarterly* 18, no. 2 (June 1959): 120–33.
History of Morgan County, Illinois. Chicago, 1878.
Holm, April. *A Kingdom Divided: Evangelicals, Loyalty, and Sectionalism in the Civil War Era.* Baton Rouge: Louisiana State University Press, 2017.
Howard, Victor B. "The Black Testimony Controversy in Kentucky, 1866–1872." *Journal of Negro History* 58, no. 2 (Apr. 1973): 140–65.
——. "Negro Politics and the Suffrage Question in Kentucky, 1866–1872." *Register of the Kentucky Historical Society* 72, no. 2 (Apr. 1974): 111–33.
Hudson, J. Blaine. *Fugitive Slaves and the Underground Railroad in the Kentucky Borderland.* Jefferson, NC: McFarland, 2002.
An Illustrated Atlas of Mason County, Kentucky. Philadelphia, 1876.
Johnson, Michael P. "Denmark Vesey and His Co-conspirators." *William and Mary Quarterly* 58, no. 4 (Oct. 2001): 915–76.
Kahan, Paul. *Amiable Scoundrel: Simon Cameron, Lincoln's Scandalous Secretary of War.* Lincoln: University of Nebraska Press, 2016.
Kleber, John E., ed. *The Kentucky Encyclopedia.* Lexington: University Press of Kentucky, 1992.
Lard, Moses E. "Patterson Institute, at North Middletown, Ky." *Lard's Quarterly: Devoted to the Propagation and Defense of the Gospel* 4 (July 1867): 285.
Lewis, Alvin Fayette. *History of Higher Education in Kentucky.* Washington, DC, 1899.

Lewis, Dio. *The New Gymnastics for Men, Women, and Children.* Boston, 1862.

Livingston, John. *Biographical Sketches of Distinguished Americans, Now Living.* New York, 1853.

———. *Portraits of Eminent Americans Now Living.* Vol. 4. New York, 1854.

Lucas, Marion B. *A History of Blacks in Kentucky.* Vol. 1: *From Slavery to Segregation, 1760–1891.* Frankfort: Kentucky Historical Society, 1992.

Marrs, Elijah P. *Life and History of the Rev. Elijah P. Marrs.* Louisville, 1885.

Marshall, Anne E. "Kentucky's Separate Coach Law and African American Response, 1892–1900." *Register of the Kentucky Historical Society* 98, no. 3 (Summer 2000): 241–59.

Meininger, J. C. "School Girls Dream" (piano piece). Cincinnati, 1880.

Milewski, Melissa. "From Slave to Litigant: African Americans in Court in the Postwar South, 1865–1920." *Law and History Review* 30, no. 3 (Aug. 2012): 723–70.

Miller, Caroline R. *Slavery in Mason County, Kentucky: A Century of Records 1788–1888.* 2 vols. Maysville, KY: National Underground Railroad Museum, 2001.

Miller, Patricia. *Bringing Down the Colonel: A Sex Scandal of the Gilded Age, and the "Powerless" Woman Who Took on Washington.* New York: Farrar, Straus and Giroux, 2018.

Milligan, Robert. *Second Annual Announcement of Kentucky University.* Harrodsburg, KY, 1860.

Minutes of the Annual Conferences of the Methodist Episcopal Church, South for the Year 1862. Nashville, TN, 1862.

Minutes of the Fifty-First Session of the Kentucky Annual Conference of the Methodist Episcopal Church, South. Cincinnati, 1871.

Minutes of the Fifty-Second Session of the Kentucky Annual Conference of the Methodist Episcopal Church, South. Louisville, KY, 1872.

Minutes of the Forty-Ninth Session of the Kentucky Annual Conference of the Methodist Episcopal Church, South. Shelbyville, KY, 1869.

Minutes of the Forty-Seventh Session of the Kentucky Annual Conference of the Methodist Episcopal Church, South. Shelbyville, KY, 1867.

Minutes of the Kentucky Conference of the Methodist Episcopal Church, South. Shelbyville, KY, 1878.

Minutes of the Sixty-Eighth Session of the Kentucky Conference of the Methodist Episcopal Church, South. Frankfort, KY, 1888.

Northrop, Henry Davenport, et al. *The College of Life or Practical Self-Educator: A Manual of Self-Improvement for the Colored Race . . . Giving Examples and Achievements of Successful Men and Women of the Race.* [No place of publication], 1896.

Norwood, John Nelson. *The Schism in the Methodist Episcopal Church 1844: A Study of Slavery and Ecclesiastical Politics.* Alfred, NY: Alfred University Press, 1923.

Parrish, C. H. *Golden Jubilee of the General Association of Colored Baptists in Kentucky: The Story of 50 Years' Work from 1865–1915.* Louisville, KY: Mayes Printing, 1915.

Perrigo, Lynn Irvin. *Gateway to Glorieta: A History of Las Vegas, New Mexico.* Santa Fe, NM: Sunstone Press, 2010.

Perrin, William Henry. *History of Bourbon, Scott, Harrison, and Nicholas Counties, Kentucky.* Chicago, 1882.

Peters, Anne. "From War Horse to Saddle Horse." *American Saddlebred Magazine,* Nov.–Dec. 1998.

———. "Pedigree Analysis: Grey Eagle." *Bloodhorse,* Jan. 9, 2015. At http://www.bloodhorse.com/horse-racing/articles/109985/pedigree-analysis-grey-eagle.

Pope, Richard M. *Lexington Theological Seminary: A Brief Narrative.* Lexington, KY: Lexington Theological Seminary, 1973.

Proceedings of the State Convention of Colored Men Held at Lexington, Kentucky, in the A. M. E. Church, November 26th, 27th, and 28th, 1867. Frankfort, KY, 1867.

Ragan, O. G. *History of Lewis County.* Cincinnati, OH: Jennings and Graham, 1912.

Raitz, Karl, and Nancy O'Malley. *Kentucky's Frontier Highway: Historical Landscapes along the Maysville Road.* Lexington: University Press of Kentucky, 2012.

Rammelkamp, Charles H. "The Reverberations of the Slavery Conflict in a Pioneer College." *Mississippi Valley Historical Review* 14, no. 4 (Mar. 1928): 447–61.

Report of the Adjutant General of the State of Illinois. 1900–1902. At http://www.old-new-orleans.com/ILLINOIS_CW_reghist.pdf.

Report of the Commissioner of Education Made to the Secretary of the Interior for the Year 1882. Washington, DC, 1883.

Rhyne, Michael. "'We Are Mobed & Beat': Regulator Violence against Free Black Households in Kentucky's Bluegrass Region, 1865–1867." *Ohio Valley History* 2, no. 1 (Spring 2002): 30–41.

Schmidt, Carl, and Ellen Puerzer. "More about Octagons." *Lexington Herald-Leader,* Dec. 26, 1998.

Second Annual Announcement of Kentucky University. Harrodsburg, KY, 1860.

Short, Roy Hunter. *Methodism in Kentucky.* Rutland, VT: Academy Books, 1979.

Simpson, Matthew, ed. *Cyclopedia of Methodism, Embracing Sketches of Its Rise, Progress, and Present Condition.* Philadelphia, 1883.

Smith, Martin H. *History of the Maysville Baptist Church.* Maysville, KY, 1875.

Spencer, John H. *A History of Kentucky Baptists.* 2 vols. Cincinnati, 1885.

Stevens, Walter B. *Centennial History of Missouri.* 6 vols. St. Louis, MO: S. J. Clarke, 1921.

Stevenson, W. R. "Capture of Holly Springs, Miss." *Confederate Veteran Magazine* 9 (1901): 134.

Swift, David E. "Conservative versus Progressive Orthodoxy in Latter 19th-Century Congregationalism." *Church History* 16, no. 1 (Mar. 1947): 22–31.

Tallant, Harold D. *Evil Necessity: Slavery and Political Culture in Antebellum Kentucky.* Lexington: University Press of Kentucky, 2003.

———. "Slavery." In *The Kentucky Encyclopedia,* edited by John E. Kleber, 827–29. Lexington: University Press of Kentucky, 1992.

Tenkotte, Paul A., and James C. Claypool, eds. *The Encyclopedia of Northern Kentucky* Lexington: University Press of Kentucky, 2009.

Todd, Jan. *Physical Culture and the Body Beautiful: Purposive Exercise in the Lives of American Women 1800–1870.* Macon, GA: Mercer University Press, 1998.

Twelfth Report of the Railroad Commissioners of Kentucky, for the Year 1891. Frankfort, KY, 1891.

Wadsworth, William H. *Speech of Hon. W. H. Wadsworth, at Flemingsburg, Kentucky, June 13, 1868.* Washington, DC, 1868.

Walsh, Margaret. *The Rise of the Midwestern Meat Packing Industry.* Lexington: University Press of Kentucky, 2015.

Warren, William F. *Ministry of Evil: An Examination of the Popular Bitter-Sweet Theology.* New York, 1859.

Watson, J. Madison. *Watson's Manual of Calisthenics: A Systematic Drill-Book without Apparatus, for Schools, Families, and Gymnasiums, with Music to Accompany the Exercises.* New York, 1864.

Webb, Ross A. *Benjamin Helm Bristow: Border State Politician.* Lexington: University Press of Kentucky, 1969.

———. "Bristow, Francis Marion." In *Kentucky Encyclopedia*, edited by John E. Kleber, 124–25. Lexington: University Press of Kentucky, 1992.

White, Alma Bridwell. *The Story of My Life.* Vol. 1. Zarephath NJ: Pillar of Fire, 1919.

Williams, Kenneth H., and James Russell Harris. "Kentucky in 1860: A Statistical Overview." *Register of the Kentucky Historical Society* 103, no. 4 (Autumn 2005): 743–64.

Winchell, Alexander. *Adamites and Preadamites.* Syracuse, NY, 1878.

Wright, George C. *A History of Blacks in Kentucky.* Vol. 2. Frankfort: Kentucky Historical Society, 1992.

Index

Index

Index

Index

Index

Index